# Love to the Little Ones

*The Trials and Triumphs of Parents
through the Ages*

—

*In Letters and Diaries, Memoirs
and Essays*

# Love to the Little Ones

## The Trials and Triumphs of Parents
## through the Ages

—

### In Letters and Diaries, Memoirs
### and Essays

Louisa Lane Fox

**F**

FRANCES LINCOLN LIMITED
PUBLISHERS

Frances Lincoln Ltd
4 Torriano Mews
Torriano Avenue
London NW5 2RZ
www.franceslincoln.com

A catalogue record for this book is available from the British Library.

ISBN 978-0-7112-2940-2

Printed and bound in China

1 2 3 4 5 6 7 8 9

*For Henry, Tara and my grandson Max LF*
*Martha LF and Christopher GB*
*John J and Lily J*

# CONTENTS

# ACKNOWLEDGEMENTS

This anthology owes much to my friends: Sarah Hawkins, who has not only helped me to organise and shape the book, but, for over forty years of selfless friendship, has helped me organise and shape my life. Special thanks to Kirsty Hudson for encouraging me from the start, reading an early draft and making wise suggestions. Harriet Crawley urged me to get on with it and Laurence Colchester insisted that I finish it.

I am grateful to the following: my cousin Arabella Heathcoat Amory for the letters from her husband's family papers; Jonathan Keates for his grandmother's letter; John Julius Norwich for the letters of my great-aunt Diana Cooper; Elisa Segrave for her father's letter; and Richard Eyre for allowing me to quote the opening lines from his book *Utopia & other places*. My thanks to John Nicoll, friend and best publisher, and Jo Christian, editor at Frances Lincoln. Serena Dilnot, copy editor, made all the difference to the book and to me. The staff at Kensington and Chelsea Central Library have always been friendly and helpful.

I started this book for fun. It is a jackdaw work: full of little bits that sparkled appealingly to me; what I have done is to try to make a pattern out of other people's labours, within a subject that has always interested and amused me. This is owing, in part, to my having been so very lucky in my children, their other halves, and my stepchildren: I thank them all, just as I thank my husband Charles Jencks, the optimist who changed my life.

# INTRODUCTION

In this anthology I have tried to show some of the ways in which mothers and fathers have thought about and written to their children over the last four hundred years, using examples from letters, diaries, memoirs and books of advice. At the start of the twenty-first century, parents may believe that they face worse problems and demands in bringing up their children than ever before. They are certainly given more advice: from professional child-care experts, from other parents and from governments. There are weekly pages in the newspapers on the subject, quantities of books published, television series made and self-help groups begun. Although this country is a safer place in which to grow up than it ever was, there has never been more anxiety among parents. Letters and diaries from the past are reassuring because they speak of familiar concerns against strikingly different historical backgrounds. The fundamental feelings of parents then and parents now seem to be unchanged: their affections, their anxieties, their hopes, their difficulties and their grief. It is a pleasure to understand the predicament of a mother trying to mediate between her son and his father four hundred years ago and to enjoy the tenderness of an eighteenth-century father who tells his friend that he should read to his pregnant wife every night.

On the other hand, there are dramatic differences between our lives as parents and the lives of earlier mothers and fathers. Many women died in childbirth; sometimes more than half the children in a family died and no one knows how many children died at birth or through miscarriage. They died in the greatest numbers in infancy, but they also died of disease or accident in their teenage years. Nevertheless, one of the most extraordinary aspects of women's lives was the number of mothers who contrived to bring up five or more children while leading a demanding life as the manager of her husband's estate, an actor or a writer. Religion dominated family life in the sixteenth and seventeenth centuries and continued to play a part right up to the twentieth century. In a similar way, fathers dominated their families although not always in the conventional fashion one might expect. In 1724 Nicholas Blundell tried hard to marry off his daughter, who rejected suitor after suitor; a situation he accepted because he did not want to be thought a harsh parent.

Early private letters and memoirs which have been preserved and published by historical societies were often written by men. They come from a tiny segment of society: those who were literate and had the time to communicate at length with their children and to reflect on their relationships. Before the twentieth century, fewer women wrote about childbirth or about how they were bringing up their children, and the private papers and letters of those who did so may not have been considered sufficiently important to be kept over time. With only a few exceptions, this anthology is about the 'survival of the richest' parents and children from the past. In recent years, it is the successful and famous who engage our attention when they reveal their attitudes to their children or those who can transform a familiar situation by their vivid writing.

I have concentrated on British parents because they seem to have had a slightly different experience of family life from other English-speaking countries. The examples I have chosen are those that interested, moved or amused me. Some of them are well known but too striking to be left out, like Thomas More's last letter to his daughter or Rudyard Kipling's letters to his son. I have also included the occasional quotation from books of advice on how to bring up children. When written by women in earlier centuries they were often presented as devotional works but the most influential over the time span were written by men. I include them when they strike me as relevant to the parents' own writings. I enjoy the feeling of recognition and sympathy that a letter written in the fifteenth century can elicit in us, as when the young Margaret Paston, pregnant in 1444, complains of having nothing to wear because she has grown so fat, or when, in the seventeenth century, Edmund Verney writes an angry and disappointed letter to his son Edmund, a student at Oxford, where he is apparently doing no work and deeply in debt.

There have always been parents who looked after their children well and those who looked after them badly, whatever theories happened to be fashionable at the time. I have included a couple of examples of overt cruelty, although I suspect that I would have found far more had I been choosing extracts from the writings of children. There are more examples of abusive mothers than fathers but this may be merely a reflection of how ruthless fathers were expected to be. It is salutary to be reminded of the level of physical violence against children that was considered acceptable right up to the second half of the twentieth century.

Nowadays parents are blamed not only for their failures as parents but also for the failures in the lives of their grown-up children. Understanding child development and psychoanalytic theory has made everyone more careful and more frightened of the influence and effect they are supposed to be going to have on children's lives. Over the last five hundred years, parents have considered their children to be small adults, sinful souls, empty pages, artless creatures of nature or troubled egos. I wonder if mothers and fathers have ever felt so responsible for every tiny change or development in their children's lives as they do at present?

Because I have chosen to focus on parents' views of themselves, we cannot be sure whether they were considered good or bad parents at the time, or whether we should consider them to be so today. There are indications of course. One of my favourite mothers is Lady Brilliana Harley, who wrote to her son Ned from the time he was sent off to Oxford, aged fourteen, to the time of her death in the Civil War five years later. We have no letters from him in return, but he preserved hers for future generations. She was a rigorously devout Protestant who showed a most beguiling and tender love for her son as well as great personal courage.

The letters and diaries remind us that most parents would claim to have had the best intentions, whatever their children might have said about it. Judging by these extracts, mothers and fathers were pretty confident about how they brought up their families. It may be the power of the professional childcare expert that has undermined our belief in our own parenting skills, or it may be that so few of us grow up with much younger siblings through whom we learn about the demands of childhood. Although the average family size in the past was only a little larger than today, on the whole the richer, more educated parents who have left us their diaries and letters had larger families. Children grew up surrounded by other children: those of their own families, stepfamilies or the household with whom they had been sent to live.

In earlier centuries, it was common for boys and girls to be sent away from home to be educated, in the broadest sense, and to develop ties to other great families. The English upper classes have been sending their young children away from home for centuries; other northern European countries gave up the practice long before we did. Only in Italy, throughout the period, did parents keep their children at home for as long as they could and, some might argue, longer than they should. It was this contrast that so shocked an Italian visitor in 1551. From the seventeenth to the twentieth centuries, daughters on the whole were kept at home or sent for a few years to school but sons were sent away to boarding schools, aged seven or eight. Brutality was a feature of school life until very recently. Parents accepted it even when they didn't like it; just as they accepted the fact that young boys fought, went to war or joined the Navy, where they faced adult responsibilities and hardship.

Today, parents from all backgrounds seem to think that, of all the dangers facing their children, drugs pose the greatest threat. But this is a significant change from the past. Until 1920, when the Dangerous Drugs Act was passed, laudanum, which was made from opium and alcohol, was freely available for babies and children as well as adults.

Despite the fundamental changes in family life over the last five hundred years a surprising number of things remain the same. Through the centuries we see fathers and mothers struggling to make their sons follow rules, work hard, strive to abide by religious principles, and carve a successful social life and career. Apart from the declining interest in religion, parents appear to want the same things for their sons through time. Attitudes to daughters have changed far more dramatically. Some parents may have given their daughters the education and confidence that enabled them to realise their lives intellectually and emotionally but the conventions of society were restrictive, quite apart from the demands of childbearing and caring.

There is a feeling that parents today are so soft on their children that they are in danger of growing up irresponsible, immature, and incapable of achieving anything without praise. This concern is not a new one: Thomas More, in the early sixteenth century, insists that excessive praise leads to 'vain glory' and, two centuries later, Lady Susan

Strangways regrets that the 'excessive praises and flattery' of her uncle, Lord Holland, made his children vain and spoilt and, in the end, a disappointment to him.

Conversely, there is also a sense that there is, among the middle classes, more pressure on children to perform academically and socially. But is it any different from Sir Henry Sidney's high expectations of his eleven-year-old son in the sixteenth century? Lord Chesterfield may have been obsessive in his desire to promote his son but, from the sixteenth century to Vita Sackville-West in the twentieth, parents have tried to persuade or force their children to be what the parents want them to be. Sometimes the children grow up to be just what their mothers and father had hoped and sometimes they grow up to be other kinds of people altogether.

In the past, children were more likely to grow up with a stepmother or stepfather than in a single-parent family. As people lived longer, children often grew up with their grandparents. 'Your children are my children' says Sydney Smith to his daughter, referring to her stepchildren, but, as happens today, parents in old age were not always shown the kind of loyalty they felt was owed them. Daniel Defoe complains of the cruelty of his children and John Milton shows little affection for his. Again, it is a foreigner, Hermann Pückler Muskau in the nineteenth century, who remarks on the odd behaviour of English families as the children grow up.

We believe that at present we are particularly open-minded and easy-going as parents but some of the eighteenth-century parents seem to have pretty similar attitudes. The 'paragon of mothers' in Harriette Wilson's *Memoirs* exhibits a fashionably relaxed attitude to nudity among her children; Lord Bessborough devotes as much time and trouble to looking after his small son as any father alive today; and many aristocratic parents accepted illegitimate grandchildren with fond tolerance.

The death of a child is no longer an ever-present threat in this country. Of all the changes in parental experience this must be the greatest. In our society, only a minority of families experience what must be the worst of all deaths. In the past almost no one escaped the anguish and desolation of the death of babies, young children, teenagers and young adults. Few of the parents can bear to write very much at the time of their child's death, which makes the exchange of letters between Charles Darwin and his wife during the last days in the life of his daughter Annie all the more important.

Because many of the extracts I have chosen come from a small segment of British society, there are often connections between families over time. In the first half of the nineteenth century, for example, Maria Josepha Stanley wrote to her daughter-in-law Henrietta, who in turn wrote about her own children, one of whom, Kate, married John Russell, Viscount Amberley. Kate filled in a diary about her experiences as a mother before her early death. One of her two surviving two sons was Bertrand Russell, who also recorded his views about his own children. I didn't know about many of these connections when I first started the anthology and, although I have not always drawn attention to them in the text, I hope readers may discover some for themselves.

I have divided the book into five chapters that parallel an individual parent's life: pregnancy and birth, childhood, adolescence, adulthood and death. Within each chapter, the extracts are arranged chronologically. With a few exceptions (notably the Paston letters), I have used the original spelling.

The extracts present a partial and personal view of the subject, a view that has been formed by my own experiences. The common reader, wrote Virginia Woolf, picking up on Dr Johnson's definition, 'reads for his own pleasure rather than to impart knowledge or correct the opinions of others. . . . he is guided by an instinct to create for himself, out of whatever odds and ends he can come by, some kind of whole.' The selections have been chosen from the point of view of a parent and with the habits of just such a 'common reader'.

# IN THE BEGINNING

## PREGNANCY

'. . . not forgetting the kicker in the dark'
*Jack Verney to his wife, 1683*

In the middle of the fifteenth century, the young Margaret Paston writes a letter of startling immediacy: she is in high spirits over her pregnancy and although she complains of how fat she is and how few suitable clothes she has to wear, her happiness is tangible. Few of the later examples seem so full of confidence and contentment: pregnancy was a frightening experience when women were always at risk of dying in childbirth.

In the seventeenth century, Mary Rich admits to having deliberately avoided a third pregnancy in her youth, out of vanity, only to find that she has left it too late when she is aged thirty-eight and both her children have died: a situation with resonance for older mothers today. Frances Boscawen, in the eighteenth century, writes from past experience when she expresses the fears and agonies of her future labour.

There is a well-known exchange of letters, written in 1847 between Edward Stanley and his wife, congratulating themselves on their luck in ending an unwanted eleventh pregnancy, but other future fathers, like George Lyttelton in 1752, are solicitous, while in 1905 Augustus John is wittily unconcerned. Coleridge correctly imagines the importance of the first nine months of life where Sydney Smith and Anthony Trollope make us laugh about it.

In more recent times, expecting a baby is less dangerous than it used to be, but is still a complicated business, whether it is a first, long-wanted child for Diana Cooper or an unexpected, unwanted one for the seventeen-year-old Lorna Sage.

Margaret Paston writes to her husband John (1421–1466) a year after they were married, when she is expecting their first child. She reminds him to send her some cloth to make a dress that will fit her now she is so fat, and she reassures him that the midwife, Elisabeth Peverel, who has bad sciatica, promises to arrive when needed, even if she has to be brought in a barrow.

14th December, 1441

Right reverend and worshipful husband,

I recommend me to you, . . . praying you to weet that my mother sent to my father to London for a gown cloth of musterdevillers [a grey woollen cloth] to make of a gown for me; and he told my mother and me, when he was come home, that he charged you to buy it after that he were come out of London. I pray you, if it be not bought, that ye will vouchsafe to buy it and send it home as soon as ye may; for I have no gown to wear this winter but my black and my green a lierre, and that is so cumbrous that I am weary to wear it.

As for the girdle that my father behested me, I spake to him thereof a little before he yede to London last, and he said to me that the fault was in you, that ye would not think thereupon to do make it [have it made]; but I suppose that is not so – he said it but for a scusation [as an excuse]. I pray you, if ye dare take it upon you, that ye will vouchsafe to do make it against ye come home; for I had never more need thereof than I have now, for I am wax so fetis [fat] that I may not be girt in no bar of no girdle that I have but of one.

Elizabeth Peverel hath lay sick fifteen or sixteen weeks of the sciatica, but she sent my mother word by Kate that she should come hither when God sent time, though she should be crod in a barrow.

John of Damme was here, and my mother discovered me to him; and he said by his troth that he was not gladder of nothing that he heard this twelvemonth that he was thereof. I may no longer live by my craft, I am discovered of all men that see me. . . .

I pray that ye will wear the ring with the image of Saint Margaret that I sent you for a remembrance till ye come home. Ye have left me such a remembrance that maketh me to think upon you both day and night when I would sleep.

Yours, M.P

Mary Rich, Countess of Warwick (1625–1678), laments the decision she made not to have more children when she was still young enough to do so. She had only two children, partly due to vanity and partly to her husband's financial position, and both had died: her daughter at one year and her son, aged twenty, from smallpox. Her arguments would be familiar to many women at the start of the twenty-first century.

At my son's death I was not much more than thirty-eight years old, and therefore many, as well as my lord and myself, entertained some hopes of my having more children. But it pleased God to deny that great and desired blessing to us, and I cannot but acknowledge a just hand of God in not granting us our petition. For when I was first married, and had my two children so fast, I feared much having so many, and was troubled when I found myself to be with child so soon, out of a proud conceit I had that if I childed so thick it would spoil what my great vanity then made me to fancy was tolerable (at least) in my person; and out of a proud opinion, too, that I had, that if I had many to provide for they must be poor; because of my lord's small estate; which my vanity made me not endure well to think of. And my husband, too, was in some measure guilty of the same fault; for though he was at as great a rate fond of his two children he had, as any father could be, yet when he had had two, he would often say he feared he should have so many as would undo a younger brother; and therefore I cannot but take notice of God's withholding that mercy from us when we so much needed it, being we were unthankful for them we had, and durst not trust to His good providence for more, if he saw fit to give them to us.

❧

John Verney (b. 1640), known as Jack, writes to his wife Elizabeth (1664–1686) when she is pregnant with her third child. Elizabeth died three years later, leaving four children.

### 1683

... everything that the Lovingest of husbands can express to the best of wives, & love to the little ones not forgetting the kicker in the dark.

Margaret, Countess of Wemyss (1659–1705) gives good advice to her pregnant daughter Anne: eat well, be confident and cheerful.

## Scotland, 1695

I long to hear if you be grown big yet and if you keep your meat well. I hope you will grow stronger and be better and better with every child till all the twenty be born that you used to wish for. . . .

My sister writes me word that you look very well. I pray God it may continue. There is nothing so good for you and the child both as to be merry, so I entreat you let not any thing that falls out disquiet and vex you for it never alters the matter that troubles us and does much displease and dishonour God.

෴

Frances Boscawen (1719–1805) was a letter writer and literary hostess. In 1742 she married Edward Boscawen (1711–1761), who ended up an admiral in the English Navy. They had five children and Frances gained a reputation as the ideal wife and mother. Even so, in this letter to her husband who was away at sea, she admits her terror of childbirth: most women must have felt just the same.

## 28th April, 1747

The near approach of my labour terrifies me and sinks my spirits to a degree that you would be sorry to be witness of. Indeed, were you here, it would not be thus. I frequently get no sleep of nights, and not through indulging in a morning, for I do not breakfast in bed, nor continue there longer than nine – seldom so long. I was obliged to send for Sandys [the doctor], and he ordered me to be blooded, which I was, and on sight of the blood he said I had very great occasion for it.

## 18th May

I thought to have increased the number of them [children] as long ago as this day se'enight. I was taken ill in the afternoon and continued in pain all night, so that at 5 a.m. I sent for Mrs Chapman . . . and, at noon, I informed the doctor how I was – but without desiring any of his assistance, for I did not think it was time for that. And I judged right, for I have continued much in the same way ever since; sometimes in pain so that I think execution is at hand; sometimes quite easy, much as I was with the boy, when (if you recollect) I sent for both nurses in a vast hurry and went three weeks. But I don't believe this will be so long. I have appointed it as next Wednesday, which completes the 39th week. I have been miserably terrified with the thoughts of it – such horrors and tremblings as were indeed dreadful. But now, since Saturday, I think nothing of it – I think of you and you only.

Her husband returned to England on 27th May and her third child was born the following morning.

֍

George Lyttelton, 1st Baron Lyttelton (1709–1773), was a politician and writer. I love this letter, written to his friend Sanderson Miller, which reminds us that not to be pregnant was often as much a cause for celebration as to be so. George Lyttelton sounds a most sympathetic friend and husband.

## February 1752

I congratulate you and condole with Mrs Miller on her being with child again. I know you think an increase of your Family an Encrease of your Blessings, but the poor little Woman who brings you those blessings has a great deal of trouble and pain to confer them on you, and you are bound in Return to read to her every night. My Wife is well and not a breeding.

֍

Mrs Hester Lynche Thrale (1741–1821) was a literary hostess, diarist and mother of twelve children; only five survived, all girls. A few days before this entry, Mr Thrale had had what Mrs Thrale believed to be a stroke.

## 11th June, 1779

Oh Lord have mercy on us! this is a horrible Business indeed. five little Girls too, & breeding again, & Fool enough to be proud of it! ah, Ideot! what should I want more Children for? God knows only to please my Husband, who now perhaps may be much better without them.

Mary Wollstonecraft (1759–1797) was a passionate believer in women's rights and author of the influential *A Vindication of the Rights of Women*, published in 1792. Mary writes to Gilbert Imlay who was a speculator, diplomat and womaniser. They had met and become lovers in Paris in 1793 during the Revolution. In September of that year she was registered at the American Embassy as his wife although they had not married, but she had become pregnant with her daughter Fanny.

## Paris, November 1793

Ever since you last saw me inclined to faint, I have felt some gentle twitches, which make me begin to think, that I am nourishing a creature who will soon be sensible of my care. – This thought has not only produced an overflowing of tenderness to you, but made me very attentive to calm my mind and take exercise, lest I should destroy an object, in whom we are to have a mutual interest, you know.

## Paris, January 1794

Considering the care and anxiety a woman must have about a child before it comes into the world, it seems to me, by a *natural right*, to belong to her. When men get immersed in the world, they seem to lose all sensations, excepting those necessary to continue or produce life! – Are these the privileges of reason? Amongst the feathered race, whilst the hen keeps the young warm, her mate stays by to cheer her; but it is sufficient for man to condescend to get a child, in order to claim it. – A man is a tyrant!

❦

Samuel Taylor Coleridge (1772–1834), the Romantic poet, had three children, in whom he sometimes took an imaginative interest.

The history of man for the nine months preceding his birth would probably be far more interesting and certain events of greater moment than all the threescore and ten years that follow it.

Sydney Smith (1771–1845) was a wit, writer and somewhat unwilling, although ultimately much admired, clergyman. He established, edited and wrote for the *Edinburgh Review*, in which he defended the emancipation of women, Catholics and the abolition of slavery. He writes the following to his friend Francis Jeffrey before the birth of his second child.

## 16th February, 1805

I am sure you will be glad to hear of Mrs. S. first. I have been expecting that she would be brought to bed every night for the last eight days, but to the amazement of the obstetric world she is still as pregnant as the Trojan Horse.

ᘛ

Edward Stanley, 2nd Baron Alderley (1802–1869) and Under-Secretary of State for Foreign Affairs, writes a frank and patronising letter to his wife Henrietta (1807–1895) on hearing that she is pregnant again. They already had ten children. She was a successful political hostess who believed strongly in women's education; after her husband's death, she helped to found Girton College, the Girls' Public Day School Trust and the Medical College for Women.

## 9th November, 1847

My dearest love,

This your last misfortune is indeed most grievous & puts all others in the shade. What can you have been doing to account for so juvenile a proceeding, it comes very opportunely to disturb all your family arrangements and revives the nursery . . . I only hope it is not the beginning of another flock for what to do with them I am sure I know not. I am afraid however it is too late to mend & you must make the best of it tho' bad is best.

Henrietta to Edward on the same day:

Dearest love,
   A hot bath, a tremendous walk & a great dose have succeeded but it is a warning.

Edward to Henrietta:

10th November

I hope you are not going to do yourself any harm by your violent proceedings, for though it would be a great bore it is not worth while playing tricks to escape its consequences. If however you are none the worse the great result is all the better.

Henrietta to Edward:

10th November

I was sure you would feel the same horror I did at an increase of family but I am reassured for the future by the efficacy of the means.

❧

The poet Elizabeth Barrett Browning (1806–1861) writes her diary before the birth of her son in March 1849. Her husband, the poet Robert Browning (1812–1889), was presumably even more anxious than many new fathers of the time, because Elizabeth had been an invalid for most of her life until she met and married Browning four years earlier.

Two days before, when I had caught cold and was not well and made him more nervous than usual about me, he wished to heaven that the living creature would exhale and disappear in some mystical way without doing me any harm.

The novelist Anthony Trollope (1815–1882) writes to his elder brother Tom on hearing that Tom is to be a father. Tom beat Anthony throughout his schooldays but Anthony was a loving father and not a beater.

### 5th October, 1852

I am glad you are to have a child. One wants some one to exercise unlimited authority over, as one gets old and cross. If one blows up one's servants too much, they turn round, give warning, and repay one with interest. One's wife may be too much for one, and is not always a safe recipient for one's wrath. But one's children can be blown up to any amount without damage, – at any rate, for a considerable number of years. The pleasures of paternity have been considerably abridged, since the good old Roman privilege of slaying their offspring at pleasure, has been taken from fathers. But the delights of flagellation, though less keen, are more enduring. One can kill but once; but one may flog daily, and always quote Scripture to prove that it is a duty. And then the gratification of disinheriting a disobedient son, and sending him adrift, with the determination that no calf shall be killed on his return!

A daughter, I fear, does not offer so much innocent enjoyment. But some fathers do manage to torment their daughters with a great degree of very evident and enviable satisfaction. I have none, and therefore have not turned my attention to that branch of the subject.

❦

Queen Victoria (1819–1901) writes to her eldest daughter Victoria (1840–1901), aged eighteen and recently married to the Crown Prince of Prussia.

### 30th June, 1858

I delight in the idea of being a grandmama; to be that at 39 (D.V.) and to look and feel young is great fun, only I wish I could go through it for you, dear, and save you all the annoyance. But that can't be helped. I think of my next birthday being spent with my children and a grandchild. It will be a treat!

Ida John (1877–1907), wife of the artist Augustus John, writes to console his mistress, Dorelia McNeill, who is expecting her first child. Ida had five children by John (whom she called Gus) and Dorelia had two; David was Ida's eldest son.

## 1905

My dear, men always seem indifferent about babies – that is, men of our sort. You must not think Gus is more so over yours than he was over mine. He never said anything about David except 'don't spill it'.

ᘙᘗ

Diana Cooper (1892–1986), beautiful and idiosyncratic muse to many writers and artists, was married to the politician Duff Cooper. For many years she failed to conceive a child. She looked back on that time in her memoir, *Trumpets from the Steep.*

. . . I had made the best of my barrenness and persuaded myself that children were sharper than serpents' teeth. Girls were sure to be plain and without virtue, boys dishonest, even queer, and certainly gambling drunkards.

But while abroad on holiday in 1929, after ten years of marriage, she suspects that she might at last be pregnant:

I could find no calm. . . . my mind was all but closed to outer things. It was totally wrapped in whether or not I was going to have a child. I was alive to that thought only. . . .

I was not long away, being every day surer of my secret and anxious to curtail the excursion. . . . I knew that Duff, not having had to invent a consolatory philosophy as I had, would be happier at the prospect than I, who was only slowly appreciating what was coming to me. I was singing the Magnificat for Duff, not yet for myself, but as the months passed I became obsessed with joy and pride. 'Late in time' made this child more to be adored.

. . . we retired from wordly labours, Duff to start his book on Talleyrand and I to marvel and dream about my child, very happy though a little apprehensive, marking auguries and omens.

Lorna Sage (1943–2001) was a literary critic and author of the memoir *Bad Blood*. In 1959, aged sixteen, Lorna is married and secretly pregnant while doing her A levels at school.

I tried to eat as little as possible, but it didn't work, and by December I was grateful for the shapelessness of school uniform and had swapped my skimpy Silhouette girdle for a heavy-duty version, bones and all. There was only one occasion when I felt close to being found out, but that is etched on my memory with panic's acids, complete with the kind of circumstantial detail that usually you don't store away because it's so ordinary and innocent. The school hall had an upper gallery that served as a corridor linking classrooms, and also as a vantage point for watching gym displays, drama rehearsals and so on. I cannot recall what was happening that day on the floor below, but one of my friends or fans – a fat girl who admired me – had dragged a stool from the biology lab to the balustrade. As I passed by she reached out, put an arm round my waist, pulled me on to her lap before I could escape and exclaimed with what sounded like triumphant malice, 'Ooh! You've put on weight!' In that moment the smell of formaldehyde from the rats pinned out on boards in the lab, and the familiar, claustrophobic feel of the closeness of other girls' bodies, inspired such fear and nausea that I was beside myself. I was an outsider, harbouring an alien, an alien myself. Having such a secret was like having cancer – a disease which couldn't be mentioned except in shamed whispers.

❧

Laurie Lee (1914–1997), writer and poet, encourages his daughter Yasmin during her pregnancy in 1963:

. . . the rarest orchids are always the most trouble to grow.

# BIRTH

Very few women celebrate the process of giving birth, however quickly they claim to forget the pain. In the past the problems and dangers were the same for everyone, but there is still no certainty for any woman that the delivery will be as free from pain or risk as they might hope, even though the use of drugs in childbirth has become widespread.

With some exceptions, it is the fathers who record the outcome: in 1659, William Blundell is unenthusiastic about the birth of his daughter and tenth child ('the thing is called Bridget') while, in the nineteenth century, Oscar Wilde shows real delight at the birth of his first son. The seventeenth-century vicar Ralph Josselin is unusual in giving a close description of his wife's many births.

In earlier centuries, mothers seldom wrote about their labour, but by the twentieth century there is a sharp contrast between an upper-class home birth, as described by Daphne Fielding, and the tough early NHS experience of Lorna Sage. Susan Hill gave birth at the same time as I did, in the 1970s; she writes with wry humour of the unforgiving English hospital delivery of that time. In this chapter I have included the only Irish writer in the book, Fergal Keane, who takes a broad, sombre view of fatherhood at the start of the twenty-first century.

Margaret Paston writes to her husband, John, to tell him the story of a neighbour and enemy of theirs, whose wife has given birth to a child by another man.

### 8th July, 1444

Heydon's wife had her child on Saint Peter's Day. I have heard since that her husband wants nothing to do with her, nor with the child she has just had either. I heard it said that he said that if she came into his presence to make her excuse, he would cut off her nose so that everyone would know what she was, and if the child came into his presence, he would kill it. He will not be persuaded to have her back on any account, so I hear.

❧

John Donne (1572–1631), poet and influential clergyman, writes to his friend Sir Robert Ker. The following year his wife Anne died in giving birth to her eleventh child.

### 17th April, 1615

... I see that I stand like a tree, which once a year bears, though no fruit, yet this mast of children ...

❧

Before the birth of her third child, Lady Mary Verney (1616–1650) writes to her husband, Sir Ralph Verney (1613–1696), who is in exile in France. Though he took the side of the Parliament during the Civil War, he went into exile rather than accept Cromwell's alliance with the Scottish and presbyters; his estates were threatened so Mary had returned to England to lobby Parliament on his behalf.

### 11th March, 1647

If itt be a boy I am resolved to have itt of thy owne name, therefore I charge you doe nott contredict itt; but if itt be a gerle I leave it wholly to thee to chuse. ... I will be governed by thee in anything but the name if it be a boy, for to tell the truth I must have itt have thy name.

Ralph to Mary:

## 7th April

Now for the name. If it bee a girle and that you have noe conceit because the other died, I desire it may bee Mary; but if it bee a boy, in earnest you must not deny mee, let it bee Richard or what you please, except my owne name. Really I shall take it ill if you contradict mee in this. If it bee a sonne I trust God will make him a better and a happier man than his father.

Mary (at the foot of a letter from her doctor to Ralph):

## 3rd June

This is onely to lett you know that I thang god I have a great boy and wish my selfe and boy with thee. I can say noe more.

Ralph to Mary:

## 20th June

My deare Budd, the longer your letters were the more they were woont to please mee, but I must confesse the three lines you writ me at the end of Dr.'s letter dated 3rd June pleased mee above any that I have yett received from you, because they assured me of thy safe delivery which is a most unspeakable blessing to us both; God make us thankful for it. If the boye's name is Richard I shall hope he may bee a happy man; but if it bee otherwise I will not prophecie his ill-fortune, but rather pray to God to make him an honest man, and then he will be happy enough.

On 17th June, the baby was christened Ralph.

William Blundell (1620–1698) was a recusant Catholic landowner. Often cruelly sarcastic about the births of his children, he seems to have brought them up with kindness and he proved a devoted grandfather. He writes to a friend, Madam Giffard, on the birth of his sixth daughter and ninth child.

## 1653

My wife hath much disappointed my hopes in bringing forth a Daughter which, finding herself not so welcome in this world as a Son, hath made already a discreet choice of a better. . . . Wherefore I am now resolved to have none hereafter but boys, goodly gallant boys for Bishops.

But bishops turned out to be in short supply, and he doesn't hide his irritation when he writes to his seventeen-year-old son Nicholas.

## 16th May, 1659

Your mother was well delivered of her tenth daughter upon the 30th of March (the thing is called Bridget) so that now you have had three sisters born in the space of thirty-two months. You may well think that this is not the way to get rich.

❧❧

Ralph Josselin (1616–1683) was a Puritan vicar who lived with his family in Essex throughout his life; he kept a diary that is considered as revealing of his time and place as Pepys' diary is of his. Here he describes the births of two of his ten children; the first entry is about the birth of his third child, Jane.

## 24th November, 1645

I had sought to god for my wife (that was oppressed with feares that she should not doe well on this child,) that god would order all providences so as wee might rejoyce in his salvacion, I had prayd with confidence of good success to her: about midnight on Monday: I rose called up some neighbours: the night was very light: goodman Potter willing to goe for the midwife, and up when I went: the horse out of the pasture, but presently found: the midwife up at Buers, expecting it had beene nearer day; the weather indifferent dry; midwife came, all things even gotten ready towards day. I called in the women by day light, almost all came; and about 11 or 12 of the clocke my wife was with very sharpe paynes deliverd. Nov: 25. of her daughter intended for a Jane, she was then 25. y of age her selfe; wee had made a good pasty for this houre, and that also was kept well, wife and child both well prais bee my good and mercifull father.

*Thirteen years and four births later, Josselin records how frightened his wife is during this long labour, how much help the neighbours give compared to the midwife, and how strongly he shares the emotion of the birth and the joy of the child's survival.*

### 12th January, 1658

Baptized my neighbour Burtons son, at night the midwife with us, my wife thinking shee might use her, but being sent for my wife let her goe, that another that was in present need might bee holpen, and it was a mercy to us so to dispose my wives heart, her going tending to save a poore womans life, but within halfe an houre, as soon as I had done family prayer, my wife had so sure a signe of her labour and speedie that put us all to a plunge, I sent 2 messengers after her and it was at least 4 houres before shee came. Mr R.H. man fetcht her, but shee came time enough for us god bee praised, my wife was wonderfully afraid and amazed but helpe was speedily with her and in particular young Mrs Harlakenden, who put forth her selfe to the utmost to helpe her, and her presence was much to my wife.

### 13th January

her pains ceased, the labour very strange to her, which sett her heart, but her eye was towards him who is the helper, my faith was up for her, shee judged at the labour it would bee a daughter. contrary to all her former experience and thought; prayer was for her; wee commended her to god and her warm bed early and all to their rests, none watching this night as formerly. her sleep was a comfort to her mixed with pain, feare, which made her quake and tremble

14th January

and so increased on her by two of the clocke in this morning that I called up the midwife, and nurse, gott fires and all redie, and then her labour came on so strongly and speedily that the child was borne only 2 or 3 women more gott in to her but god supplied all, young Mrs Harlakenden gott up to us very speedily, and some others; my wives labour was different from all former exceeding sharpe, shee judged her midwife did not doe her part, but god did all, and hath given us new experience of his goodnes, the child was dead when borne, I blesse god who recovered it to life, we baptized it this day by the name of Mary, young Mrs Harlakenden holding it in my wives place god hath evened my number and made up the three which he tooke from me my heart was very lightsom and joyful in the god of my mercie

⊙⥮⊙

Henry Fox (1705–1774) was a highly influential statesman of the day who made a suspect fortune as Paymaster General; he became the first Lord Holland in 1763. He writes to his brother, Lord Ilchester, on the birth of his third son Charles James Fox (1749–1806), who also became an influential statesman and politician.

14th January, 1749

After a safe quick labour, which lasted but from a little after nine till within a few minutes of twelve last night, Lady Caroline was brought to bed of a boy. He was a good deal wasted and is weakly, but likely to live. His skin hangs all shrivell'd about him, his eyes stare, he has a black head of hair, and 'tis incredible how much like a monkey he look'd before he was dressed.

Henry, 10th Earl of Pembroke (1734–1794) writes to his son George Augustus, (1759–1827) on the birth of George's first child. The congratulations are expressed in the nonchalant style of the time with a sly emphasis on his son being 'legitimately' a father.

### 4th April, 1788

Much joy to you, my dear George, & many thanks to you for the early intelligence of your being legitimately a father. My love to Elizabeth. Tell her that I shall be very fond of my grand son; but beg she will not make me kiss him till he has attained that certain age at which children leave off smelling sour.

❧

Mary Talbot sends a message to Maria, her stepmother, after her delivery. The complaint is a fair one: many mothers are unprepared for sickness when they give birth.

### 1795

Pray tell Maria she gave me but a poor idea of what I was to suffer at the time, and several things disappointed me very much, particularly as she told me it was not a sickening pain, but I was dreadfully sick for many hours before, every paroxysm brought on violent sickness.

❧

Thomas Fremantle (1765–1819), a successful naval officer, writes to his wife Betsey on the birth of their daughter. (Harriet was Betsey's sister.)

### off Cadiz, 1st October, 1805

My Dearest Betsey,

I have seen and dined with Lord Nelson, – he shows me the same kindness and attention he has ever done. . . . he told me, I should have my old place in the Line of battle, which is *his second*, this is exactly what is the most flattering to me in every point of view, he desired me to come to him whenever I chose, and to dine with him as often as I could make it convenient in short I am quite pleased with his manner towards me, he in the most friendly way delivered himself Harriets letter announcing your accouchement. – and now my Dearest Woman let me congratulate you on your recovery, . . .

. . . I find I love you not a little my ever dearest Woman, kiss the newcomer for me, . . . what is it that makes me think so much more of my Girls than my boys? Lord Nelson on presenting me with Harriet's letter asked me if I would have a Girl or a boy, I answd, the former, when he put the letter into my hand and told me to be satisfied . . .

ॐ

Augustus J.C. Hare (1834–1903) was a biographer, travel writer and storyteller, as is apparent in this extract from the story of his aunt, who adopted him after the death of his uncle, written in 1896.

. . . my father's most earnest wish was to comfort his widowed sister-in-law, and in the hope of arousing an interest which might still give some semblance of an earthly tie to one who seemed then upon the very borderland of heaven, he entreated, when I was born in the following month, that she would become my godmother, promising that she should be permitted to influence my future in any way she pleased . . .

I was baptized on the 1st April in the Villa Strozzi [in Rome] . . . Soon afterwards, my godmother returned to England . . . [where] it occurred to [her] as just possible that my parents might be induced to give me up to her altogether. In July she wrote her petition, and was almost surprised at the glad acceptance it met with. Mrs. Hare's answer was brief – 'My dear Maria, how very kind of you! Yes, certainly, the baby shall be sent as soon as it is weaned; and, if any one else would like one, would you kindly recollect that we have others.'

William Makepeace Thackeray (1811–1863) writes to his mother-in-law, Mrs Shawe, on the birth of his second daughter Jane. This is a poignant letter: Jane died the following year and in 1840, after giving birth to another daughter, Harriet, Thackeray's wife Isabella had a mental breakdown, from which she never recovered; she was confined to a home in Paris for the rest of her life.

12th July, 1838

My dear Mrs. Shawe.

We had intended to keep profoundly secret an invent wh. has just occurred. Mrs. Thack after walking to Piccadilly on Monday, and eating a tolerable dinner requested me to fetch a medical gentleman wh. I did, and on my return had the pleasure to find another Miss Thackeray arrived in my family, and her mother just as unconcerned as if nothing had happened. The child is hideous of course, but when I left home in the morning I left Isabella perfectly happy, giving her a nice milk breakfast: and as cool and as comfortable as any woman could be. . . . She produces children with a remarkable facility. . . .

Miss Thackeray on seeing her new sister wanted to poke one of her eyes out and said teedle deedle, wh. is considered very clever . . .

❧

Queen Victoria writes to her daughter Victoria, the Princess Royal, who was aged only nineteen at the birth of her first child.

23rd February, 1859

These last two days, telegrams have cheered and delighted me more than words can say. I see a decided progress, and hope each day you will feel stronger and better. Occasional lowness and tendency to cry you must expect. You of all people would be inclined to this; and I am quite agreeably surprised to hear from Sir James how little you suffered with this; for it is what every lady suffers with more or less and what I, during my two first confinements, suffered dreadfully with.

9th March

Your dear affectionate letter of the 6th reached me today and I thank you and with all my heart for it. It is quite like your own dear self again and it is a pleasure to see how you feel like me even on all those distressing subjects so painful to a woman's feelings and especially to a young child as you are! Poor dear darling! I pitied you so! It is indeed too hard and dreadful what we have to go through and men ought to have an adoration for one, and indeed to do everything to make up, for what after all they alone are the cause of! I must say it is a bad arrangement, but we must calmly, patiently bear it, and feel that we can't help it and therefore we must forget it, and the more we retain our pure, modest feelings, the easier it is to get over it all afterwards.

∾

Oscar Wilde (1854–1900), the writer and wit, writes to Norman Forbes-Robertson in ebullient spirits at the birth of his first son by his wife, Constance.

16 Tite Street, June 1885

Dear Norman, Thanks for your congratulations. Yes, come tomorrow. The baby is wonderful: it has a bridge to its nose! which the nurse says is a proof of genius! It also has a superb voice, which it freely exercises: its style is essentially Wagnerian.

Constance is doing capitally and is in excellent spirits.

I was delighted to get your telegram. You must get married *at once*!

Ever yours
Oscar

Aldous Huxley (1894–1963), a modern writer, tells Arnold Bennett (1867–1931), an Edwardian writer, of the birth of his first and only child.

### 1920

The works of nature really do put works of art in the shade.

❧

Marie Stopes (1880–1958), birth control pioneer and eugenicist, comments on the birth of her only, desperately desired child in an interview she gave to the *Daily Express*.

### 14th April, 1924

'The sister at the nursing home where he was born told me that she had never seen such a beautiful new-born baby in the whole of her career . . . That is what comes of birth control. You get your babies when you want them and at the right time. You get the good, strong babies and cut out the weaklings.'

❧

Antonia White (1899–1980) was a novelist and mother of two daughters by different fathers. She had a nervous breakdown aged twenty-two and began a lifetime of psychoanalysis in her thirties: none the less she showed a lack of imagination and understanding towards her daughters which led to difficulties in their relationship with her as they grew up. Her eldest daughter, Susan Chitty (b. 1929), edited her diaries for publication; Si was Susan's father.

### 25th June, 1938

I didn't feel the tremendous excitement and satisfaction in having a baby that most women seem to feel. I half felt it with Susan, but it was clouded by all the difficult circumstances, Si's not being there, not having it as a proper married woman, and above all the disappointment of her not being a boy. I suppose I want a book in some funny way to be a male child, something powerful, able to fertilise other people. I can understand the extraordinary satisfaction of producing a son. A woman has not a penis but she can produce a being with a real penis. I did once, anyhow, conceive a son. I wonder if the realisation of that was what made me so extraordinarily happy and peaceful after that abortion [1924] which was in so many ways a very distressing experience. It was as if after that I really recovered from insanity and collected my wits again . . . My impulse to write a novel began in the year following the beginning of menstruation. My father, as it were, killed the child. He thought of it as having been conceived in sin. Just about ten years later, I conceived a real child, about the same time of year, this time definitely 'in sin' and to my father's horrified disapproval. This time my father wishes me to go on and have the child, in very distressing circumstances, as a punishment . . . I suddenly remember something I had forgotten – I cheated him over the money, told him the injections cost £1 each time instead of 10/– . . . He was very kind to me when I was in pain and had to go to the nursing home . . . I borrowed £30 from him (he was reluctant) in connection with Susan's birth . . . He was more willing to lend money for the abortion than for the birth of a child. If Susan had been a boy, he told me he would have found it far easier to overlook the circumstances of her birth. It was a great distress to him that all his children were girls . . . I think he felt it in some ways to be a punishment . . .

⊙⦚

*Vivien Greene (1905–2003) was married to the novelist Graham Greene; she gave birth to her first child Lucy in Oxford, on 28th December, 1933. It was a traumatic and frightening experience, which she remembers many years later.*

It was like a train running slowly into the buffers. You can see the accident from afar and then the birth comes. In those days no one told you. Lucy was born in that horrible Radcliffe Hospital in Oxford. . . . Graham was just beginning to do well and we had moved to Woodstock Road. It was very bad anyway. In those days they didn't look at you beforehand. Lucy was a really bad birth. It was very bad and they were very unfriendly, horrible nurses. They didn't look at you, they didn't weigh you or take your blood pressure. I think I saw the doctor twice before I had her and I was extremely ignorant. I remember asking, 'Will it hurt much?' and he said 'We'll see.' That was Dr Shurrock. It certainly did hurt. Chloroform, after a long, long time – 28 hours was quite enough. The gas and air went wrong. It had to be a caesarean and they were so brutal about the stitches. I remember that awful head nurse or sister coming to me and saying, 'Oh this room smells' and flinging open the window and I said, 'I can't do anything about it – I can't get up.' And she came up and leant over me and said, 'Don't you talk to me like that!' It was terrifying.

❧

Daphne Fielding (1904–1997) was a writer, society beauty and mother of the present Marquis of Bath. In her autobiography, *Mercury Presides*, she describes the experience of an upper-class home birth.

My third son Valentine was born in 1937. One forgets the experience of giving birth so quickly. This time I was determined to remember it and, from this detailed account which I wrote immediately afterwards, I am able to recapture the moment:

'For several days I had been having contractions in my stomach and quite a few little pains, recurring about every twenty minutes, only to stop after a while. Always I welcomed them, eagerly thinking the battle was on, but always they vanished into nothing. I told no one but Henry about them, because I feel foolish and a fraud when Nanny B. and Mr. Gilliatt sit waiting and nothing happens.

'On the evening of November 4th we went to the cinema to see *Stella Dallas*, very appropriate, Locke's drama of maternal love triumphant, full of sacrifice and selflessness. My nose bled and I blubbed. I looked hideous; my one and only skirt clung to my vastness like a glove. My once swagger coat was like a bum-freezer. When pregnant, my wretched legs are dwarfed to sparrow-like proportions by the hugeness of my stomach, which the poor spindly things can barely support.

'I took off my hateful maternity clothes for the last time. Before I got into bed I felt little niggly pains – very faint and undisturbing. I read for a bit and they continued vaguely grumbling. I went to sleep until 2.30, and woke up with them still going on at regular intervals of half an hour. I read *The Tatler* over and over again, advertisements and all, and tried to keep very quiet and not wake Henry because I was still not convinced that the pains had come to stay, and I wanted to surprise him with them well started.

'Henry woke up at about 3.30 and would not go to sleep again. He kept on asking me how I was and trying to do a cross-word puzzle aloud. He insisted on waking up Nanny B. after an hour.

'When she arrived all dressed in her war-paint, white starched cap and comforting, creaking waist-belt, I felt that the curtain had really gone up and the pains would soon open in full orchestra. The baby was kicking, which I thought showed character.

'Nanny B. and Henry became terribly busy, unpacking sterilized things and putting out enamel bowls and dust sheets. The house was woken up and I decided I might as well have a bath. After this I was draped in Nanny B.'s red flannel dressing-gown, and sat reading *Richard II* in front of the fire. I opened it at John of Gaunt's dying speech, but never seemed able to get beyond the first few lines before a pain came crashing in to interrupt "This teeming womb of royal kings".

'We drank lots of cups of tea. There is something physically comforting in the mere sound of the words "nice cup of tea", especially in the way darling Nanny B. says it.

'Some bad pains began to come, seizing the pit of my back like a relentless beast, gripping my vitals in its teeth, and then slowly letting go.

'I can never decide how it is best to meet the pains – in what position – lying, sitting, standing or kneeling.

'There is no moving once a pain has its teeth in you, because the strength for movement just isn't there. It is all concentrated on wrestling with the pain.

'Mr. Gilliatt came at seven on the morning of the 5th. He felt the contractions of my stomach. They were coming good and strong and I welcomed them knowing that I would soon be given chloroform. Mr. Gilliatt sounded me, listening for the baby's heart.

'I thought something was a little wrong because he could not hear it for a time and it seemed to me that it might be the same thing as Timmy [her second child, born with a failed lung, who died at eleven months]. He did a lot of telephoning to get an anaesthetist; there seemed to be some difficulty. He had breakfast with Henry at 8 o'clock and stayed downstairs about half an hour, which seemed endless. The pains were coming heavy and fast. They just gave me time to walk once round my bed before they caught me again. I was wet with sweat. 'My body is the slave of pain' I kept on saying. Some cats screamed in the street and the noise seemed to be the song of my pain.

'Mr. Gilliatt came up. "I can't bear it any more", I said. "And neither shall you", he replied. (Actually I could have borne a little more).

'They started giving me chloroform. Nanny B. did not give it well; it was either too much or too little, and the cotton wool seemed to smother me and burn my nose, nevertheless it was balm. Roy Saunders arrived to give me the anaesthetic. I vaguely took him in; he had helped with Christopher's birth. Whenever they let me come round the pains seemed to be crushing me and all my strength pressed down to fight them out. Roy Saunders is really a gynaecologist but gave the chloroform beautifully. How I love it – the buzzing, swimming feelings, the dreams which solve every thing. I become a Jimmy-Know-All in the ether.

'I came to in my own big bed, crying, and wanting to see Henry. "Lady Weymouth, you have got a beautiful little boy . . . a beautiful little boy . . . a beautiful little boy . . . " Another boy? I wished it was triplets, or black . . . or a furry little animal, different in some way . . . not just a boy. But the baby was there, a new person . . . I opened my eyes, sat up quickly and asked for the child. Unutterably sweet was the new little son shown to his mother. Even then the pain began to be forgotten.'

❦

The writer Lorna Sage gave birth as a young, poor, unknown mother in a National Health hospital in 1960. She was aged seventeen and still at school doing her A levels; Vic was her husband.

When we got there, around 3.30, I stepped down into a puddle of my own making, in a state of panic. The Sister on duty, who seemed instantly to know that I was late on purpose, briskly slapped me in the face two or three times, sent Vic off back to Whitchurch with the ambulance and hauled me into the Delivery Room.

There, time caught up with me. While the slap-happy Sister woke the doctor, I lay where she'd put me and watched the clock on the wall between my knees. Things were happening too fast. 'Don't push!' she yelled (she wanted the doctor to be there) but I couldn't stop pushing, and although it felt as if I was being torn apart (I was) and the second hand loitered round the dial as slowly as it does for someone on speed, the adrenalin of my fright and my seventeen-year-old's abdominal muscles soon brought an end. The ruffled, sleepy Indian locum who arrived, pinning up her thick plait of hair, was too late, the Sister was already crooking my nerveless arm around a baby girl (girl!) wrapped in a blanket, her face streaked with blood (I remember thinking, whose? mine?) and whisking her away again. Then it was all over except for the stitches, which hurt like hell, so they gave me some gas and air, and left me alone until the real morning came. I watched the clock, fascinated. It was still only 4.15, the liminal pre-dawn hour, and I'd never felt so awake, as though I'd died and been born again knowing how to tell the time. Ages later an orderly pushed a mop into the room and, seeing me there, brought me a cup of hot, sweet tea under telepathic orders from my mother, and I was immediately, violently sick (never mind, said she, mopping it up) and fell asleep.

❧

Laurie Lee's wife and his illegitimate daughter Yasmin gave birth on the same day. He and his wife Kathy (Lee spells her name with a C) had been married for thirteen years. He was besotted with their child in the way middle-aged fathers often are. He writes about the births in his diary:

Monday Sept 30, 1963, two girls, daughter & granddaughter.

Of his daughter:

She was wrinkled & purple, her head bruised darkly from the birth, skinny, with an old woman's hands & tiny bent legs. She curled back her lips to wail and I saw Cathy's mouth. . . . I kissed her forehead & she lay still. The first flattery.

Laurie wrote later:

The birth of my child meant a farewell to the child bride who bore her.

Kenneth Tynan (1927–1980), influential theatre critic, had three children: two daughters and a son. He writes his diary after the birth of his son. Even on this occasion, Tynan is capriciously egocentric.

9th June, 1971

At 3.30 pm., a son – 7lb. 3½ oz. – to be called Matthew (after K.'s father) Blake (after William Blake and James Blake, the American convict author) Tynan. I had thought I could sire only girls and rather wanted a third. She would have been exquisitely named Angelica Tiffany Tynan and when the nurse told me the child was a boy, I spoke aloud a short farewell to Angelica Tiffany, who had emerged briefly from the shadows and now receded into them. What I feared was a husky thug of a boy: I do not like male competition – in fact I am not all that crazy about men *per se* – so I was much relieved to find that Matthew is sensitive, almost *girlish* – looking – resembles Roxana when she was born. So long as he develops my feminine streak he will be very welcome. I shall shortly buy him a few pretty frocks and enter him for Sadler's Wells Ballet School. K. is positively glowing with earth-motherliness. She has always wanted a boy and now she *has* one. I begin to feel almost superfluous. The problem about this child will not be that *Roxana* may feel overshadowed, but that *I* may – a situation of which Freud had omitted to warn me.

❧

Rebecca West (1892–1983), novelist, gave birth to an illegitimate son by H.G. Wells in 1914. Reflecting on motherhood in old age, she makes an implicit contrast with her own creative writing.

18th February, 1971

Life makes itself. I cannot see that childbirth is creative at all, one is just an instrument, and it's none the worse for that.

Susan Hill (b.1942), novelist, describes giving birth on the NHS in 1977, a time when procedures were dominated by medical mechanics.

Whenever I think about that day, 14 July 1977, I reflect that ten years or so later, things would probably have been very different . . . women now have so much more choice about labour, that routine induction for convenience and 'social reasons' is now rarer. Women can walk about, sit, stand, kneel, adopt whatever position is comfortable for them in labour, within safe and sensible margins – can even give birth under water, in some circumstances. A happier environment in the labour room, belief that interference by machines and drugs should be the exception and when necessary, not the norm; the practice, in many hospitals, of making sure that the woman in labour is looked after by the same midwife throughout, whenever possible, not by a procession of new and strange ones. So much of this is taken for granted now, even if it may not be absolutely universal. . . .

As it was, from the moment we arrived, shortly after nine o'clock in the morning, technology and the efficient routine took over. I was undressed and got into one of those unflattering, billowing shrouds which fall open all the way down the back, exposing your backside to the world, and taken into the delivery room. It looked like an operating theatre – high narrow couch, tiles, gleaming instruments, gas and air machine, huge lights, sink, chrome taps with long arms; it was painted green and cream – of course – and there was a tall window at the far end, frosted over so that it let in a curiously deadened, greyish light. The whole reminded me of the dentist's surgery as much as anything – and I'd had some pretty horrendous times in *those* in the past.

I stepped onto a stool to help me climb onto the delivery bed and as I did so, my waters broke; gallons of warm wetness, it seemed, gushed down my legs and all over the floor, messy, embarrassing – though no one minded, everyone took it for granted.

More indignities to come: internal examination, shaving of pubic hair – routine, then, rarely done for normal deliveries now. For some reason, Stanley was asked to leave the room while this went on, and only allowed back when I was decent again. I lay on my back, feeling vaguely unsafe, as if I might easily roll off the narrow bed, and uncomfortable, too – flat on your back is the most miserable of positions during late pregnancy and, of course, the least efficient position in which to give birth. But that was the way it had to be – nobody's fault particularly, except that of the system.

༜

*Fergal Keane (b.1961) is a writer and journalist. He writes a letter to his son Daniel Patrick, shortly after the baby's birth on 4th February, 1996 in Hong Kong.*

My dear son, it is six o'clock in the morning on the island of Hong Kong. You are asleep cradled in my left arm and I am learning the art of one-handed typing. Your mother, more tired yet more happy than I've ever known her, is sound asleep in the room next door and there is soft quiet in our apartment.

Since you've arrived, days have melted into night and back again and we are learning a new grammar, a long sentence whose punctuation marks are feeding and winding and nappy changing and these occasional moments of quiet.

When you're older we'll tell you that you were born in Britain's last Asian colony in the lunar year of the pig and that when we brought you home, the staff of our apartment block gathered to wish you well. "It's a boy, so lucky, so lucky. We Chinese love boys," they told us. One man said you were the first baby to be born in the block in the year of the pig. This, he told us, was good Feng Shui, in other words a positive sign for the building and everyone who lived there.

Naturally your mother and I were only too happy to believe that. We had wanted you and waited for you, imagined you and dreamed about you and now that you are here no dream can do justice to you. Outside the window, below us in the harbour, the ferries are ploughing back and forth to Kowloon. Millions are already up and moving about and the sun is slanting through the tower blocks and out on to the flat silver waters of the South China Sea. I can see the contrail of a jet over Lamma Island and, somewhere out there, the last stars flickering towards the other side of the world.

We have called you Daniel Patrick but I've been told by my Chinese friends that you should have a Chinese name as well and this glorious dawn sky makes me think we'll call you Son of the Eastern Star. So that later, when you and I are far from Asia, perhaps standing on a beach some evening, I can point at the sky and tell you of the Orient and the times and the people we knew there in the last years of the twentieth century.

Your coming has turned me upside down and inside out. So much that seemed essential to me has, in the past few days, taken on a different colour. Like many foreign correspondents I know, I have lived a life that, on occasion, has veered close to the edge: war zones, natural disasters, darkness in all its shapes and forms.

In a world of insecurity and ambition and ego, it's easy to be drawn in, to take chances with our lives, to believe that what we do and what people say about us is reason enough to gamble with death. Now, looking at your sleeping face, inches away from me, listening to your occasional sigh and gurgle, I wonder how I could have ever thought glory and prizes and praise were sweeter than life.

And it's also true that I am pained, perhaps haunted is a better word, by the memory, suddenly so vivid now, of each suffering child I have come across on my journeys. To tell you the truth, it's nearly too much to bear at this moment to even think of children being hurt and abused and killed. And yet looking at you, the images come flooding back. Ten-year-old Andi Mikail dying from napalm burns on a hillside in Eritrea, how his voice cried out, growing ever more faint, when the wind blew dust on to his wounds. The two brothers, Domingo and Juste, in Menongue, southern Angola. Juste, two years old and blind, dying from malnutrition, being carried on seven-year-old Domingo's hack. And Domingo's words to me, 'He was nice before, but now he has the hunger'.

Last October, in Afghanistan, when you were growing inside your mother, I met Sharja, aged twelve. Motherless, fatherless, guiding me through the grey ruins of her home, everything was gone, she told me. And I knew that, for all her tender years, she had learned more about loss than I would likely understand in a lifetime.

There is one last memory. Of Rwanda, and the churchyard of the parish of Nyarabuye where, in a ransacked classroom, I found a mother and her three young children huddled together where they'd been beaten to death. The children had died holding on to their mother, that instinct we all learn from birth and in one way or another cling to until we die.

Daniel, these memories explain some of the fierce protectiveness I feel for you, the tenderness and the occasional moments of blind terror when I imagine anything happening to you. But there is something more, a story from long ago that I will tell you face to face, father to son, when you are older. It's a very personal story but it's part of the picture. It has to do with the long lines of blood and family, about our lives and how we can get lost in them and, if we're lucky, find our way out again into the sunlight.

It begins thirty-five years ago in a big city on a January morning with snow on the ground and a woman walking to hospital to have her first baby. She is in her early twenties and the city is still strange to her, bigger and noisier than the easy streets and gentle hills of her distant home. She's walking because there is no money and everything of value has been pawned to pay for the alcohol to which her husband has become addicted.

On the way, a taxi driver notices her sitting, exhausted and cold, in the doorway of a shop and he takes her to hospital for free. Later that day, she gives birth to a baby boy and, just as you are to me, he is the best thing she has ever seen. Her husband comes that night and weeps with joy when he sees his son. He is truly happy. Hungover, broke, but in his own way happy, for they were both young and in love with each other and their son.

But, Daniel, time had some bad surprises in store for them. The cancer of alcoholism ate away at the man and he lost his family. This was not something he meant to do or wanted to do, it just was. When you are older, my son, you will learn about how complicated life becomes, how we can lose our way and how people get hurt inside and out. By the time his son had grown up, the man lived away from his family, on his own in a one-roomed flat, living and dying for the bottle.

He died on the fifth of January, one day before the anniversary of his son's birth, all those years before in that snowbound city. But his son was too far away to hear his last words, his final breath, and all the things they might have wished to say to one another were left unspoken.

Yet now, Daniel, I must tell you that when you let out your first powerful cry in the delivery room of the Adventist Hospital and I became a father, I thought of your grandfather and, foolish though it may seem, hoped that in some way he could hear, across the infinity between the living and the dead, your proud statement of arrival. For if he could hear, he would recognize the distinct voice of family, the sound of hope and new beginnings that you and all your innocence and freshness have brought to the world.

# NURSING

*She was only rather dirty till last night,*
*when she was quite drunk.*
*Georgiana Duchess of Devonshire, 1783*

Feeding babies turns out to be fraught with all kinds of difficulties, from the sixteenth century to the present. Men still dominate the records (although the Duke of Buckingham is the only one to invent his own feeding bottle) and they lead the endless debate about the rights and wrongs of wet-nursing.

Mothers describe their trouble with nurses, but it is only recently that they could articulate the intricate sensations of breast or bottle feeding. In the twentieth century, women finally begin to reflect on their experiences of looking after a new baby: one of the best examples is written by the contemporary novelist Rachel Cusk, who digs deeply and powerfully into the complex emotions of a mother's relationship to her first child.

༺༻

This is an odd story about the Duke of Buckingham (1647–1721), told in a roundabout fashion by Peter Wentworth, writing to his brother, Lord Wentworth; the Duke could be thought of as ahead of his time in his design for a feeding bottle, however unsuccessful, or just perverse for his refusal to recognise that his child was dying.

31st October, 1710

. . . and now I shall tell you a pleasant story accation'd by the death of this child. Lady Dotchester [Dorchester] says the Duke kill'd it with over care, he wou'd not let it suck [from a wet nurse] from the apprehention he had that there was no sound woman to be mett with, nor be fed with a Spoon because he designed the Dutchess when she was well enough should give it suck herself, so he had an invention of a Sucking bottle wch was so managed in short the child was starved, then they were in hunt for a Nurse. Mr. Walpool had a child at nurse, that nurse got herself recommended there, the Duke examin'd her Breast himself and told her he like't her but would see the child that suckt her wch she brought without asking Walpool's leave, snd the Duke made her undress the child and he examined it all over strake naked and found it without any spot so he said he wou'd have her. She went with joy to her Master Walpool and told him all that had past and begged pardon she had gone without his leave; he said he would not have her loose her place, but charged her to tell the Duke, that all the soundest Nurses in England cou'd never [make] a child of his sound, and if he had a mind to have a sound one there was no way but to desire him to get it. The child was open'd and Lady Dorchester [the Duchess's mother] said they cou'd see nothing but that it was starved.

❧

James Nelson (1710–1794) was a doctor and writer who observed the behaviour of upper-class women with some sympathy.

A man cannot be conversant in life, and not see that many a sensible woman, many a tender mother, has her heart yearning to suckle her child, and is prevented by the misplaced authority of her husband.

❧

Lord Orrery (1707–1762) writes from the country to his wife who has recently given birth in London. She has told him that in the doctor's opinion her baby should not be weaned until May. He wants her to join him but only if they can make love, which he would not do if she went on feeding the child because intercourse was considered liable to spoil the milk and endanger the baby.

14th April, 1741

Let me meet you as a Husband, tho' I stay a month longer for the happiness. Consider what it is to be banish'd for so many months. Consider I love only You. Consider – oh! consider nothing at all but obey me. You promised it at Marriage, I now put you to the execution of that Promise. Dr. Barry will tell you the Girl has been suckled long eno'. Believe him if you will not regard me, and wean her my Dear, wean her.

### 3rd June

Yours [your letter] my dearest Life from London made me happy yesterday more from the sight of the Hand than from the contents, since you seem'd to fear Kitty will be the worse for being wean'd. Seriously Dr. B told me a child ought not to be suckled too long – but recall all I've said if she runs the least hazard. I cannot bear to hurt our child. I assure you I am under the most uneasiness about it. Let your Answer ease me if possible.

☙❧

William Cadogan (1711–1797) was a doctor at Bristol Royal Infirmary. His 'Essay upon Nursing, and the Management of Children' (addressed to one of the governors of the Foundling Hospital in London) contained plenty of good advice about letting children have more liberty, kindness and freedom. He thought that childcare should be based on scientific principles not on old wives' tales, which makes his opinion of women predictable if absurd.

### 1748

It is with great Pleasure I see at last the Preservation of Children become the Care of Men of Sense. . . . The Foundling Hospital may be of more Use to the World, than was perhaps at first perhaps imagin'd by the Promoters of it; it will be a Means not only of preventing the Murder of many, but of saving more, by introducing a more reasonable and more natural Method of Nursing. In my Opinion, this Business has been too long fatally left to the Management of Women, who cannot be supposed to have proper Knowledge to fit them for such a task, notwithstanding they look upon it to be their own Province.

J.G. Stedman (1744–1797) writes in his journal expressing a note of personal grievance that makes me a little suspicious about the failure of four nurses in a row.

Four different wet-nurses were alternately turn'd out of doors on my account, and to the care of whom I had been entrusted, my poor mother being in too weak a condition to suckle me herself. The first of these bitches was turn'd off for having nearly suffocated me in bed; she having slept upon me till I was smothered, and with skill and difficulty restored to life. The second had let me fall from her arms on the stones till my head was almost fractured, and I lay several hours in convulsions. The third carried me under a moulder'd old brick wall, which fell in a heap of rubbish just the moment we had passed by it, while the fourth proved to be a thief, and deprived me even of my very baby clothes. Thus was poor Johnny Stedman weaned some months before the usual time.

❧

Lady Caroline Fox (1723–1774), one of the four famous Lennox sisters, was married to Henry Fox, with whom she had four sons. She writes to her sister Emily about a relation of theirs who has just given birth. The quality of the wet nurse was always considered important.

3rd November, 1760

Lady George was yesterday brought to bed of a fine large girl, who I hope will do well, tho' it runs a great risk, poor thing! she having provided no wet nurse; one was to be got from the lying-in hospital yesterday. They must, you know, in that case take what they can get, and a nurse got in such a hurry and in London I'm afraid the chance is much against. I feel very angry at her. I own I was pretty near as young as her, and yet I was very anxious to provide a good nurse. I think it a duty and the only way one can justify to one's own mind not nursing one's child oneself.

Georgiana Duchess of Devonshire (1757–1806), beauty and political hostess, describes the nurse whom she has employed to look after her first child in a letter to her mother. This is just one example of many where the nurse proved unreliable and ill qualified to look after a child.

## 1783

She was only rather dirty till last night, when she was quite drunk. . . . My Dr little girl sleeps in bed with me after her first suckling as it is cold to move her, and the Rocker was to turn her dry and lay her down to sleep. I perceiv'd she had made the bed stink of wine and strong drink whenever she came near it . . . this morning I learnt that she had been so drunk as to fall down and vomit . . . I have therefore sent her 10 guineas and told her I would pay her journey up to town, and that I parted with her because I wanted her no longer.

❦

Benjamin Haydon (1786–1846) was a portrait painter and diarist; he is writing here about his daughter Fanny. This is the first of two examples of how, owing to extreme poverty, a wet nurse tried to nurture another's child at the expense of her own.

## 18th November, 1831

This day my dear little child Fanny died, at half-past one in the forenoon, aged two years, nine months, and twelve days. The life of this child has been one continued torture: she was weaned at three months from her mother's weakness and attempted to be brought up by hand. This failed, and she was reduced to a perfect skeleton; one day when I was kissing her she sucked my cheek violently. I said, 'This child wants the bosom even now.' Our medical friend said it was an experiment, but we might try it. I got a wet nurse instantly, and she seized the bosom like a tigress; in a few months she recovered, but the woman who came to suckle her weaned her own child.

I called on the nurse before she came, and found a fine baby, her husband and herself in great poverty. I said, 'What do you do with this child?' She replied, 'Wean it, sir. We must do so: we are poor.' I went away. 'Is this just,' thought I, 'to risk the life of another child to save my own?'

I went home tortured about what I should do, but a desire to save my own predominated.

The nurse came, Fanny was saved, but the fine baby of the poor nurse paid the penalty. I was never easy. 'Fanny never can, and never will prosper,' thought I. What right had I to take advantage of the poverty of this poor woman to save my own child, when I found out she had an infant of her own? When the nurse's time was up, Fanny withered, the bosom was again offered, and refused. From that moment she daily sank in spite of all medical advice, and to-day, after two convulsive fits, expired without a gasp.

❧

On learning of the death of the child of his daughter's wet nurse, whom she had left behind to come to nurse his baby, Mr Watson of Hampstead writes:

1840

It is a melancholy reflection that our own child's life should be sustained, as it were at the expense of the life of another infant. . . . The same thing happened to Mrs Cooper who suckled our Margaret.

❧

William Cobbett (1763–1835), now best known for his book *Rural Rides*, was a polemicist and landowner. Here he writes against wet-nursing, from his essay 'To a father'.

1829

Who has not seen these banished children, when brought and put into the arms of their mothers, screaming to get from them, and stretch out their little hands to get back into the arms of the nurse, and when safely got there, hugging the hireling as if her bosom were a place of *refuge*? Why, such a sight is, one would think, enough to strike a mother dead. And what sort of a husband and father, I want to know, must that be, who can endure the thought of his child loving another woman more than its own mother and his wife?

Charles Darwin (1809–1882), author of *On the Origin of Species*, was the father of ten children, of whom the surviving seven were unusually successful for the children of a world-famous father. In his diary, Darwin reflects, with scientific curiosity, on the early behaviour of his first child, William (1839–1914).

It was surprising how slowly he acquired the power of following with his eyes an object if swinging at all rapidly; for he could not do this well when seven and a half months old. At the age of 32 days he perceived his mother's bosom when three or four inches from it, as was shown by the protrusion of his lips and his eyes becoming fixed; but I much doubt whether this had any connection with vision; he certainly had not touched the bosom. Whether he was guided through smell or the sensation of warmth or through association with the position in which he was held, I do not at all know.

🂱

George du Maurier (1834–1896) was an illustrator, cartoonist and novelist. He wrote to his mother a week or so after the birth of his first child, a daughter. I have no idea what all this licking is about.

January 1864

Everything is going on splendidly; Pem has vanquished the difficulties of the commissariat department [breastfeeding], though not without terrific pain, and the little giant's energy of suction is terrific. It is a wonderfully fine child; about that there are not two opinions. . . . Her voice when she is not screaming too loud has the sweetest tones imaginable. The nurse may bring her to me every morning in bed, that I may lick it 'with the fasting tongue' – I enjoy the operation so much that I shall persevere till it reaches the age of discretion.

🂱

John Russell, Viscount Amberley (1842–1876), was a politician, writer and father of Bertrand Russell, the philosopher. John Russell fills in his wife Kate's journal two days after the birth of their first child. The baby would not breastfeed so Russell has a go at suckling to see how difficult it might be for the baby. He writes up the experience without any signs of prudishness.

Monday, 14th August, 1865

Tho' perfectly well K. had much trouble today from baby not sucking. He would not or could not do it. Another baby took a little but K. still suffered much pain in her breasts. In the evg. b.d. I sucked a little thinking it might do good, but I could not get much. Since I had to apply all my sucking power to get any milk it is no wonder the infant found it too hard for him. The milk was not nasty, but much too sweet to be pleasant; like the sweetest of syrup. It seems very badly managed by nature that little babies should not always find it as easy to suck as little puppies; but if this is one of the arrangements that was made in consequence of Original Sin of course we must not complain of it.

❧

Kate Amberley writes to Georgiana Russell, her sister-in-law; she has just sacked the nanny, Davies. Bad nannies had different cruel and dangerous strategies to control small babies, which sometimes went undiscovered; unlike Kate, many parents never bothered or perhaps couldn't bear to find out what was going on in the nursery.

24th October, 1865

My wetnurse (Lizzy) told me that Davies was very unkind to the child. It makes my blood boil for my precious little darling to think what he has had to bear. I am too furious. When he cried she used to shake him – when she washed him she used to stuff the sponge in his little mouth – push her finger (beast!) in his dear little throat – say she hated the child, wished he were dead – used to let him lie on the floor screaming while she sat quietly by & said screams did not annoy her it was good for his lungs, besides she liked me to hear him scream as she thought otherwise I should think she had nothing to do & as soon as I came into the room she would take him into her arms & cant over him as if she loved him dearly.... She would not let the wetnurse suckle him before he came to me, that he might scream & that I might know what a trouble he was – she sat in her room most of the day I find reading novels & never nursed the baby or spoke to it.
... She always put it on wet diapers ... then she gave it an empty bottle in its cot to suck the tube & keep it quiet so making it suck in only wind – No wonder it cried & was so unhappy.

Jane Carlyle (1801–1886), a great letter writer with no children of her own, commiserates.

### 7th November, 1865

What a mercy you *found out* that Ogresse before she had done any irreparable mischief! Poor little child! I can especially sympathize with him under the *gin*; for my own Nurse used to put me into dead sleep with *whisky*, when she had assignations outside! And my Mother was always of the opinion that my sleeplessness in after life was owing to having been *drunk* so often as a Baby!!

In her journal, Kate writes:

### 15th March, 1866

Baby cut his first tooth this mg.; he cried very violently yesterday and this mg. over it. The doctor (Brown) came to see him. I asked him for Amberley what was a good and safe narcotic and he advised me to give him 20 drops of chloroform on a pocket handkerchief and let him inhale it for 5 or 10 minutes, on no account longer, and it will produce a lulling effect which will be followed by sleep.

❧

Thomas James Cobden-Sanderson (1840–1922), bookbinder and printer, reflects on the metaphysical questions that finding a new nurse for his first child, Richard, seem to inspire in him.

### 9th June, 1885

Annie is upstairs with Ellen, nursing Richard who has the earache and wakes up. Poor Annie, she gets pale with fear when anything ails him. And what will she do when Ellen, the comforter, is gone? Whom shall we have in her place? Some girl now living somewhere, undreaming of us, as we of her. What game of chess are we to play to get her? Will she be good or bad? And then? And so on to the end, the all-silence, the universal nurse and comforter of all of us.

Rachel Cusk (b.1967) is a novelist. In her book about the birth of her first child, she depicts the relationship of a mother to her permanently crying new baby; the problems of feeding the child and, at the heart of this struggle, the profound transformation that occurs between them.

I have no difficulty in understanding what I read of the early relationship between mother and child. The child's yearning to be repossessed by the mother's body, its discovery of desire and satisfaction, its exploration of the limits of itself, and of another person and the fact of that person's own will; the mother's impulse both to protect and to expose, to yield and to separate, her responsibility both to love and to sort of steer everything in the right direction: I can see it all. The problem is that this vision doesn't much seem to resemble my situation. The baby's objections seem both comprehensive and startlingly personal; my own responses random, off-key and profoundly unmagical. It is not only difficult to believe that I am the object of the baby's desire, an object she is unresting in her attempts to enslave to her own will; it is in fact quite possible that she doesn't like me at all. . . .

I wake to find her red and rigid on the bed beside me, the room vibrating with sound. It is 9.30 am. I have been up many times in the night to feed her, and at some late point we clearly slumped jointly into an unexpected sleep. Other people have gone to work, to school, while we slept: the world is at its desk. We are in the housewifely slurry of everything that is both too late and too early, of madness and morning television. The day lies ahead empty of landmarks, like a prairie, like an untraversable plain. The baby is roaring. It is the sort of sound that permits no pause between deep sleep and full activity. I leap to my feet, pick her up and am pacing the reeling room with her within seconds. Dimly I remember feeding her perhaps two hours earlier, but decide to feed her again anyway while I think of something else I can do. My thoughts have become rat-like and rudimentary with guesswork, with lack of sleep. Feeding is something I do with a measure of confidence only because I have done it several times before, not because I understand particularly when and how it should be done. This morning she won't feed. Suddenly it is like trying to feed a kitchen appliance, or a shoe, bizarre and apparently inappropriate. Her body is ramrod-straight, her open mouth a furnace of noise, her face blue and red with fury. Milk runs in untasted rivulets down her affronted cheek. I decide on a change of scene. We go to the bathroom, where I intend to change her nappy. Again, this strategy has worked before, although I am unsure why. I lie her down on the mat. Immediately the crying stops. Delighted at the speed with which I have disarmed her, I sit down on the bathroom floor and lean back against the wall. I trill at the baby as she lies there watching me. Presently I change her nappy. I pick her up. Immediately she roars. I put her down again. She stops. I clean my teeth, I get into the bath, I get out. I get dressed. I try picking her up again in the hope that something has changed, but it hasn't. She roars. When I put her down, she stops. I wonder whether it is possible to spend the whole day in the bathroom. The telephone rings in the next door room and I go to answer it. Back in the bathroom, she roars. I turn on my heel and go back in. I pick her up. She stops.

I meet a woman who tells me kindly that one day, when the baby is about three months old, the crying will stop. From one day to the next, just like that. By now the fact of the baby's crying, if not its hours, has become predictable, although its causes remain unknown. She has cried in her sling on walks, in her pram when I am trying to shop, on the bus, on the tube, at the houses of friends and relations, in mine and others' arms. She has cried from one end of many dark afternoons to the other, when she and I were alone in the house and there was nothing to do, or it was raining, or I was too tired to do anything but sit with her in a chair while she cried. I have given up trying to contain the crying within a vision of adult normality, of competence. I have run home with her bawling in my arms, pulling the pram crazily behind us while people stare. I have jumped off buses in the middle of nowhere. I have bolted from cafés. I have ended telephone conversations without explanation. I have cried myself. I have shouted, making her tiny frame jump. I have sat for long evenings while her father paced the kitchen with her, offering advice. It was better when you were doing that jiggling thing, I say; or, try that thing you did the other night when you held her face down, with your other hand on her back. I have put her in a safe place and tried to leave the room, but before I could reach the door her crying has brought me back. We have even taken her to Italy, where for three days she cried beside Lake Garda while boats glided silently beneath the mountains over the pale water and the warm air was filled with the chattering of birds and children.

One evening, sitting outside in the garden in the dusk, I realise that three months have passed and that summer has come. My daughter is lying on a rug looking at the leaves above her. She wriggles and kicks her legs and laughs at things that I can't see. She has red hair and bright eyes. I know that in some inarticulable way I have over the past weeks witnessed again her birth; that the sound of her agony, her despair, was the sound of a terrible, private process of creation. I see that she has become somebody. I realise, too, that the crying has stopped, that she has survived the first pain of existence and out of it wrought herself. And she has wrought me, too, because although I have not helped or understood, I have been there all along and this, I suddenly and certainly know, is motherhood; this mere sufficiency, this presence. With every cry she has tutored me, in what is plain and hard: that my affection, my silly entertainments, my doting hours, the particular self I tried to bring to my care of her, have been as superfluous as my fury and despair. All that is required is for me to be there; an 'all' that is of course everything, because being there involves not being anywhere else, being ready to drop everything. Being myself is no compensation for not being there. And accordingly, the whole peopled surface, the occupation of my life has been swept away by her cries. That she has stopped crying I take as an indication that she judges my training to have been successful and the rank of mother attained; a signal that we can now, cautiously, get on with the business of living together.

# CHILDHOOD

> . . . though tis mine owne I must needs say he is
> an extreame witty child.
> *Mary Verney to her husband, 1647*

The English used to have a reputation for not being particularly affectionate to their children and an Italian visitor confirms this view as far back as the sixteenth century. However, there are plenty of examples which show quite the opposite to be the case. Thomas More is an unusually devoted father in the early sixteenth century and the Earl of Lauderdale, a century later, is an exemplary grandfather. Nearly three hundred years ago, Mary Robinson delights in the moment her daughter says her first words: the same first words that many children still say today. More recently, Charles Darwin continues his close observation of his first child with a mixture of scientific detachment and endearing affection.

There were conflicting views on how to look after babies and small children. Parents divide between the severe, attentive restrictions advocated by John Locke in the seventeenth century and the benign neglect recommended by Jean Jacques Rousseau in the eighteenth. There are good parents, abusive parents and anxious parents. Lord Nelson shows a touching concern for his daughter's safety, William Lamb resigns himself to his failure to control his children or even his dogs and Queen Victoria expresses a familiar sentiment about the difficulties of bringing up children successfully.

Over the centuries, many mothers (and fathers) regret the custom of sending young boys away to boarding school. More recently, E.M. Delafield describes the attitudes of a 1930s prep-school master, which might be recognisable to some parents today, but it is Frances Partridge, in the 1940s, who writes most convincingly about the pressures and consequences for the child.

I particularly enjoy Maureen Lipman's marvellous parallel between the behaviour of a tribe in the Kalahari Desert and today's worried mothers and fathers.

Edmund Stonor (d.1382) is sent a letter by his chaplain, Thomas Mull, telling him about his son (another Edmund) who has been ill at school. English boys have been sent away to boarding school for centuries.

c.1380

My Lord and faithful to God, you should know, if you please, that I saw your son Edmund, and I considered his condition for two nights and a day: his illness decreases from day to day, and he is not lying in bed, but when the fever attacks him he lies down feeling somewhat weak for less than two hours, after which he gets up, and as the time requires he goes to school, eats and walks in good health and good spirits, in such a way that he seems to be in no danger. And of his own accord, he sent his greetings to you and to his lady mother and various and other members of the household. And he is beginning to learn Donatus [a grammatical manuscript] slowly and carefully as he ought to do. He has the copy of Donatus which I feared was lost. I never saw a boy be so well cared for during his illness. The master and his wife would like some of his clothes to be taken home because he has too many, fewer would be sufficient as they may be dirtied and spoilt.

*(translated from the Latin)*

❧

Geoffrey Chaucer (1340–1400), author of the *Canterbury Tales*, writes to a young boy, probably his son Lewis, aged ten. In response to the boy's 'busy prayer' Chaucer gave him an astrolabe, which was a six-inch-diameter sphere with a moving part, designed to show how the stars looked at a specific time and to teach basic astronomy. This letter forms part of the Prologue to Chaucer's Treatise on the Astrolabe, which accompanied the instrument.

1391

Litell Lowys my sone, I haue perceiued well by certeyne euidences thine abilite to lerne sciencez touchinge noumbres & proporciouns; & as wel considere I thy bisi preyere in special to lerne the tretis of the astrelabie. . . . therfor haue I geuen thee a suffisaunt astralabie as for owre orizonte, compowned after the latitude of Oxenford vp-on which, by mediacion of this litel tretis, I purpose to teche the a certein nombre of conclusiouns . . .

On his banishment from England, the Duke of Suffolk (1396–1450) writes a farewell to his young son, John, aged eight, the great-grandson of Geoffrey Chaucer. After charging him to obey the Commandments and to be a true Liege man to the King, he shows his confidence and trust in his wife.

## April 1450

Thirdly, in the same wise, I charge you, my dear Son, alway as ye be bounden by the Commandment of God to do, to love, to worship, your Lady and Mother; and also that ye obey alway her commandments, and to believe her counsels and advices in all your works, the which dread not but shall be best and truest to you.

❧

Thomas More (1478–1535), described by Erasmus as 'the wittiest man in Europe', was a writer, statesman and martyr. During his lifetime he was also admired as a father. Here he writes to his four children: Margaret, Elizabeth, Cicely and John (all under the age of twelve).

## Flanders, 1515

This one letter, designed to reach all four of my children,
  Carries a father's wish thus to preserve them from ill.
  Still as I plod on my way, and am drenched to the skin by the rain-
storms,
  Still as my labouring horse frequently sticks in the mud,
  This is the verse that I make for you in the midst of my hardships,
  Hoping that you may be pleased, rough as I know it to be.
  This is a proof to you all of your father's love, for it shows you
  How much dearer are you e'en than the sight of his eyes,
  . . . he cannot be torn from you, but in constant affection
  Proves he remembers you well, no matter where he may be. . . .
  It's no wonderful thing if my heart embraces you wholly,
  Thinking with awe as I do, 'I am the source of their life.' . . .
  Here is the source, do you see? of my mind's known tender
indulgence,
  Prone upon least excuse softly to fondle you all.
  Here is why cake looms large in my thoughts of you, which are frequent,

Why fine pears (apples, too) figure as favourite gifts,
Why I so often have dressed you in silks, in Cathaian refulgence,
Why, too, the sight of your tears weakens my sternest resolves.
Well you know how often I kissed you, how rarely I spanked you,
– Yes, with a peacock's tail doing its best as a whip!
And what is more, it was wielded in light soft blows, with compunction
Lest it should leave but a bruise scoring a tender behind.
    Ah, what a beast is the man, unworthy the name of a father,
Who, when his children weep, weeps not in instant response!
Others may do as they will, but you are aware – and profoundly –
How in my dealings with you I show affectionate care.
All of my children alike have I loved with eagerness always,
And, as a father should be, I have been light on the rein:
Yet in amazement I find that love to have yielded an increase
Such that I seem to myself not to have loved you before. . . .
*(translated from the Latin)*

More advises his children's tutor, William Gunnell, that he should teach the children in a way in which they will not grow proud through constant praise. More demanded a great deal from his children, but some of what he says still rings true today.

For myself I consider it so hard to shake from us this plague of pride that we ought the more to endeavour to do it from our very infancy. I think there is no other cause why this mischief doth stick so fast to us, but that it is ingrafted in us even by our nurses as soon as we have crept out of our shells, fostered by our masters, nourished and perfected by our parents, whilst no one proposeth anything good to children, but they at once bid them expect praise as the reward of virtue, whence they are so used to esteem much of praise, that seeking to please the greater number, who are always the worst, they are ashamed to be good with the few. And that this plague may be banished from my children, I desire that you, my dear Gunnell, their mother, and all their friends, would still sing them this song, hammer it into their heads on every occasion, that vain glory is to be despised, nor anything more excellent than the humble modesty so much praised by Christ, which prudent charity will so guide and direct that it will teach us rather to desire virtue than to upbraid others for their vices, and make them rather love those who correct their faults than hate them for their good counsel, to obtain which nothing is more available than to read them the precepts of the Fathers, whom they know not to be angry with themselves, and with whose authority they must be moved because they are venerable for their sanctity.

If, therefore, you will read the works of such to Margaret and Elizabeth besides their lessons in Sallust, as they, being the eldest, are of riper age, than John and Cicely, you will make both them and me every day more beholden to you; moreover you will then make my children, dear in the order of nature, more dear for learning, and by their increase in virtue most dear unto me. Farewell – From the Court, this Whitsun Eve.

*(translated from the Latin)*

❧

'A Relation, or rather a True Account, of the Island of England; . . . about the year 1500' by an Italian visitor is a famous text which has been used as evidence for a lack of affection in English parents.

## c.1500

The want of affection in the English is strongly manifested towards their children; for after having kept them at home till they arrive at the age of 7 to 9 years at the utmost, they put them out, both males and females, to hard service in the houses of other people, binding them generally for another 7 or 9 years. And these are called apprentices, and during that time they perform all the most menial offices; and few are born who are exempted from this fate, for every one, however rich he may be, sends away his children into the houses of others, whilst he, in return, receives those of strangers into his own. And on inquiring their reason for this severity, they answered that they did it in order that their children might learn better manners. But I, for my part, believe that they do it because they like to enjoy all their comforts themselves, and that they are better served by strangers than they would be by their own children. Besides which the English being great epicures, and very avaricious by nature, indulge in the most delicate fare themselves and give their household the coarsest bread, and beer, and cold meat baked on Sunday for the week, which, however, they allow them in great abundance. That if they had their own children at home, they would be obliged to give them the same food they made use of for themselves. That if the English sent their children away from home to learn virtue and good manners, and took them back again when their apprenticeship was over, they might, perhaps, be excused; but they never return, for the girls are settled by their patrons, and the boys make the best marriages they can, and, assisted by their patrons, not by their fathers, they also open a house and strive diligently by this means to make some fortune for themselves . . .

⟡

*Sir Henry Sidney (1529–1586) writes to his son Philip, aged about eleven, who had been sent away to school: the advice he gives reminds us how docile and diligent children had to be compared to most eleven-year-olds today. Philip's efforts proved worthwhile: he grew up to be a poet and favourite of Elizabeth I.*

c.1565

Son Philip,

I have received two letters from you, one written in Latin, the other in French; which I take in good part, and will you to exercise that practice of learning often; for that will stand you in most stead in that profession of life that you are born to live in. And now, since this is my first letter that ever I did write to you, I will not that it be all empty of some advices which my natural care of you provoketh me to wish you to follow, as documents to you in this your tender age. . . .

*After encouraging his son to pray, study and show humble good manners, Sir Henry continues:*

Use moderate diet, so as, after your meal, you may find your wit fresher and not duller, and your body more lively and not more heavy. Seldom drink wine; and yet sometimes do, lest, being enforced to drink upon the sudden, you should find yourself enflamed. Use exercise of body, yet such as is without peril of your bones or joints: it will increase your force and enlarge your breath. Delight to be cleanly, as well in all parts of your body as in your garments: it shall make you grateful in each company – and otherwise loathsome.

Give yourself to be merry; for you degenerate from your father if you find not yourself most able in wit and body to do anything when you are most merry. But let your mirth be ever void of all scurrility and biting words to any man; for a wound given by a word is oftentimes harder to be cured than that which is given by the sword.

*Sir Henry instructs Philip to be modest in society, not to swear and to be discreet.*

Above all things, tell no untruth; no, not in trifles. The custom of it is naughty. And let it not satisfy you that for a time the hearers take it for a truth; for after it will be known as it is, to your shame. For there cannot be a greater reproach to a gentleman than to be accounted a liar.

Well, my little Philip, this is enough for me, and too much, I fear, for you. But if I shall find that this light meal of digestion nourish in anything the weak stomach of your capacity, I will, as I find the same grow stronger, feed it with other food. . . .

*Philip's mother, Lady Mary Sidney (1535?–1586), adds a postcript to the letter, which begins:*

Your noble careful father hath taken pains with his own hand to give you, in this letter, so wise, so learned and most requisite precepts for you to follow with a diligent and humble, thankful mind, as I will not withdraw your eyes from beholding . . . And therefore, at this time, I will write unto you no other letter than this; . . . have always before the eyes of your mind these excellent counsels of my lord, your dear father, and that you fail not continually, once in four or five days, to read them over.

Dr John Dee (1527–1609), astrologer, magician, mathematician, navigator and scientific adviser to Elizabeth I, had eight children. He kept a detailed diary from 1554 to 1601.

1st January, 1588

About nine of the clok afternone Michel, going chilyshly with a sharp stik of eight inches long and a little wax candell light on the top of it, did fall upon the playn boards in Marie's chamber and the sharp point of the stik entered through the lid of his left eye towards the corner next the nose, and so persed throwgh, in so much that great abundance of blood cam out under the lid, in the very corner of the said eye; the hole on the outside is not bigger than a pyn's head; it was anointed with St John's oyle. The boy slept well. God spede the rest of the cure! The next day after it apperid that the first towch of the stikes point was at the very myddle of the apple of the ey, and so (by God's mercy and favor) glanced to the place where it entred; with the strength of his hed and the fire of his fullness.

An enormous number of children died from accidental causes but here Dee records the casual violence that parents could inflict on their small children.

19th April, 1589

Katharin by a blow on the eare given by her mother did bleed at the nose very much, which did stay for an houre and more; afterward she did walk into the town with her nurse; upon her coming home, she bled again.

Elizabeth Joceline (1596–1622) was extremely well educated – in religion, languages, art and history – and 'one of the most notable young women of the times of James I'. She continued to study and write poetry after marrying in 1616, and wrote 'The Mother's Legacie, To her unborne Childe' when she became pregnant, after six childless years, because of her fear of dying in childbirth. She explained to her husband, 'I thought theare was som good office I might doo for my childe more then only to bring it forth (though it should pleas god to take me)'.

## 1622

I desire her bringing vp may bee learning the Bible, as my sisters doe, good houswifery, writing, and good workes: other learning a woman needs not: though I admire it in those whom God hath blest with discretion, yet I desired not much in my owne, hauing scene that sometimes women haue greater portions of learning, than wisdome, which is of no beter vse to them than a main saile to a flye-boat, which runs it vnder water. But where learning and wisdome meet in a vertuous disposed woman, she is the fittest closet for all goodnesse. She is like a well-ballanced ship that may beare all her saile. She is – Indeed, I should but shame my selfe, if I should goe about to praise her more.

She died a few days after giving birth to a daughter.

❦

Sir Ralph Verney, in exile in France with the two eldest children, Edmund aged eleven and Bess aged eight, writes to his wife Mary about the clothes she has sent for them.

## 11th August, 1647

As for Mun's gray stockings they are about a handful too short and almost an inch too Little, soe I have layed them upp for your sonn John, and you must buy Mun more. . . . Besse is as well fitted, for Luce sent her 2 paire of Shooes that will come as soon uppon her head as uppon her Heeles; soe we laugh at you both.

Mary Verney has returned to England to see their youngest son John (Jack), aged nearly seven, who is being looked after by his grandparents at the family home, Claydon House, while she is abroad with her husband.

### 10th August

For Jack his leggs are most miserable, crooked as evor I saw any child's, and yett thank god he goes very strongly, and is very strayte in his body as any child can bee; and is a very fine child all but his legges, and truly I think would be much finer if we had him in ordering, for they lett him eate anythinge that he hath a mind toe, and he keepes a very ill diett; he hath an Imperfection in his speech, and of all things he hates his booke, truly tis time you had him with you for he learns noething heare. You would be much pleased with his Company, for he is a very ready witted child and is very good company, and is soe fond of the name of his father and mother; he is allwayes with me from the first hour thatt I came, and tells me that he would very fayne goe into france to his father; he sings prettely.

Ralph Verney replies:

### 5th September

I long to see poor Jack, truly the Crookedness of his Leggs grieves my very Hart, aske some advise about it at London, but doe not Tamper with him.

Mary writes again:

### 7th September

Jack is a very gallant boy, butt truly if he stay at Claydon a little longer he will be utterly spoyled . . . he hath noe fault in him besides his leggs, for though tis mine owne I must needs say he is an extreame witty child.

Sir Ralph Verney writes to his god-daughter Nancy, aged twelve, child of his friend Dr William Denton. Ralph Verney, a loving and attentive father and godfather, held the conventional view of women's education but fortunately Dr Denton was more imaginative about his intelligent daughter.

## 27th July, 1652

My dear Childe, – nothing but yourselfe, could have beene soe welcome as your letter, nor have surprized mee more, for I must confesse I did not think you had beene guilty of soe much learning as I see you are; and yet it seems you rest unsatisfied or else you would not threaten Lattin, Greeke, and Hebrew too. Good sweet hart bee not soe covitous; beleeve me a Bible (with yr Common prayer) and a good plaine cattichisme in your Mother Tongue being well read and practised, is well worth all the rest and much more suitable to your sex; I know your Father thinks this false doctrine, but bee confident your husband will bee of my oppinion. In French you cannot bee too cunning for that language affords many admirable bookes fit for you as Romances, Plays, Poetry, Stories of illustrious (not learned) Woemen, receipts for preserving, makinge creeames and all sorts of cookeryes, ordring your gardens and in Breif all manner of good housewifery.

☙

The Earl of Lauderdale (1616–1682), politician and favourite of Charles II, writes to his friend the Earl of Tweeddale about his grandson Charles, aged fifteen months, who has suddenly been taken ill. His wife is also ill and his daughter has just given birth to her second child. For a grandfather, he seems to manage remarkably well.

## 1668

And for a new and sharp affliction to me, our dear little man Charles grew sick on Tuesday, but the causes are so apparent that neither the physicians nor I were any thing apprehensive of it, for he hath four great teeth broken the flesh, and his gums for his eye-teeth [are] much swelled, and [he keeps] his finger continually in his mouth. His frowardness and great heat made me conclude him sick, but I apprehended nothing till Tuesday about six o'clock at night when I was talking with the physician about my wife; a sudden alarm comes in that my dear baby Charles had taken a convulsion. The physicians and I run in to his chamber and found him stiff with his arms out and his eyes staring. Never did I see a convulsion before (for never child of mine had it) and it was a dreadful sight. By God's providence the physicians were present; they presently undressed him, made him be rubbed and went to write their prescriptions. The women said he was out of the fit, but the doctors said No, or if he was it was another. Always, before their prescription was written he was clearly out of it. So whether it was two fits or one the convulsions lasted not half a quarter of an hour. They made all the directions, especially forbidding him his nurse's breast, which was obeyed. He was well watched all night; sure I slept little. When the doctors and I talked together, they said they liked it the better that it came by the pain of so many teeth, but if it had come by the beginning of smallpox or measles, they would not be so apprehensive. He slept ill all night, was most impatient for the breast, and was in a cruel heat. When the physicians came yesterday morning they found him in a great fever, but within an hour they did see apparent signs of the smallpox. They were pleased with it, appointed him to suck again, which strangely recovered the child's humour. All this while the mother and grandmother knew nothing, for the physicians positively forbade it. My first care was to remove the other child and nurse with maids to another side of the house, where they are very well. My babe Charles grew much better, his smallpox struck out handsomely, and in the afternoon and towards the evening he plays as merrily as ever. He slept well and sucked well all night and the most part of this day, only he is more froward than when in health, but his fever is much abated and the smallpox strike out finely and seem not to be many, I cannot see twenty or thirty in his face. We have now told my wife of the smallpox, but not a word of the convulsion; my daughter knows nothing of neither. My wife being still kept in bed, I have chosen to shut my self up here, so does *nostre fils* [son-in-law] at nights, but he goes abroad in the afternoons, though not to Court. I sent my excuse to the King, and that I would not presume to wait on him, the smallpox being in my house and I compelled by my wife's sickness and my daughter's lying in to stay here.

Two days later:

Our dear little man Charles looks hopefully for his condition. He hath little or no fever, his pox come on finely and are of a good colour, his eye is very sharp and well though his pain is great which makes him froward often. Yet he is at fits and often as merry as ever. Last night I was playing with him, and called him pockie rogue; presently he pointed to his pox with his little finger distinctly one by one. This he did repeat again before the doctors this day, and I wondered to see him understand that word. The Doctors give him nothing, only they appoint his nurse to drink a posset constantly with hartshorn and marigold flowers and other things of that nature in it. In a word by God's great mercy he is yet in a hopeful condition. *Nostre fille* [daughter] mends well and knows nothing of all this. The little one is very well. Never was I so free of business and yet never so unwilling to write. Here I am in a troublesome government going to and again from one sick one to another and attending doctors, surgeon apothecaries and nurses; a government I was never shaped for and of which I am most heartily weary.

Hartshorn and marigold did the trick, and the child recovered.

⟡

John Locke (1632–1704), philosopher, believed the child's mind was a blank sheet, so that in order to achieve his full potential he had to be brought up to have a healthy body, a virtuous disposition and a proper intellectual education. Locke never married and had no children of his own. *Some Thoughts Concerning Education* was one of the three or four most influential works on education ever written in English.

## 1693

Of all that looks soft and effeminate, nothing is more to be indulg'd Children, than *Sleep*. In this alone they are to be permitted to have their full Satisfaction; nothing contributing more to the Growth and Health of children, than *Sleep*. . . .

. . . But some time between seven and fourteen, if they are too great Lovers of their Beds, I think it may be seasonable to begin to reduce them by Degrees to about eight Hours, which is generally Rest enough for healthy grown People. . . . They should constantly be call'd up and made to rise at their early Hour; but great Care should be taken in waking them that it be not done hastily, nor with a loud or shrill Voice, or any other sudden violent Noise. This often affrights Children, and does them great Harm; and sound *Sleep* thus broke off, with sudden Alarms, is apt enough to discompose any one. When Children are to be waken'd out of their *Sleep*, be sure to begin with a low Call, and some gentle Motion, and so draw them out of it by degrees, and give them none but kind Words and Usage 'till they are come perfectly to themselves, and being quite dress'd, you are sure they are thoroughly awake. The being forc'd from their *Sleep*, how gently soever you do it, is Pain enough to them; and Care should be taken not to add any other Uneasiness to it, especially such that may terrify them.

I don't see how anyone could argue with these rules for bringing up healthy children, except, of course, the need for cold wet feet.

And thus I have done with what concerns the Body and Health, which reduces itself to these few and easily observable Rules: Plenty of *open Air*, *Exercise*, and *Sleep*; plain *Diet*, no *Wine* or *strong Drink*, and very little or no *Physick*, not too warm and strait *Clothing*, especially the *Head* and *Feet* kept cold, and the *Feet* often us'd to cold Water and expos'd to wet.

Locke writes with very good sense, in my opinion, about the disastrous effects of indulging children.

The Fondling must be taught to strike and call Names, must have what he cries for, and do what he pleases. Thus Parents, by humouring and cockering them when *little*, corrupt the Principles of Nature in their Children, and wonder afterwards to taste the bitter Waters, when they themselves have poison'd the Fountain. For when their Children are grown up, and these ill Habits with them; when they are now too big to be dandled, and their Parents can no longer make Use of them as Playthings, then they complain that the Brats are untoward and perverse; then they are offended to see them wilful, and are troubled with those ill Humours which they themselves infus'd and fomented in them; and then, perhaps too late, would be glad to get out those Weeds which their own Hands have planted, and which now have taken too deep Root to be easily extirpated. For he that hath been us'd to have his Will in every Thing, as long as he was in Coats, why should we think it strange, that he should desire it, and contend for it still, when he is in Breeches? Indeed, as he grows more towards a Man, Age shews his Faults the more; so that there be few Parents then so blind as not to see them, few so insensible as not to feel the ill Effects of their own Indulgence. He had the Will of his Maid before he could speak or go; he had the Mastery of his Parents ever since he could prattle; and why, now he is grown up, is stronger and wiser than he was then, why now of a sudden must he be restrain'd and curb'd? Why must he at seven, fourteen, or twenty Years old, lose the Privilege, which the Parents' Indulgence 'till then so largely allow'd him? Try it in a Dog or an Horse or any other Creature, and see whether the ill and resty Tricks they have learn'd when young, are easily to be mended when they are knit; and yet none of those Creatures are half so wilful and proud, or half so desirous to be Masters of themselves and others, as Man.

⊙⊙

Lady Wentworth writes to her son Thomas Wentworth, Earl of Stafford (1672–1739). Sounding unpleasantly smug, she refers to the terrible story of how Lady Abergavenny (who she calls Lady Abargane) murdered her own daughter. If the description is accurate, there is something especially horrible about the father's failure to prevent his child's murder.

### 8th January, 1712

My dearist and best of children, a thoussand thancks to you for the kyndness of yours of the 12 of this instent, but I shall never thinck it possable for any dog to compaer to charming Perl, I never goe anywhear without her except to church. Hear is a straing unnaturell reporte of Lady Abargane that she has in pation kild her own child about seven year old, she having been a great while whiping it, my Lord being greeved to hear it crye soe terryably went into the roome to beg for it, and she threw it with such a forse to the ground she broack the scul; the girle leved but fower howers after it. I am sure never any letter from me was half soe welcome as this will be, although I never will yeeld that any creeture can lov you better then, dear soul, your moste infenit affectionat mother.

Lady Mary Wortley Montagu (1689–1762) was an adventurous traveller and writer. Her husband was ambassador in Istanbul, where she learnt about inoculation against smallpox. Her own children were treated and she was the first person to introduce the practice into England. Her remark about doctors' revenue strikes home today as it must have done then.

1st April, 1717

The small-pox, so fatal, and so general amongst us, is here entirely harmless, by the invention of ingrafting, which is the term they give it. There is a set of old women, who make it their business to perform the operation, every autumn, in the month of september, when the great heat is abated. People send to one another to know if any of their family has a mind to have the small-pox; they make parties for this purpose, and when they are met (commonly fifteen or sixteen together) the old woman comes with a nut-shell full of the matter of the best sort of small-pox, and asks what vein you please to have opened. She immediately rips open that you offer to her, with a large needle (which gives you no more pain than a common scratch), and puts into the vein as much matter as can lie upon the head of her needle, and after that, binds up the little wound with a hollow bit of shell, and in this manner opens four or five veins. . . . The children or young patients play together all the rest of the day, and are in perfect health to the eighth. Then the fever begins to seize them, and they keep their beds two days, very seldom three. They have very rarely above twenty or thirty in their faces, which never mark, and in eight days time they are as well as before their illness. Where they are wounded, there remains running sores during the distemper, which I don't doubt is a great relief to it. Every year thousands undergo this operation, and the French ambassador says pleasantly that they take the small-pox here by way of diversion, as they take the waters in other countries. There is no example of any one that has died in it, and you may believe I am well satisfied of the safety of this experiment, since I intend to try it on my dear little son. I am patriot enough to take pains to bring this useful invention into fashion in England, and I should not fail to write to some of our doctors very particularly about it, if I knew any one of them that I thought had virtue enough to destroy such a considerable branch of their revenue, for the good of mankind.

Susanna Wesley (1669–1742) was the mother of John Wesley (1703–1791), Anglican clergyman and founder of the Methodist movement in the Church of England. She had nineteen children, of whom nine died as infants. The family was extremely poor and she was harsh with her children, but they were, boys and girls alike, highly educated.

## 24th July, 1732

According to your desire, I have collected the principal rules I observed in educating my family; which I now send you as they occurred to my mind. . . . When turned a year old (and some before) they were taught to fear the rod, and to cry softly; by which means they escaped abundance of correction they might otherwise have had; and that most odious noise of crying children was rarely heard in the house. As soon as they were grown pretty strong, they were confined to three meals a day. At dinner, their little table and chairs were set by ours, where they could be overlooked; and they were suffered to eat and drink (small beer) as much as they would, but not to call for anything. . . . Drinking and eating between meals was never allowed, except in case of sickness, which seldom happened. At six, as soon as family prayer was over, they had their supper; at seven the maid washed them; and, beginning at the youngest, she undressed and got them all to bed by eight: at which time she left them in their several rooms awake; for there was no such thing allowed of in our house, as sitting by a child until it fell asleep. They were so constantly used to eat and drink what was given them, that when any of them was ill, there was no difficulty in making them take the most unpleasant medicine; for they durst not refuse it, though some of them would presently throw it up. . . . There was no such thing as loud talking or playing allowed of; but everyone was kept close to their business for the six hours of school. Rising out of their places, or going out of the room was not permitted except for good cause; running into the yard, garden, or street, without leave, was always esteemed a capital offence.

Frances Boscawen writes to her husband, Admiral Boscawen. Although conscious of conceit, as she was, most parents think the same about their own children.

21st March, 1747

I must have one observation in [this letter] that savours of vanity, but upon so true a foundation that it ought to excite your gratitude. The comparison of our children with your brother George's. I went directly from our boy to his girl. What a difference! In every circumstance, and in nothing more than behaviour. She would not come near me, and is as far from an agreeable child as she is from a pretty one. Ours is both, in the highest degree, and so everybody thinks.

Frances Boscawen may boast about her children, but she certainly devotes herself to them.

January 1748

All three children have been ill at once. The two girls had coughs and fevers occasioned by teeth, which were lanced immediately. The boy had a violent and never-ceasing cough, which I am inclined to believe he caught from his sisters' breath. It totally deprived him of rest, so that, by the 3rd night, he too was in a fever. By this time, you may imagine, we had decreed them for the measles; all three coughs, all three fevers, resembled it too much. You can imagine the state I was in. For poor Fanny I trembled, her breath and lungs being already so oppressed that 'twas pain to hear her, and the slut would not drink anything, though she was dying with thirst. There was no sort of liquor I did not try her with. Tea I made in her sight; water with a roast apple; mingled a drop of wine in warm water; milk; jelly. No, nothing would do, and she still persisted to cry, 'No, no, no, can't.' This she had occasion to repeat twenty times a day, sometimes when nobody asked. As to the medicines, the few we gave her we threw down by force, but you know it must be a trifle that could be obtained that way of drink.

As to the dear boy, he would at all times take anything I brought him; but then I dreaded a bleeding, which would have been necessary in the measles. I did not doubt my being able to persuade him to it. I had even got his promise. But I distrusted myself. I doubted my being able to stay in the room, and the least signs of fear in me would have inspired and justified his.

In short, my dearest husband, I have endured a great deal, and can never be enough thankful to the gracious providence that has comforted me and cured them. The boy and the little one come now downstairs. Frances keeps chamber still; but they have been purged, and to-morrow the two eldest begin asses' milk. Bess, as you know, has provision of that sort nearer at hand!

Bess, aged nine months, was still being breastfed.

Nearly forty years after Mary Wortley Montagu advocated smallpox inoculation, Frances Boscawen writes to her husband about having her children immunised.

20th April, 1755

Pray Papa! Pray to God to bless us, for we are inoculated. This day exactly at noon it was done; no fuss, no rout, no assistance. Nobody with me but the servants. I held the child myself and so effectually employed his eyes and attentions (by a bit of gold lace which I was putting into forms to lace his waistcoat) that he never was sensible of the first arm. For the second, he pretended to wince a little, but I had a sugar plum ready, which stopped the whimper before it was well formed. And he is now (Mr. Hawkins gone) tattling here by my bureau with some cards and papers, etc., for the weather is so very hot that I reckon the chief service I can do him is to provide him such amusements as will keep him still and quiet. . . . The nurse-maids are both inoculated too.

I have now, I think, two great stakes! My husband sails, my child is inoculated; both in the same day. There is but one way to look. Towards the blessing which can protect on the fields of battle, or on the bed of sickness!

Lady Caroline Fox writes to her sister about her son, Charles James Fox, aged ten.

## 21st June, 1759

. . . you can have no idea how companiable a child he is, nor how infinitely engaging to us he is. If Mr Fox and I are alone, either of us, or only us two, he never leaves one, enters into any conversation going forwards, takes his book if we are reading, is vastly amused with any work going on out of doors or indoors, furniture or anything that's going forwards; will sit and read by me when my stomach is bad and I lie down between sleeping and waking, and is in every respect the most agreeable companion. I know you'll make allowances for my partiality, for these same qualities so pleasing to us often make him troublesome to other people. He will know everything, watches one if one wants to speak to anybody, and is too apt to give his opinion about everything, which tho' generally a very sensible one, makes him appear pert to other people . . .

❧

The Earl of Chesterfield (1694–1773) was a statesman and diplomat but is most famous for his letters to his illegitimate son, Philip Stanhope (1732–1768). Here, he gives good advice to his seven-year-old godson, also Philip Stanhope (1755–1815), a third cousin once removed; he adopted his godson and made him his heir after his son's death.

## 1762

As I know you desire to be a well bred gentleman, and not a two-legged bear. . . . I send you some general rules for your behaviour. . . . whoever you speak to, to whosever speaks to you, you must be sure to look them full in the face. . . . You must call every gentleman, Sir or My Lord, and every woman Madame. You must never on any account put your fingers in your nose, for that is excessively ill-bred, very nasty, and will make your nose bleed and be very sore. What is your handkerchief for? When you are at dinner you must sit upright in your chair, and not loll. . . . When you first come into company, and also when you go out of it you must never look sullen or pouting, but have a cheerful, easy countenance.

James Boswell (1740–1795), friend and biographer of Dr Samuel Johnson (the Mr Johnson referred to here), had two legitimate daughters, born in 1773 and 1774. He debates whether to leave his estate to a male cousin or to his daughters. (Later, he also had an illegitimate son and daughter, but he had no surviving sons at this date.)

### 28th July, 1774

Mr. Wood the surgeon . . . very earnestly spoke to me to agree to make such a settlement of the estate of Auchinleck as my father chose, that my wife and children might have provisions secured to them in case of my death; and he said it was his opinion my father's chance of life was better than mine. This struck me much. But I felt a firmness in my old male feudal principles, though honest Wood could not see them but as wild romantic fancies. I have a strong conflict in my mind between my concern for my valuable wife, who in case of my death would be left in a miserable state of dependence, and those principles which are interwoven with my very heart, and which I hold myself bound in honour to maintain, as my great-great-grand-uncle gave the estate to his nephew, my grandfather, in prejudice of his own four daughters; so that all who receive it as a male fief should faithfully transmit it as such. Mr. Johnson confirmed me in that principle and inculcated upon me that the chance of my wife and children being in a bad situation was nothing in the general calculation of things. I shall therefore be steady, conscious of my sincere affection for my wife and children, and trusting that I may have it in my power to make them all easy.

As it turned out, Boswell's anxieties were unnecessary: his wife died before him.

Richard Lovell Edgeworth (1744–1817) was a writer, inventor and father of twenty children, by four wives. His books on child education were influenced by Jean Jacques Rousseau but his own experiment in following Rousseau's method was unsuccessful and, unsurprisingly, his son grew up to be wild and unmanageable.

My eldest son was born at Black-Bourton, in Oxfordshire, in 1764. . . . I formed a strong desire to educate my son according to the system of Rousseau. His Emile had made a great impression upon my young mind, as it had done upon the imaginations of many far my superiors in age and understanding. His work had then all the power of novelty, as well as all the charms of eloquence; and when I compared the many plausible ideas it contains, with the obvious deficiencies and absurdities, that I saw in the treatment of children in almost every family, with which I was acquainted, I determined to make a fair trial of Rousseau's system. My wife complied with my wishes, and the body and mind of my son were to be left as much as possible to the education of nature and of accident. I was but twenty-three years old, when I formed this resolution; I steadily pursued it for several years, notwithstanding the opposition with which I was embarrassed by my friends and relations and the ridicule by which I became immediately assailed on all quarters.

I dressed my son without stockings, with his arms bare, in a jacket and trowsers such as are quite common at present, but which were at that time novel and extraordinary. I succeeded in making him remarkably hardy: I also succeeded in making him fearless of danger, and, what is more difficult, capable of bearing privation of every sort. He had all the virtues of a child bred in the hut of a savage, and all the knowledge of *things,* which could well be acquired at an early age by a boy bred in civilized society. I say knowledge of *things,* for of books he had less knowledge at four or five years old, than most children have at that age. Of mechanics he had a clearer conception, and in the application of what he knew more invention, than any child I had then seen. He was bold, free, fearless, generous; he had a ready and keen use of all his senses, and of his judgment. But he was not disposed to *obey*: his exertions generally arose from his own will; and, though he was what is commonly called good-tempered and good-natured, though he generally pleased by his looks, demeanour, and conversation, he had too little deference for others, and he shewed an invincible dislike to control. With me, he was always what I wished; with others, he was never any thing but what he wished to be himself. He was, by all who saw him, whether of the higher or lower classes, taken notice of; and by all considered as very clever. I speak of a child between seven and eight years old . . .

I must not here omit a remarkable circumstance, which ought to be recorded in justice to Rousseau's penetration in judging of children. In passing through Paris at this time, we went to see him: he took a good deal of notice of my boy; I asked him to tell me any thing that struck him in the child's manners or conversation. He took my son with him in his usual morning's walk, and when he came back, Rousseau told me, that, as far as he could judge from two hours observation, he thought him a boy of abilities, which had been well cultivated; and that in particular his answers to some questions on history proved, contrary to the opinion given in Emilius and Sophia, that history can be advantageously learned by children, if it be taught reasonably, and not merely by rote. 'But,' said Rousseau, 'I remark in your son a propensity to party prejudice, which will be a great blemish in his character.'

I asked how he could in so short a time form so decided an opinion. He told me, that, whenever my son saw a handsome horse, or a handsome carriage in the street, he always exclaimed, 'That is an English horse, or an English carriage!' And that, even down to a pair of shoe-buckles, every thing that appeared to be good of its kind was always pronounced by him to be English. 'This sort of party prejudice,' said Rousseau, 'if suffered to become a ruling motive in his mind, will lead to a thousand evils: for not only will his own country, his own village, or club, or even a knot of his private acquaintance, be the object of his exclusive admiration; but he will be governed by his companions, whatever they may be, and they will become the arbiters of his destiny.'

In fact, the boy had the species of party spirit, which Rousseau remarked, and this prophecy, as after events proved, shewed his sagacity.

Mrs Hester Lynche Thrale wrote a book of anecdotes about her close friendship with Dr Samuel Johnson (1709–1784). Here she reports a conversation with him.

'Who,' he [Dr Johnson] said, 'might be very good children if they were let alone; but the father is never easy when he is not making them do something which they cannot do; they must repeat a fable, or a speech, or the Hebrew alphabet; and they might as well count twenty, for what they know of the matter: however, the father says half, for he prompts every other word. But he could not have chosen a man who would have been less entertained by such means.'

'I believe not!' cried Mrs. Thrale; 'nothing is more ridiculous than parents cramming their children's nonsense down other people's throats. I keep mine as much out of the way as I can.'

'Yours, madam,' answered he, 'are in nobody's way; no children can be better managed or less troublesome; but your fault is a too great perverseness in not allowing anybody to give them anything. Why should they not have a cherry or a gooseberry as well as bigger children?'

'Because they are sure to return such gifts by wiping their hands upon the giver's gown or coat, and nothing makes children more offensive. People only make the offer to please the parents, and they wish the poor children at Jericho when they accept it.'

A propos her father:

Rakish men seldom make tender fathers, but a man must fondle something.

Mrs Thrale has not been considered a good mother, but most of us would sympathise with this complaint.

How little do these wise Men know or feel, that the crying of a young child, or the perverseness of an elder or the danger however trifling of any one – will soon drive out of a female parent's head a conversation concerning wit, science or sentiment, however she may appear to be impressed with it at the moment; besides that to a Mere de Famille doing something is more necessary & suitable than even hearing something; and if one is to listen all evening and write all morning what one has heard – where will be the time for tutoring, caressing, or what is still more useful, for having one's children about one: I therefore charge all my neglect to my young one's account.

Mrs Thrale rightly thought Dr Burney a goose-cap for not allowing his daughter Fanny (1752–1840) to learn Latin.

## July 1781

Dr. Burney did not like his daughter should learn Latin even of Johnson, who offered to teach her for friendship, because then she would have been as wise as himself forsooth, and Latin was too masculine for Misses. A narrow-souled goose-cap the man must be at last, agreeable and amiable all the while too, beyond almost any other human creature. Well, mortal man is but a paltry animal! the best of us have such drawbacks both upon virtue, wisdom, and knowledge.

❧

Matthew Boulton (1728–1809) was a manufacturer, engineer and partner to James Watt, the inventor of the steam engine. Boulton writes from Cornwall, to his son Matthew, aged twelve, about examining the rocks and minerals that he has found locally.

## 28th October, 1782

There is nothing could add to this pleasure so much as the having your assistance in making solutions precipitations filtrations evaporations & chrystalizations; but previous to the exercising of any art or science it is necessary to learn it, and previous to that, it is necessary you should learn certain languages such as your own, the latin, the french; and then go to the university to learn science & then you come to the more agreeable part: viz: the application of that knowledge . . .

Mary Robinson (1756/8?–1800), famous actress and author, describes the occasion when her daughter says her first word. At the time, she and her child were living in the Fleet prison with her husband, who had been imprisoned for debt.

It was during one of these night walks that my little daughter first blessed my ears with the articulation of words. The circumstance made a forcible and indelible impression on my mind. It was a clear moonlight evening; the infant was in the arms of her nursery maid; she was dancing her up and down, and I was playing with her; her eyes were fixed upon the moon, to which she pointed with her small forefinger; – on a sudden a cloud passed over it, and the child, with a slow falling of her hand, articulately sighed, *"all gone!"* This had been a customary expression with her maid, whenever the infant wanted any thing which it was deemed prudent to withhold or to hide from her. These little nothings will appear insignificant to the common reader; but to the parent whose heart is ennobled by sensibility, they will become matters of important interest. I can only add, that I walked till near midnight, watching every cloud that passed over the moon, and as often, with a rapturous sensation, hearing my little prattler repeat her observation.

❧

Lord Bessborough (1758–1844) writes to his wife on a journey to Europe, with his small son, aged six. He is pretty casual about the fact that France and England are at war, but his attention is on the boy (although his enthusiasm for reading aloud depends on the circumstances).

Ostend, 23rd August, 1793

I write one line to tell you we are arrived here safe. Willy was very sick at one time but slept a good deal & is not the worse. We were 11 hours. He is much entertained with everybody he has seen here. We heard a good deal of firing near Dunkirk. They say we have defeated some part of the French army near there. We shall come on piano piano.

25th August

We mean to sleep tomorrow at Bonn. . . . [Willy] is very entertaining & has mighty odd expressions. His great rage is at present to go into a nunnery to see the nuns. He says he understands after he is 7 they will not let him in.

30th August

[Willy] has his own sheets & mattress, and never wakes from the time he goes to bed till we call him, & he is always in bed by ½ past 8, so you need be under no concern about him. . . . We stuff a great deal, for I dine with him between 1 & 2, & then drink tea when he sups, and have my supper after he is in bed.

Munich, 5th September

Dear Willy is perfectly well but we have had some sad quarrells, a little in the stile of Caro's [the future Caroline Lamb], when he grows tired. I wrote you word he was to be Governor during the journey, it is a very arbitrary Government, I have been made to read today 3 volumes thro' aloud in the chaise of his books, & being hoarse or choked with dust is not admitted as an excuse, & having read them thro' several times is no reason why they should not be read over again. Mrs Jennet is the one I am most afraid of, as there are 96 pages.

❧

Sydney Smith writes to Mrs Beach. How did babies and children ever survive the medical treatments they were given?

July 1802

Mrs. Smith is much better, and my little girl perfectly recovered from a severe attack of the croup. By the bye, it may be worth while to inform you that she was saved from this fatal and rapid disease by taking two grains of calomel every hour till the symptoms subsided, and then gradually lessening the doses; so that she took in twenty-four hours thirty-two grains, besides bleeding and blistering and emetics; and is not yet six months old.

A year later, he writes to Lady Caroline Fox, after moving from Edinburgh to London. Saba was his daughter.

### 24th August, 1803

The children are two of the stoutest animals I ever saw. The Waiters on the road all called little Saba the Boy. What can you possibly mean by saying that Country air is the best for children?

❦

Samuel Taylor Coleridge writes to Thomas Poole about his son David Hartley, aged seven.

### 14th October, 1803

Hartley is what he always was – a strange strange Boy – "*exquisitely wild*"! An utter Visionary! like the Moon among thin Clouds, he moves in a circle of Light of his own making – he alone, in a Light of his own. Of all human Beings I never yet saw one so utterly naked of *Self* – he has no Vanity, no Pride, no Resentment and tho' *very passionate*, I never yet saw him *angry with* any body. He is, tho' now 7 years old, the merest Child, you can conceive – and yet Southey says, that the Boy keeps him in perpetual Wonderment – his Thoughts are so truly his own. [He is] not generally speaking an *affectionate* Child but his Dispositions are very sweet. A great Lover of Truth, and of the finest moral nicety of Feeling – apprehension all over – & yet he is always Dreaming. He said very prettily about half a year ago – on my reproving him for some inattention, & asking him if he did not see something – 'My Father!' quoth he with flute-like Voice – 'I see it – I saw it – I see it now – & tomorrow I shall see it when I shut my eyes, and when my eyes are open & I am looking at other Things; but Father! it's a sad pity – but it can't be helped, you know – but I am always being a bad Boy, because I am always *thinking of my Thoughts*.' – He is troubled with Worms – & to night has had a clyster of oil & Lime water, which never fails to set him to rights for a month or two – . If God will preserve his Life for me, it will be interesting to know what he will be – for it is not my opinion, or the opinion of two or of three, but all who have been with him, talk of him as of a thing that cannot be forgotten.

Four years later Coleridge's expectations of his son, now aged ten, have veered from the poetic to the hopelessly unrealistic. Apparently even the most radical poets want their children to conform and succeed in society when they are young.

## 3rd April, 1807

You are by nature very kind and forgiving, and wholly free from revenge and sullenness; you are likewise gifted with a very active and self-gratifying fancy, and such a high tide and flood of pleasurable feelings, that all unpleasant and painful thoughts and events are hurried away upon it, and neither remain in the surface of your memory nor sink to the bottom of your heart. So far all seems right and matter of thanksgiving to your Maker; and so all really *is* so, and will be so, if you exert your reason and free will. But on the other hand the very same disposition makes you less impressible both to the censure of your anxious friends and to the whispers of your conscience. Nothing that gives you pain dwells long enough upon your mind to do you any good, just as in some diseases the medicines pass so quickly through the stomach and bowels as to be able to exert none of their healing qualities. In like manner, this power which you possess of shoving aside all disagreeable reflections, or losing them in a labyrinth of day-dreams, which saves you from some present pain, has, on the other hand, interwoven with your nature habits of procrastination, which, unless you correct them in time (and it will require all your best exertions to do it effectually), must lead you into lasting unhappiness.

You are now going with me (if God have not ordered it otherwise) into Devonshire to visit your Uncle G. Coleridge. He is a very good man and very kind; but his notions of right and of propriety are very strict, and he is, therefore, exceedingly shocked by any gross deviations from what is right and proper. I take, therefore, this means of warning you against those bad habits, which I and all your friends here have noticed in you; and, be assured, I am not writing in anger, but on the contrary with great love, and a comfortable hope that your behaviour at Ottery will be such as to do yourself and me and your dear mother *credit*.

First, then, I conjure you never to do anything of any kind when out of sight which you would not do in my presence. What is a frail and faulty father on earth compared with God, your heavenly Father? But God is always present. Specially, never pick at or snatch up anything, eatable or not. I know it is only an idle, foolish trick; but your Ottery relations would consider you as a little thief; and in the Church Catechism *picking* and *stealing* are both put together as two sorts of the same vice, "And keep my hands from picking and stealing." And besides, it is a dirty trick; and people of weak stomachs would turn sick at a dish which a young *filth-paw* had been fingering.

Next, when you have done wrong acknowledge it at once, like a man. Excuses may show your ingenuity, but they make your *honesty* suspected. And a grain of honesty is better than a pound of wit. We may admire a man for his cleverness; but we love and esteem him only for his goodness; and a strict attachment to truth, and to the whole truth, with openness and frankness and simplicity is at once the foundation stone of all goodness, and no small part of the superstructure. Lastly, do what you have to do at once, and put it out of hand. No procrastination; no self-delusion; no 'I am sure I can say it, I need not learn it again,' etc., which *sures* are such very unsure folks that nine times out of ten their sureships break their word and disappoint you.

Among the lesser faults I beg you to endeavour to remember not to stand between the half-opened door, either while you are speaking, or spoken to. But come *in* or go out, and always speak and listen with the door shut. Likewise, not to speak so loud, or abruptly, and never to interrupt your elders while they are speaking, and not to talk at all during meals. I pray you, keep this letter, and read it over every two or three days.

Take but a little trouble with yourself, and every one will be delighted with you, and try to gratify you in all your reasonable wishes. And, above all, you will be at peace with yourself, and a double blessing to me, who am, my dear, my very dear Hartley, most anxiously, your fond father,

S.T. Coleridge.

P.S. I have not spoken about your mad passions and frantic looks and pout-mouthing; because I trust that is all over.

Captain Fremantle, a close friend of Lord Nelson, writes to his wife Betsey at the turn of the nineteenth century. Families are thought to have been as child-centred then as they are today, but Thomas Fremantle's experiences in the Navy may well have made him favour a tougher approach than his wife.

### Bantry Bay, 5th November, 1803

You will I am sure consider that your conduct will form a very leading feature to your Sisters who are now living with you, and that you will not indulge them in Idleness, – but if there is any subject on which I feel diffident, it is that your kindness and affection for the Children will lead you to take *too much care* of them, believe me that nothing tends more to health than exercise and Air, and that the more they are out of the house the better. I have this day been in several of the Cottages, where the poor wretches of Children of a year and a half old take care of themselves, and are infinitely more healthy than any Gentleman's Children I ever saw, if you Nurse them too much be assured they will ever have cause to lament it, and they will not be able to undergo the vicissitudes of this life, – If I thought any man could have a more real or sincere Love for his family than I have I should not have ventured to have expressed what I now do. Consider what your boys must undergo before they arrive even at Manhood, and I am sure you will agree with me that it is not wise to bring them up too tenderly.

❧

Lord Nelson (1758–1805) writes attentively to Horatia (1801–1881), his daughter by Emma Hamilton (1761–1815).

### 1803

My dear Horatia,

I feel very much pleased by your kind letter, and for your present of a lock of your beautiful hair. I am very glad to hear that you are so good, and mind everything which your Governess and Lady Hamilton tell you. I send you a lock of my hair, and a one-pound note to buy a locket to put it in, and I give you leave to wear it when you are dressed and behave well; and I send you another to buy some little thing for Mary and your Governess. As I am sure for the world, you would not tell a story, it must have slipt my memory that I promised you a watch, therefore I have sent to Naples to get one, and I will send it home as soon as it arrives. The Dog I never could have promised, as we have no Dogs on board ship.

*Nelson, keenly aware of the dangers of drowning and the difficulty of making your way in the world without money or influence, does his best to protect his daughter on both counts.*

### off Toulon, 14th March, 1804

. . . I also beg, as my dear Horatia is to be at Merton, that a strong netting, about three feet high, may be placed round the Nile [the local river], that the little thing may not tumble in; and, then, you may have ducks again in it. I forget, at what place we saw the netting; and either Mr. Perry, or Mr. Goldsmid, told us where it was to be bought. I shall be very anxious until I know this is done. . . .

I shall, when I come home, settle four thousand pounds in trustees' hands, for Horatia; for I will not put it in my own power to have her left destitute; for she would want friends, if we left her in this world. She will be independent of any smiles or frowns.

*Soon after Nelson's death on 21st October 1805, Emma writes about Horatia, then aged five, and recently pulled down by chickenpox. Emma regards her daughter with sad sentimentality.*

### 1806

My dearest Horatia is so well and strong and now eats and drinks and sleeps well, and creates universal interest, – altho' Princess Charlotte is here she is left, and all come to look at Nelsons angel. She improves in languages, musick, & accomplishments, but my heart bleeds to think how proud wou'd her glorious Father have been, he that lived only for her, whose last words & thoughts to her – she wou'd have been every thing, 'tis dreadfull to me.

A few years later, two letters addressed to Horatia, aged twelve, suggest that Emma thinks her less obliging as she grows into adolescence. Emma was an inconsistent and histrionic mother who, owing to her daughter's illegitimacy, spent much of Horatia's childhood pretending to be her aunt.

### 18th April, 1813

Ah, Horatia! if you had grown up as I wish'd you, what a joy, what a comfort might you have been to me! for I have been constant to you, and willingly pleased for every manifestation you shew'd to learn and profit of my lessons, and I have ever been most willing to overlook injuries. But now 'tis for myself I speak & write. Look into yourself well, correct yourself of your errors, your caprices, your nonsensical follies, for by your inattention you have forfeited all claims to my future kindness. I have weathered many a storm for your sake, but these frequent blows have kill'd me. Listen, then, from a mother who speaks from the dead! Reform your conduct, or you will be detested by all the world, & when you shall no longer have my fostering arm to sheild you, whoe betide you! you will sink to nothing Be good, be honourable, tell not falsehood, be not capricious, follow the advice of the mother whom I shall place you in at school, for a governess must act as mother. I grieve & lament to see the increasing strength of your turbulent passions; I weep & pray you may not be totally lost; my fervent prayers are offered up to God for you; I hope you will yet become sensible of your eternal wellfare. I shall go join your father & my blessed mother & may you on your death-bed have as little to reproach yourself as your once affectionate mother has, for I can glorify, & say I was a good child. *Can Horatia Nelson say so? I am unhappy to say you CANNOT. . . .*

P.S. Look on me now as gone from this world.

### 31st October

Horatia, – Your conduct is so bad, your falsehoods so dreadfull, your cruel treatment to me such that I cannot live under these afflicting circumstances; my poor heart is broken. If my poor mother was living to take my part, broken as I am with grief and ill-health, I should be happy to breathe my last in her arms. I thank you for what you have done to-day. You have helped me on nearer to God, and may God forgive you.

The following year, Emma, as insecure financially as she was as a mother, writes to Sir William Scott, trying to provide for her daughter's future.

If my dear Horatia were provided for I should die happy, and if I could only now be enabled to make her more comfortable and finish her education, oh God how I would bless them that enabled me to do it! She already reads, writes, and speaks Italian, French and English, and I am teaching her German and Spanish. Music she knows but all must yet be cultivated to perfection, and then our own language, geography, arithmetic, etc. etc., she knows. . . .

Horatia is adored, she dances all those dances, and speaks French like a French girl. She is good, virtuous and religious.

❧

Dora Jordan (1761–1816), a remarkable woman and famous comic actress, was the mistress of the Duke of Clarence, by whom she had ten children. Boys were sent off to the Navy and to war at a frighteningly young age; her son Henry (1797–1817) was sent to be a midshipman at the age of eleven.

Two years is a long time to lose the society of so dear a child as Henry, but we must give up our children to the World, for our own sakes, and I will reconcile myself to the separation as well as I can.

❧

Sydney Smith writes to John Allen about his son Douglas, aged nine.

10th March, 1814

We are all very well; tho' Douglas alarmed us the other night with the croup. I darted into him all the mineral, and vegetable resources of the shops, cravatted his throat with blisters, and fringed it with leeches, excited now the Peristaltic, now the Antiperistaltic motion . . . and set him in 5 or 6 hours to play at marbles, breathing gently and inaudibly . . .

Sydney Smith adopts a characteristically teasing tone in the last doubtful phrase.

There is more happiness in a multitude of children than safety in a multitude of counsellors and if I were a rich man, I should like to have and would have 20 children. The haunts of happiness are varied and rather unaccountable; but I have more often seen her among little children, and home firesides, and in country houses, than anywhere else – at least, I think so.

ᘛᘚ

William Lamb (1779–1848), who became the prime minister, Lord Melbourne, married Caroline, who was notorious for her volatile behaviour and her later infatuation with Lord Byron.

Before I was married, whenever I saw the children and the dogs allowed, or rather caused, to be troublesome in any family, I used to lay it all to the fault of the master of it, who might at once put a stop to it if he pleased. Since I have married, I find that this was a very rash and premature judgment.

ᘛᘚ

Harriette Wilson (1786–1846) was a courtesan and the mistress of the Duke of Wellington. She writes with ironic amusement of the liberal-minded way in which her sister brings up her children.

1825

. . . I drove to the house of a married sister of mine, whose name we will call Paragon, since she was the very paragon of mothers, having drawn up a new patent system of education for her children, better than Jean Jacques Rousseau's, and unlike everybody's else.

Her family consists of two boys and two girls. The eldest daughter was then nearly seven years of age: her son and heir had scarcely attained his fifth year. "They shall never go to school," said my sister Paragon, "nor will I suffer them to be left, one instant, to the care of nurses or servants, to learn bad grammar and worse morals. . . . They shall never obtain what they want by tears, nor rudeness, after the age of two; and it shall depend on the politeness and humility of their deportment, whether they have any dinner or not; and nothing shall be called indecent, which is natural, either in words or deeds. So much for the minds of my children; and, with regard to their bodily health, I shall make them swallow one of Anderson's Scots Aperient Pills every night of their blessed lives! *et il n'y aura rien à craindre!*"

. . . the children were all running about stark naked, as they were born, laughing, romping, and playing with each other. Little Sophia, who was not yet two years of age, did nothing but run after her beautiful brother Henry, a dear little laughing boy, who was about to celebrate his fourth birthday. Little Sophia, bred in the school of nature, handled her brother rather oddly, I thought.

"Surely it is Nature's own sweet work!" said Paragon.

"Mamma! mamma!" called out little Henry.

"What is the matter, my love?" said Paragon.

"Is Sophy to have my did—dle to keep?"

"No, my love," answered mamma with calm dignity, "not to keep, only to play with!"

❧

William Cobbett gives a clear example of the influence of Jean Jacques Rousseau in his belief that children should be brought up naturally and free of all constraint.

## 1829

Besides *sweet air*, children want *exercise*. Even when they are babies in arms, they want tossing and pulling about, and want talking and singing to. They should be put upon their feet by slow degrees, according to the strength of their legs; and this is a matter which a good mother will attend to with incessant care. If they appear to be likely to *squint*, she will, always when they wake up, and frequently in the day, take care to present some pleasing object *right before*, and *never on the side* of their face. If they appear, when they begin to talk, to indicate a propensity to *stammer*, she will stop them, repeat the word or words slowly herself, and get them to do the same. These precautions are amongst the most sacred of the duties of parents; for, remember, the deformity is *for life*; a thought which will fill every good parent's heart with solicitude. All *swaddling* and *tight covering* are mischievous. They produce distortions of some sort or other. To let children creep and roll about till they get upon their legs of themselves is a very good way. I never saw a *native American* with crooked limbs or hump-back, and never heard any man say that he had seen one. And the reason is, doubtless, the loose dress in which children, from the moment of their birth, are kept, the good food that they always have, and the sweet air that they breathe in consequence of the absence of all dread of poverty on the part of the parents.

᷐᷐

The Countess of Sutherland writes to her husband about how to look after their children in the event of her death.

As to the children, pray get my mother . . . to take care of the girls and if I leave my boys too little to go to school . . . a man can't take care of little children as a woman can. Don't be as careless of the dear children as when you relied on me to take care of them.

᷐᷐

Elizabeth Gaskell (1810–1865) was a novelist and mother of five children. This letter was sent to her sister-in-law, Anne Robson, to explain her anxieties over the care of her eldest daughter, Marianne (MA), aged six, in the event of her own death. (Meta was her daughter Margaret, aged three, and William was Elizabeth's husband.)

23rd December, 1840

I have of course had MA more with me during this delicacy of hers, and I am more and more anxious about her – not exactly her health; but I see hers is a peculiar character – *very* dependent on those around her – almost as much so as Meta is *in*dependent & in this point I look to Meta to strengthen her. But I am more and more convinced that love & sympathy are very *very* much required by MA. The want of them would make MA an unhappy character, probably sullen and deceitful – while the sunshine of love & tenderness would do everything for her. She is very conscientious, and very tender-hearted – Now Anne, will you remember this? It is difficult to have the right trust in God almost, when thinking about one's children – and you know I have no sister or near relation whom I could entreat to watch over any peculiarity in their disposition. Now you know that dear William feeling most kindly towards his children, is yet most reserved in *expressions* of either affection or sympathy – & in case of my death, we all know the probability of widowers marrying again, – would you promise, dearest Anne to remember MA's peculiarity of character, and as much as circumstances would permit, watch over & cherish her. The feeling, the conviction that you were aware of my wishes and would act upon them would be *such* a comfort to me.

ॐ

William Thackeray writes to his mother about his daughter Anne (1837–1919), aged two.

1st–2nd December, 1839

. . . from six o'clock until ten last night Miss Thackeray roared incessantly in a hearty furious fit of passion wh. wd. have done your heart good to hear. I don't know what it was that appeased her but at the expiration of these four hours the yowling stopped and Miss began to prattle as quietly and gaily as if nothing had happened. What are the mysteries of children? how are they moved I wonder? – I have made Missy lots of pictures, and really am growing quite a domestic character. Kemble's child can sing twelve tunes but it is as ugly as sin in revenge. However we must n't brag: for every body who comes into the house remarks Missy's squint that strange to say has grown quite imperceptible to me.

. . . There is a grand power of imagination about these little creatures, and a creative fancy and belief that is very curious to watch: it fades away in the light of common day: I am sure that the horrid matter-of-fact child-rearers Miss Edgeworth and the like, with their cursed twopenny-halfpenny realities do away with the child's most beautiful privilege. I am determined that Amy shall have a very extensive and instructive store of learning in Tom Thumbs, Jack-the-Giant-Killers &c what use is there in the paltry store of small facts that are stowed into these poor little creatures' brains?

Charles Darwin continues to observe the behaviour of his son William as he grows older. His observations were not published until 1877, nearly forty years after they were made.

## 1841

*Anger.* – It was difficult to decide at how early an age anger was felt; on his eighth day he frowned and wrinkled the skin round his eyes before a crying fit, but this may have been due to pain or distress, and not to anger. When about ten weeks old, he was given some rather cold milk and he kept a slight frown on his forehead all the time that he was sucking, so that he looked like a grown-up person made cross from being compelled to do something which he did not like. When nearly four months old, and perhaps much earlier, there could be no doubt, from the manner in which the blood gushed into his whole face and scalp, that he easily got into a violent passion. A small cause sufficed; thus, when a little over seven months old, he screamed with rage because a lemon slipped away and he could not seize it with his hands. When eleven months old, if a wrong plaything was given to him, he would push it away and beat it; I presume that the beating was an instinctive sign of anger, like the snapping of the jaws by a young crocodile just out of the egg, and not that he imagined he could hurt the plaything. When two years and three months old, he became a great adept at throwing books or sticks, &c., at anyone who offended him; and so it was with some of my other sons. On the other hand, I could never see a trace of such aptitude in my infant daughters; and this makes me think that a tendency to throw objects is inherited by boys.

*Fear.* – This feeling is probably one of the earliest which is experienced by infants, as shown by their starting at any sudden sound when only a few weeks old, followed by crying. Before the present one was 4½ months old I had been accustomed to make close to him many strange and loud noises, which were all taken as excellent jokes, but at this period I one day made a loud snoring noise which I had never done before; he instantly looked grave and then burst out crying. Two or three days afterwards, I made through forgetfulness the same noise with the same result. About the same time (*viz.* on the 137th day) I approached with my back towards him and then stood motionless; he looked very grave and much surprised, and would soon have cried, had I not turned round; then his face instantly relaxed into a smile.

It is well known how intensely older children suffer from vague and undefined fears, as from the dark, or in passing an obscure corner in a large hall, &c. I may give as an instance that I took the child in question, when 2¼ years old, to the Zoological Gardens, and he enjoyed looking at all the animals which were like those that he knew, such as deer, antelopes &c., and all the birds, even the ostriches, but was much alarmed at the various larger animals in cages. He often said afterwards that he wished to go again, but not to see 'beasts in houses'; and we could in no manner account for this fear. May we not suspect that the vague but very real fears of children, which are quite independent of experience, are the inherited effects of real dangers and abject superstitions during ancient savage times? It is quite conformable with what we know of the transmission of formerly well-developed characters, that they should appear at an early period of life, and afterwards disappear. . . .

A little later (2 years and 7½ months old) I met him coming out of the dining room with his eyes unnaturally bright, and an odd unnatural or affected manner, so that I went into the room to see who was there, and found that he had been taking pounded sugar, which he had been told not to do. As he had never been in any way punished, his odd manner certainly was not due to fear, and I suppose it was pleasurable excitement struggling with conscience. A fortnight afterwards, I met him coming out of the same room, and he was eyeing his pinafore which he had carefully rolled up; and again his manner was so odd that I determined to see what was within his pinafore, notwithstanding that he said there was nothing and repeatedly commanded me to 'go away,' and I found it stained with pickle-juice; so that here was carefully planned deceit. As this child was educated solely by working on his good feelings, he soon became as truthful, open, and tender, as anyone could desire.

Lady Charlotte Elizabeth Guest (1812–1895), writer and scholar, muses over the misery of having to send her sons to public school, after a journey in which she passed through Eton and Windsor.

### 5th September, 1845

When I thought of all the sorrow and temptations my poor boys would have to go through in that place I quite shuddered and prayed that assistance might be granted them from above. It seems a sad prospect, but everybody says it is the only way to bring up boys; and what is to be done? How can I, a poor weak woman, judge against all the world

⚬⚭⚬

Henrietta Stanley writes to her mother-in-law after visiting the house at Eton to which one of her sons will go. Generations of parents have tolerated the most surprising irregularities at the boarding schools to which they have sent their children.

### 13th April, 1850

I saw Mr. Coleridge yesterday, he called, & I was quite enchanted with his manners & conversation, he looks so firm & yet so kind. He has such a very good set of boys in his house. He says he thinks there is no place any where like Eton for the advantage of public & private education, but there are fearful stories of drunkenness & people do not scruple to name two of the masters as not being free from that vice.

⚬⚭⚬

William Thackeray writes to his daughter Anne, aged twelve. In his letters, Thackeray often beguiled his daughters with a combination of jokes and admonitions. (Miss Trulock was the governess.)

### 22nd(?) May, 1850

Miss Trulock has had a good offer of 100 [shillings] a year and Im afraid must leave us – there will be the business to do over again, the same perplexities botherations uncertainties Why dont you get a little older and do without a governess? You will some day when you'll spell excursion with an S not a T.

Don't make doggrel verses and spell badly for fun. There should be a lurking prettiness in all buffoonery even, and it requires an art which you dont know yet to make *good* bad verses – to make bad ones is dull work.

And don't scribble faces at the bottom of your letters to ladies – They shouldn't be done unless they are clever – they are not respectful or ladylike else do you understand? I like you to make jokes to me because I can afford to tell you whether they are bad or good or to scold you as now: but Mrs Brookfield is too kind to do so: and when you write to her or to any other lady you should write your very best – I dont mean be affected and use fine words, but be careful grateful and ladylike.

ෆ෦ි

Charles Darwin writes to his cousin, William Darwin Fox. For a man of creative and scholarly genius, Darwin was an unusually solicitous and thoughtful father, but in the matter of education he shows, after a bit of a struggle, a characteristic preference for convention.

4th September, 1850

My wife and all my children are well; & they, the children, are now seven in number; to what I am to bring up my four Boys, even already sorely perplexes me. My eldest boy is showing the hereditary principle, by a passion for collecting Lepidoptera. We are at present very full of the subject of schools; I cannot endure to think of sending my Boys to waste 7 or 8 years in making miserable Latin verses, & we have heard some good of Bruce Castle School . . . so that on Friday we are going to inspect it & the Boys. I feel that it is an awful experiment to depart from the usual course, however bad that course may be. – Have you, who have something of an omniscient tendency in you, ever heard anything of this school?

10th October

We were very glad to get the sentence about Bruce Castle school, for we are still in an awesome state of indecision between Rugby & it. I knew you were just the man to apply to to get information upon any out of the way subject. – We have taken much pains in making enquiries, &

upon the whole the balance is decidedly favourable; yet there is so much novelty in the system that we cannot help being much afraid at trying an experiment on so important a subject. At Bruce castle, they do not begin Latin, till a Boy can read, write, spell & count *well*: they have no punishments except stopping premiums on good behaviour. I do not see how we are ever to come to a decision; but we must soon. – Willy is 11 this coming Christmas, & backward for his age; though sensible and observant. I rather think we shall send him to Bruce C. School.

A year and a half later, Willy, aged twelve, went to Rugby; Darwin wrote that he had not had the courage to break away from 'the old stereotyped classical education'. He changed his mind after Willy's experience and his other sons were sent to Clapham Grammar School. He writes to Willy in his first term.

24th February, 1852

My dear old Willy

I have not for a very long time been more pleased than I was this morning at receiving your letter with the *excellent* news at your having got so good a place. We are both rejoiced at it, & give you our hearty congratulations. It is in every respect a very good thing, for you will be amongst an older set of Boys. Your letter was a very good one, & told us all that we liked to hear: it was well expressed & you must have taken some pains to write it. We are so very glad to hear that you are happy & comfortable; long may you keep so my dear Boy. – What a tremendous, awful, stunning, dreadful, terrible, bothering steeple-chase you have run: I am astonished at your getting in the 5th. When next you write, explain how it came that you, a new Boy, & Erny, an old Boy, came to run together? What boys run, all those in your house? or in your Form? . . .

Next Sunday when you write here, tell us who your master is, & what Books you are in; & give us a History of the last Friday. The more you can write, the better we shall be pleased. All the servants enquire about you; and so they did at Aunt Sarah's. I was there the other day & saw the pretty little grey Hens. We are doing nothing particular; one day is like another: I go my morning walk & often think of you, & Georgy draws every day many Horse-guards; and Lizzie shivers & makes as many extraordinary grimaces as ever, & Lenny is as fat as ever. We shall probably come & see you during the first week in April. Have you seen anything of Cator?

Farewell my dear Willy; may you go on as well as you have begun. All here send their best loves to you.

> Your affectionate Father
> C. Darwin

Give my Love to Erny

I was saying before Georgy [aged seven] that he did not much like reading, when he said "No, I hate reading, but I like money." – I suppose he thought this made up for his not liking reading. –

⚛

Prince Albert writes to Queen Victoria, putting forward a convincing argument for her failure to enjoy the company of her children.

1st October, 1856

It is indeed a pity that you find no consolation in the company of your children. The root of the trouble lies in the mistaken notion that the function of a mother is to be always correcting, scolding, ordering them about and organising their activities. It is not possible to be on happy friendly terms with people you have just been scolding.

⚛

Samuel Palmer (1805–1881), the visionary painter, writes to his friend George Richmond after his family has recovered from scarlet fever. Palmer's daughter had died in December 1847, at the age of three.

December 1859

But the atmosphere! Would that I could send it in a bag to be let off under the nose of the Austrians in Venice! The single item of pain suffered for sick children, of anxiety terror and sometimes inconsolable grief – are a very very abundant offset to the desolateness of celibacy which people talk so much about. But as a man is to be full of misery . . . It is perhaps better for our souls to suffer the larger portion of that misery in sympathy for our poor suffering children – than like the bachelor chiefly on account of his own annoyances – His buttered muffins won't sit on his stomach his corns keep shooting like Enfield rifles – and withal he is miserable and don't know what's the matter with him –

Well! He comes to me and says 'Shall I marry? You're fond of children, you know the pleasure of yearning over them and loving them with all your heart'. What can I say to him but this? 'My dear friend I have had my heart once broken and this day I might have been the most miserable of men. In every single illness of those dear ones I have outsuffered your whole life with its shooting corns and buttered muffins.'

☙❧

David Livingstone (1813–1873), the explorer and missionary, had three children, two sons and a daughter, who were born in Africa; in 1852 they were taken back to England where they lived with their mother. Livingstone writes to his daughter Agnes, aged twelve.

River Shire, 1st June, 1859

The country is quite a Highland region, and many people live in it. Most of them were afraid of us. The women ran into their huts and shut the doors. The children screamed in terror, and even the hens would fly away and leave their chickens. I suppose you would be frightened too, if you saw strange creatures, say a lot of Trundlemen, like those on the Isle of Man pennies, come whirling up the street. . . . We saw the sticks [the slave traders] employ for training any one whom they have just bought. One is about eight feet long, the head, or the neck rather, is put into the space between the dotted lines and shaft, and another slave carries the end. When they are considered tame they are allowed to go in chains.

I am working that in the course of time this horrid system may cease. All the country we travelled through is capable of growing cotton and sugar, and the people cultivate a good deal. They would grow much more if they could only sell it. At present we in England are the mainstay of slavery in America and elsewhere by buying slave-grown produce. . . But all is in the hands of the all-wise Father.

My dear Agnes, you must take Him to be your Father and Guide. Tell him all that is in your heart, and make Him your confidant. . . .

My kind love to Grandma and all your friends. I hope your eyes are better and that you are able to read books for yourself. Tell Tom that we caught a young elephant in coming down the Shire, about the size of the largest dog he ever saw, but one of the Makolo, in a state of excitement, cut its trunk, so that it bled very much, and died in two days. Had it lived we would have sent it to the Queen, as no African* elephant was ever seen in England.

Later in his life he writes in his diary:

## 1870

I often ponder over my missionary career among the Bakwains and though conscious of many imperfections, not a single pang of regret arises in the view of my conduct, except that I did not feel it to be my duty, while spending all my energy in teaching the heathen, to devote a special portion of my time to play with my children. But generally I was so much exhausted with the mental and manual labour of the day, that in the evening there was no fun left in me. I did not play with my little ones while I had them, and they soon sprung up in my absences, and left me conscious that I had none to play with.

ॐ

Queen Victoria writes to her daughter Victoria, the Crown Princess of Prussia. It seems an odd idea to us that children should be objects of admiration for their prettiness, but otherwise she sums up precisely what many parents will always feel.

## 9th March, 1870

You are wrong in thinking that I am not fond of children. I am. I admire pretty ones – especially peasant children – immensely but I can't bear their being idolised and made too great objects of – or having a number of them about me, making a great noise.

*Livingstone was wrong about the elephant. An African elephant arrived in England in 1255 and Matthew Paris drew it. See *Cet étrange colosse* (2008) by Alan Hutchison.

## 5th January, 1876

You will find as the children grow up that as a rule children are a bitter disappointment – their greatest object being to do precisely what their parents do not wish and have anxiously tried to prevent.

## 19th January

Most extraordinary it is to see that the more care has been taken in every way the less often they succeed! And often when children have been less watched and less taken care of – the better they turn out!! This is inexplicable and very annoying.

❧

*Thomas James Cobden-Sanderson follows John Locke's recommendations on the best way to bring up children. His first son, Richard (Dickie), was aged nineteen months.*

## 5th June, 1886

Here I must enter something about Dickie. Our anxiety for his future makes us careful in ridding him of bad habits and making his will 'supple,' as Locke – whom we are now reading – would say. The other night he cried after being put to bed, not of course from pain, but mere contrariness. I tried to induce him to be quiet and failed. I then took him out of bed and whipped him, and as he cried out even more, pressed him close to me and held his head and bade him be quiet. In a moment, after a convulsive sob or two, he became quite quiet. I put him back in his cot, told him to be quiet and to go to sleep, and left him. Not a sound more did he make, and he went to sleep. The next day at noon he cried again when put to bed. I went to him, told him he must not cry, that he must lie down – he stands up in bed on such occasions and usually is found arranging his blanket over the rails of his cot – be quiet and go to sleep. I placed him properly in bed, spread the clothes over him and left him. He became and remained perfectly quiet, and went to sleep. He now goes to bed noon and night and to sleep without a cry. If this can be done, how much more may not be done? What a responsibility! What a superb instrument, gymnast of virtue and of beautiful conduct, may not a man be made early in life! Further, when he first came to sleep with us he used to wake at 5 a.m., and after that hour there was no rest for us. We thought it necessary to provide him with toys to play with in his cot. These he soon got tired of. This after a time was found to be unendurable, neither Annie nor I could stand the fatigue. Moreover, could he? Now he wakes about 6 a.m.; but at whatever hour he wakes he remains quiet, lying down, only saying 'a word' now and then, or touching the side of his cot with his hand, till 7 o'clock. If, mistaking the time, he lifts his head – for some time I lie awake to watch and be down on him – before that time, I say, 'Lie down, Dickie,' and his head falls back again at once; sometimes, it is true, with a little murmur, but this in turn I immediately attack and silence.

❧

*Oscar Wilde writes to Oscar Browning.*

16 Tite Street, July 1889

My dear O.B.,

 I am so disappointed, but I must put off my visit to Cambridge. One of our little boys is not at all well, and my wife, who is very nervous, has begged me not to leave town. You are so fond of children that I am sure you will understand how one feels about things of this kind, and I think it would be rather horrid of me to go away. . . .

*Oscar Wilde writes to a friend, More Adey, from H.M. Prison, Reading. His son, Cyril, was aged twelve at the time. The letter expresses a universal truth, which society now accepts, about the relationship between a parent and a child.*

8th March, 1897

As regards my children, I sincerely hope I may be recognised by the Court as having some little, I won't say right, but claim to be allowed to see Cyril from time to time: it would be to me a sorrow beyond words if I were not. I do hope the Court will see in me something more than a man with a tragic vice in his life. There is so much more in me, and I always was a good father to both my children. I love them dearly and was dearly loved by them, and Cyril was my friend. And it would be better for them not to be forced to think of me as an outcast, but to know me as a man who has suffered. Pray let everything be done on my behalf that is possible. A little recognition from the Court would help me so much. And it is a terrible responsibility for the Law to say to a father that he is unfit to see his own children: the consciousness of it makes me unhappy all day long.

*In the same year Wilde writes to Lord Alfred Douglas with reference to his wife agreeing not to divorce him. The letter of which this is a small part was later published as De Profundis.*

### January–March, 1897

I could not bear the idea of being separated from Cyril, that beautiful, loving, loveable child of mine, my friend of all friends, my companion beyond all companions, one single hair of whose little golden head should have been dearer and of more value to me than, I will not merely say you from top to toe, but the entire chrysolite of the whole world: was so indeed to me always, though I failed to understand it till too late.

❦

*Rudyard Kipling (1865–1936), novelist and poet, writes to his son John (1897–1915), aged ten, after leaving him at boarding school in Rottingdean for the first time.*

### 18th September, 1907

My Son:

I have just got back from Rottingdean. It was a drive full of careless dogs. We nearly killed one in Lewes coming down the steep hill and another only just saved his silly life at the end of the Broyle. Strange as it may seem I did not sing very much on the road home. No – it was not a cheerful drive. However I bucked up when I thought of that par-tic-u-larly interesting dormitory of yours and I hoped you had got hold of *The Cruise of Cachalot* and were settling down to read it till the boys came. It did not seem to me that you would want a *specially* large tea after what you tucked away at Aunt Georgie's. Mummy and Elsie and Miss Blaikie were waiting for me in the hall – awfully keen to know how you had got on and whether I was sure I had taken you all over the school. I answered:–

"By Allah, we ceased not to walk up and down and round and about that school till we had examined every apartment thereof"; and I related to them all that I had seen and I ceased not to narrate till Elsie went to bed. (I am not changing for dinner tonight. Hurrah! I wave my gaitered legs with delight.) . . .

This is not exactly a letter but merely a note full of no news just to tell you of things in general. Also, I want to know whether I have written plainly enough for you. IF NOT I CAN, OF COURSE, WRITE LIKE THIS BUT IT TAKES ME EVER SO MUCH LONGER TO WRITE. KINDLY LET ME KNOW WHICH ONE OF THE TWO STYLES OF WRITING YOU PREFER. I think myself that the easy flowing hand is the best. I have told Miss Blaikie to send you the telescope so you may view the ships at sea.

8 p.m. The bell has just gone for dinner and I must stop. I expect you have been asleep for this last half hour    but no matter. I will continue my letter tomorrow. . . .

Kipling was born in India, where his father was professor of architectural sculpture at the newly founded Sir Jamsetjee Jeejeebhoy School of Art and Industry in Bombay. Aged six, Kipling was sent, with his three-year-old sister, to be looked after by a couple in England who were professional foster parents to children whose parents lived in India. For six years, Kipling was treated with cruel severity and lack of understanding, until his parents returned home.

12th October, 1907

Dear Sir – My esteemed Son – O John, etc.

We reached this place last night and found your first letter from school waiting from us. It had been sent on from Montreal. You can just imagine how delighted we were to get it and how we read it over and over again.

I am very pleased to know that you like school – I feel sure that you will like it more and more as time goes on and you settle down and make your own friends. But I know exactly how homesick you feel at first. I can remember how I felt when I first went to school at Westward Ho! But my school was more than two hundred miles from my home – my Father and Mother were in India and I knew I should not see them for years. The school was more than two hundred boys of all ages from eighteen to twelve. I was nearly the youngest – and the grub was simply beastly.

Now with you, you are not thirty miles from home – you are by no means the youngest chap there – and they look after you in a way that no one ever dreamed of doing when I was young. . . .

෨෯

Sir John Eldon Gorst (1835–1916) was a statesman and writer with a lifelong interest in the well-being of the children of the poor. In his book *The Children of the Nation: How their health and vigour should be promoted by the state*, he urged the government to take more direct responsibility for all children's education and health.

## 1913

The independent rights of children are scarcely recognized or acknowledged by the governing classes. It has become customary to regard them as mere appendages of their parents; the idea that a child has any legal right of its own is startling and unacceptable.

෨෯

Augustus John (1878–1961), a conventionally irresponsible artist, writes mischievously to a friend after the death of his wife Ida in 1907. He is arranging for people to look after his five children temporarily.

Everyone is asking for a baby and really there aren't enough – but I should like Mrs Chowne to have a little one *if I can find one* . . .

෨෯

Bertrand Russell (1872–1970), the philosopher, had two sons and a daughter.

Parental feeling, as I have experienced it, is very complex. There is, first and foremost, sheer animal affection, and delight in watching what is charming in the ways of the young. Next, there is the sense of inescapable responsibility, providing a purpose for daily activities which scepticism does not easily question. Then there is an egotistical element, which is very dangerous: the hope that one's children may succeed where one has failed, that they may carry on one's work when death or senility puts an end to one's own efforts, and, in any case, that they will supply a biological escape from death, making one's own life part of the whole stream, and not a mere stagnant puddle without any overflow into the future. All this I experienced, and for some years it filled my life with happiness and peace.

৩৮৩

Gwen Raverat (1885–1957), an illustrator, wood engraver and author of the childhood memoir *Period Piece*, written in 1952, was the mother of two daughters. Her father was George Darwin, son of Charles Darwin, and her mother Maud de Puy, an American.

My own private theory is, that it is better to let children's teeth or morals suffer from *laisser-aller,* than to be too vigilant about them. But no doubt people who have been really hurt by neglect in their youth will disagree with me. For this is a matter in which it is impossible ever to be in the right.

Dear Reader, you may take it from me, that however hard you try – or don't try; whatever you do – or don't do; for better, for worse; for richer, for poorer; every way and every day:

THE PARENT IS ALWAYS WRONG

So it is no good bothering about it. When the little pests grow up they will certainly tell you exactly what you did wrong in their case. But, never mind; they will be just as wrong themselves in their turn. So take things easily; and above all, *eschew good intentions.*

As well as giving her own views, Gwen Raverat also describes her mother's views on raising children.

Another health theory was that, as sea-bathing was wholesome, salt in our bath-water would do just as well as a visit to the seaside. So some handfuls of Dr. Tidman's Sea Salt – little round pebbles – were put into the tub we had in front of the day-nursery fire, twice a week. As the salt was only put in when we got in ourselves it did not have time to melt; and we disliked it exceedingly, because the pebbles were so painful to stand or sit on. I suppose this was pure magic? I must put on record here a cure for chilblains, which a friend tells me was practised by her father's nurse. A red-hot poker was put into 'that which is beneath the bed', and, as the nurse said, 'it was most mysteerus', but a certain cure. And even in the year 1947 *a fried mouse* was most earnestly recommended to me as a cure for whooping cough. I dare say it is as good as any other cure; the only difficulty is to believe in it. . . .

My mother's theories of education were so revolutionary and sensible, that modern thought has hardly caught up with them even now. I find her writing, before I was six months old: '*I believe in every girl being brought up to have some occupation when they are grown-up, just as a boy is; it makes them much happier. Gwen is to be a mathematician.*' But, later on she, for once, was defeated; and, strange to say, retired baffled before my obvious mathematical idiocy. This was most exceptional, for as a rule she was quite convinced that anyone could do anything they wished to do.

❦

Kenneth Grahame (1859–1932), author of *The Wind in the Willows*, was the father of one son, Alistair (known as Mouse), who was blind in one eye. Mouse is aged eleven when this was written.

12th January, 1911

. . . Mouse and I had a wonderful bit of luck one morning in November, when the hounds ran into their fox at our very feet and we saw every detail of the kill and the 'breaking up' and then Mouse shyly asked the huntsman to 'blood' him – do you know the nasty process? And this the good-natured man did and presented him with the brush as well, and he was proud indeed.

❦

Wilfred Thesiger (1910–2003), explorer and travel writer, is only three years old when his father writes this letter to his mother.

Billy goes out shooting every day but does not get much as his only weapons are a tennis bat and empty cartridge case which he hits at the birds. He says he can't get them flying but if they would only sit for him he is sure he could kill one. His sporting instincts are very strongly developed.

❧

The life of the opera singer, Gervase Elwes (1866–1921), was written by his wife, Winefride. She included a few pages of description about each of their eight children. Of her fourth son, Valentine, she writes, quite conventionally for the time, of their fear that his gentleness might turn into softness, presumably code for homosexuality. They determined to send him off to Naval College. He grew up to become a priest and papal prelate.

What am I to say about Val except that he was the most sweet-natured, unselfish and winning person? He had all the high spirits of the others but with a sort of considerate gentleness of his own. To make sure that this quality should not degenerate into softness, we sent him into the Navy through Osborne and Dartmouth, where he did very well. He was full of initiative, and would promote entertainments on board ship, and even got up an orchestra containing all sorts of curious improvised instruments which he would lead with his violin.

❧

Ludo Heathcoat Amory (1881–1918) was a Staff Captain fighting in France in the First World War when he wrote these letters. His wife Mary (1881–1977) is pregnant with their third child and has sent him photographs of his two sons: Patrick, aged just under three, and Michael, nearly two. Gerald was born in August.

3rd February, 1917

You don't know how I loved getting those photos. They make me very homesick. I'd like to play one game of rabbits with them. I'm afraid they are giving you an awful time with no one there to protect you or divert attention, little chap [wife]. I like both photos but the one where they're standing up best. The other's nice but not very like P.G. It doesn't look bad enough for him but it's very good of Mich in the cart. It's lovely having them – they sit on my wood plank (dressing table) beside the old one of you and P.G. and I have them in front of me all the time I am shaving and dressing. Those two seem to belong to a world a million miles away from this miserable torn-up country.

## 28th April

. . . I was thinking of you all about tea time yesterday. I expect you had tea on the lawn – suppose P.G. shouted with excitement all the time. It's wretched what a lot of him I'm missing at his loveliest time . . .

## near Dranoutre, 30th May

. . . I wish you and I were P.G.'s and Mich's ages and could grow up together. I can see P.G. rushing about in blue all over the place and bending over the water lily pond.

Ludo was killed the following year. Mary brought up their sons alone but by 1944 they had all died: Michael in a plane crash, aged twenty-two, and Gerald and Patrick, aged twenty-seven and thirty, in the Second World War.

❧

D.H. Lawrence (1885–1930), novelist and poet, writes to Lady Cynthia Asquith (1887–1960). Lawrence had no children of his own.

## 3rd June, 1918

We are here with my sister, and two children – a very delightful boy of three, and a girl of seven. I am surprised how children are like barometers to their parents' feelings. There is some sort of queer, magnetic psychic connection – something a bit fatal, I believe. I feel I am all the time rescuing my nephew and my niece from their respective mothers, my two sisters: who have jaguars of wrath in their souls, however they purr to their offspring. The phenomenon of motherhood, in these days, is a strange and rather frightening phenomenon.

Iris Tree (1897–1968), daughter of Sir Herbert Beerbohm Tree, was a Bohemian poet and actor of whom her father said that when she was on stage, she had 'lying legs'; her ambitions for her children, however, seem straightforward.

If by the grace of heaven I ever have children I shall send them for about a year at the age of 10 to some farm, alone with healthy brown peasants, where they can be in the mud and steal pears and get killed as much as they want to.

She had one son.

∾

Harold Nicolson (1886–1968), diplomat, politician and author, was married to the writer Vita Sackville-West. They had two sons: Benedict (1914–1978) and Nigel (1917–2004). Here he writes to Nigel, then aged nine.

Gulahek, Persia, 16th July, 1926

I do hope that you won't make Mummy nervous by being too wild. Of course men must work and women must weep, but all the same, I hope you will remember that Mummy is a frightful coward and does fuss dreadfully about you. It is a good rule always to ask before you do anything awfully dangerous. Thus if you say, 'Mummy, may I try and walk on the roof of the greenhouse on my stilts?', she will probably say, 'Of course, darling', since she is not in any way a narrow-minded woman. And if you say, 'Mummy, may I light a little fire in my bed?' she will again say, 'Certainly, Nigel'. It is only that she likes being asked about these things beforehand.

Marie Stopes was not as advanced in her views on bringing up children as she was on how to avoid having them. She had her only child aged forty-two, but she was unable to have any more. When her son is two, she writes to her solicitor, asking him to approach the matron of the Foundling Hospital.

## 1924

I do not wish it to be known that the adoption is for me and I should be much obliged if you would write to the Matron . . . in somewhat the following terms:

'A Client in a very good position is desirous of adopting (complete adoption) a little boy between the ages of 20 months and 2¼ years. Illegitimacy is not objected to so long as it was a love child and not a rape, and so long as the mother was entirely healthy and normal during pregnancy and there is no inherited disease on either side. The child must be absolutely healthy, intelligent and not circumcised.'

. . . it would be an exceptional opportunity for any child; that he would be brought up in the nursery as a brother with the son and heir, and if the child's intelligence warranted it, he would receive a University education and a suitable start in life.

Four years later, the first six-year-old boy arrived, but he was returned to the care of his elderly aunts after a very short time. One of his aunts wrote to Marie Stopes.

## 3rd July, 1930

To speak quite plainly, it pained us very much to hear you describe him repeatedly as 'a dreadful little liar' . . . I have pictured to myself many times a day, with great distress of mind, the little fellow being 'thrashed' for insubordination. Is it the only thing to do?

Three more children were chosen and returned, each after a few months during which time Stopes discovered them all to be unsuitable companions for her perfect son. She wrote to the impecunious father of the third boy, aged around ten.

27th May, 1935

I should feel inclined to say every time he is dirty he is sent home to be thrashed. A night or two ago . . . when I looked into his bedroom when he was having his bath, his underpants were absolutely soaked with urine and of course smelling horribly. It is quite inexcusable and renders him unfit for a decent household.

His mother wrote back:

29th May, 1935

I see that you have decided to send him home this weekend for a thrashing – well – he shall be punished and very severely – but he won't be thrashed.

The child was not returned to Marie Stopes.

❦

E.M. Delafield (1890–1943) wrote an autobiography disguised as comic fiction, *The Diary of a Provincial Lady*. Her real married name was de la Pasture and she had two children, Lionel and Rosamund, whose names she disguised as Robin and Vicky; she gave her husband the name Robert.

2nd September, 1930

Robert brings home Robin, and friend called Micky Thompson, from station . . . Micky Thompson is attractive and shows enchanting dimple whenever he smiles, which is often.

(*Mem*: Theory that mothers think their own children superior to any others Absolute Nonsense. Can see only too plainly that Micky easily surpasses Robin and Vicky in looks, charm, and good manners – and am very much annoyed about it.)

4th September

Micky Thompson continues to show himself a charming child, with cheerful disposition, good manners, and excellent health. Enquiry reveals that he is an orphan, which does not surprise me in the least. Have often noticed that absence of parental solicitude usually very beneficial to offspring.

Anyone who has had anything to do with old-fashioned private schools will recognise the absurd situation played out by the form-master and the mother in this later episode.

### 25th June

Vicky arrives by green bus from Mickleham, carrying circular hat-box of astonishing size and weight, with defective handle, so that every time I pick it up it falls down again, which necessitates a taxi. She is in great excitement, and has to be calmed with milk and two buns before we proceed to station, meet Robert, and get into the train . . .

. . . in due course Robin appears and is received by Vicky with terrific demonstrations of affection and enthusiasm, to which he responds handsomely. (Reflect, as often before, that Fashion in this respect has greatly altered. Brothers and sisters now almost universally deeply attached to one another, and quite prepared to admit it. *O tempora! O mores!*) We are conducted to the playing-fields, where hurdles and other appliances of sports are ready, and where rows and rows of chairs await us.

Parents, most of whom I have seen before and have no particular wish ever to see again, are all over the place. . . .

Crowds of little boys all look angelic in running shorts and singlets, and am able to reflect that even if Robin's hair *is* perfectly straight, at least he doesn't wear spectacles.

Headmaster speaks a few words to me – mostly about the weather, and new wing that he proposes, as usual, to put up very shortly – I accost Robin's Form-master and demand to be told How the Boy is Getting On, and Form-master looks highly astonished at my audacity, and replies in a very off-hand way that Robin will never be a cricketer, but his football is coming on, and he has the makings of a swimmer. He then turns his back on me, but I persist, and go so far as to say that I should like to hear something about Robin's work.

Form-master appears to be altogether overcome by this unreasonable requirement, and there is a perceptible silence, during which he evidently meditates flight. Do my best to hold by the Power of the Human Eye, about which I have read much, not altogether believingly. However, on this occasion, it does its job, and Form-master grudgingly utters five words or so, to the effect that we needn't worry about Robin's Common-entrance exam, in two years' time. Having so far committed himself he pretends to see a small boy in imminent danger on a hurdle and dashes across the grass at uttermost speed to save him, and for the remainder of the day, whenever he finds himself within yards of me, moves rapidly in opposite direction.

ᦕᦕ

Rumer Godden (1907–1998), novelist, was the mother of two daughters. In her memoir she writes about her second child, Paula, who was born prematurely in September 1938.

Paula was a wisp of a child with flaxen hair and the . . . bluest of blue eyes. She was still tiny but she had a body as graceful as an elf's and as wiry; she walked and even ran before she was a year old and in that autumn I was able to dispense with Nurse.

Paula was, too, one of those uncanny children who seem not to need much sleep; I had been one myself and remember the misery of being forced to lie still in the dark and not put on the light, so that I let Paula be as, in the next generation, we let my grand-daughter Emma, though it is eerie to see, at one o'clock in the morning, a small figure tripping downstairs and going quite happily to write or draw at her desk.

ᦕᦕ

In her diary, Antonia White writes insensitively about her daughters, in particular Susan, aged nine.

1938

My children certainly *are* a responsibility but one that I am becoming inured to gradually. I do want (faintly) to do the best for them . . . I expected them to be . . . more interested in me . . . I see Susan daily dissipating her quite remarkable powers of understanding in dull, monotonous fantasies. She leads a complete other life as a horse. 'Susan on four legs' . . . the horse that can run faster than any other horse but is always cruelly treated. Both children really *feel the need* of harsh treatment sometimes. I want Susan to have every opportunity of *real* achievement; that is why I want her to go to a school where she will have rivals worthy of her . . .

☙❧

Sir Henry (Chips) Channon (1897–1958), Conservative politician, diarist and socialite, had one son, Paul (1935–2007), who also became an MP. No one would write in this ornate, egocentric and painfully revealing style any longer.

### 7th August, 1939

My boy is enchanting, so gentle and gay, I hold him in my lap, and see my own dark eyes reflected. That Fate should be kind to him is my deepest wish . . . If anything happened to him it would kill me.

All this week there have been war scares.

### 4th September

Tomorrow I leave by car for Geneva to attend the League of Nations Assembly. Me at Geneva! It is almost a Bateman joke, as I have always scoffed and ridiculed that absurd Assembly. But there I go. . . . And meanwhile, Kelvedon [the family home], that sleeping waterlily of a place, must await my return, as must my white dogs, and my glorious dark-eyed, angelic, glamorous, 'super' son. I love him with every fibre of my body, and he is all mine.

☙❧

In 1941, Laurie Lee is living in a caravan in West Sussex, visited occasionally by his mistress Lorna Wishart (married to Ernest Wishart) and their child Yasmin, aged one.

L. came this morning and caught me all behind as my mother would say. She had just taken Yasmin to the doctor's where he removed several yards of wool from her nose . . . sad proof of a hereditary recurrence of the nose-stuffing that has made our family a thing of wonder and fear for many generations.

Diana Cooper, married to Duff Cooper, Minister of Information, sent her eleven-year-old son John Julius to the United States during the Second World War. It was an unpopular decision as she admits in her autobiography. She writes to Kaetchen Kommer, the friend who was going to look after John Julius.

## 2nd July, 1940

Here is my child and here is Nanny armed with £25, and now they belong to you for the duration. He shall go to some Canadian school. Establish him in Long Island with the hospitable Paleys until the term starts and overlay them with my gratitude. Never have I put more in your dear gesticulating hands, never have I taken your order 'Use me' more literally.

If we are killed you will know best what to do for his good. If a miracle ends this war victoriously for us, then what a glorious jaunt he will have had! If a miracle subjugates and occupies this land beneath Hitler and we are in prison or Duff is fled to Ottawa with King and Council, he might, if here, become a hostage to force Duff's hand or mine. It is for this reason, not because of bombs, that he leaves. You'll be glad to hear that my spirit is unexpectedly high, but of course I am very unhappy. Perhaps this citadel island will have fallen before this reaches you and all will be over. If it is, you know that I am certain no one ever had a better friend than I had in you and no one loved you better.

## London, 10th July

Please, Kaetchen, do not let my little boy get spoiled by riches; buses not taxis, drug-stores not restaurants, and not too many cinemas. He is a very good child and will give no trouble, I am confident. If you see him in any way fresh with Americans or if he is not perfectly mannered, reprove him with all your might. Do not let him be loaded with presents; keep your own hands from your pockets. Nanny will buy him clothes cheaply – from Bloomingdale's please, not at Saks. You must be tolerant of my idiosyncrasies and conform to them. I feel very strongly that it must never be said that English children are living on charity, so I would like my suggested money arrangements done almost legally immediately. . . . Keep me in his mind a bit and teach him to admire Duff. Tutor him hard in American history and current events (war and peace). I'd like him to be braver than most and not to be taught 'Safety first.'

Frances Partridge (1900–2004) was one of the last members of the Bloomsbury Group. She kept a diary throughout her life, although the first extract below is part of a résumé of a period of more than a year when, unusually, she did not keep it up. Here she describes her eleven-year-old son's unhappiness at boarding school.

. . . in the late summer of 1946, Burgo left Newbury Grammar School and went as a weekly boarder to a conventional boys' prep school . . . Surprisingly happy and successful there at first, he wasn't a conventional little boy, and to our dismay he suddenly began quietly taking to the road and walking in the direction of home. 'What was wrong?' we asked, scenting bullying and other horrors. But he had no complaints. There had been a bad thunderstorm, and at length he confessed that he had got it into his head that Ralph and I might have been struck by lightning and be dead. The pattern repeated itself, and there followed many uneasy months for us all, for there is nothing that wrings the entrails more savagely than one's child's inarticulate misery. There were more escapes, and all Burgo could say was that the moment he left the school gates and started 'running away' a feeling of intense happiness invaded him.

A later addition to the text comments on the diary entry for 19th January, 1948, which records Burgo's return to boarding school:

Most parents of my generation had been brought up impersonally by nurses and in the belief that father and mother knew best, so that when the war handed us responsibilities for our own beloved children for which we were ill-prepared, many of us worried too much whether we were doing right – a worry not diminished by knowing something of the theories of Freud.

I hope I have conveyed . . . that Burgo was a happy, funny, original if sensitive little boy before the guillotine fell that took him away from home. I have noticed the same change in many other children. Before the prep school age they are unselfconscious, amusing, and so full of energy and high spirits that they cannot walk along a pavement, but need to let off steam by going hoppity-skip. Then what happens? They are forced into the company of their contemporaries, undiluted except for a few adults of a special species among whom are to be found love of power, paedophilia, and – with luck – one or two born teachers gifted to stimulate budding intelligences. Under the influence of transplantation from the flower-pot of home to an environment fraught with fear and bewilderment, what a sad change takes place! They become fidgety, competitive, suspicious, wanting to be exactly like everyone else, and ready to bang or punch the other boys before they have it done to them. I am of course exaggerating and over-generalizing, but there is some truth in my picture.

I suggest that our English system of packing children off to boarding-school at the age of eight or even six is brutally cruel, as can be seen from watching the departure of any school train at the start of the year. Of course children should learn to mix with their contemporaries, and can have glorious fun and laughter with them – if only they are allowed back to base in the evenings until they are old enough and firm enough not to be battered out of their original shape.

৩৵৩

Rebecca West gave birth to her son Anthony (1914–1987) in the second year of her ten-year affair with the writer H.G. Wells.

## 1946

I made a great mistake by not sending Anthony away for the first year to some nearby place – round the corner would be best – and not getting on with my work. As it was I had to work hard later on, so that I could not give Anthony all the time he needed when he was a little older.

৩৵৩

Jessica Mitford (1917–1996) describes how she cleverly won round her daughter Constantia (Dinky) Romilly, after the birth of Benjamin, her son by her second husband Bob Treuhaft.

## 1947

At the beginning of our life in Oakland . . . [I was] preoccupied with the birth of our son Benjamin, a lovely fat jolly creature whose upbringing was quickly assumed by Dinky, now aged six. A firm religious believer in those days, she had been praying for a baby: 'Your prayers have been answered,' I pointed out. 'Here it is, so be an angel and look after it.' Dinky watched over the adored newcomer, fed him his breakfast, rushed home after school to play with him and taught him his first words: 'Dinky's always right, Benjy's always wrong.'

⚭

Stephen Spender (1909–1995), poet, was the father of two children, Lizzie and Matthew.

## 1st November, 1951

Afternoon, went to the Hall School gym class . . . The gym instructor, in his white clothes, gave instructions. Matthew, age 6½, was in the second row, and I noticed that he never heard any orders. He just guessed, or copied what the other boys were doing. 'Hands on hips!' roared the instructor, Matthew put his on his head. Then they had to climb up a kind of gate of six bars, passing through the gap between the top two bars, and coming down the other side . . . One of the boys got stuck trying to crawl between the two top bars. He waited halfway through, shaking and trembling. All the other boys started laughing at him, until they were stopped by the instructor.

In a blessed moment while I was half attending to these things, half reading my newspaper, I could understand the state of mind of all these little boys so completely that the gap between me and them seemed paper-thin. I could easily be the Spender who did not attend, or the boy who got stuck, or the other boys who jeered at him. I was only *pretending* to be the middle-aged man reading his newspaper.

And on the way home in the bus where I sat with Matthew, one of his little friends who was seated directly in front of us suddenly turned round, pointed at me with butting finger, and said, 'Spender, is that old, white-haired man with spectacles your daddy?' 'No,' said Matthew with perfect self-possession. When we got off the bus and were at a safe distance from his little friend I asked Matthew why he had said I was not his father. 'Because you aren't,' he exclaimed passionately. 'You aren't like what he said you were.'

Doris Lessing (b.1919), the Nobel prize-winning novelist, left her first two children to be brought up by their father in Zimbabwe; after a second failed marriage, she brought up her third child alone.

## 1950s

Women who have brought up a son without a father will know how difficult it is, and those without the experience will have no idea of it. . . . the day-in, day-out slog of it all, trying to be what is impossible, a father as well as a mother.

ॐ

Kingsley Amis (1922–1995) gives his version of the facts of life to his young sons, Philip and Martin, in the mid-1950s.

. . . sex instruction in the home is often – usually? I don't know – not instruction but a formal permit. But it must be given. I shall never forget the scene when it came to my turn. I swear it began with me hearing my wife saying somewhere out of shot, 'Your father wants to speak to you in his study' – a room big enough, say, to accommodate a full-grown rhinoceros, though without giving him much room to turn round.

Philip and Martin came in, their expressions quite blank, innocent in every possible way that the most expensive film-director could have put there. They were, I suppose, seven and six years old. The short monologue I gave them slipped out of my head afterwards at the first opportunity, though I know I did conscientiously get in a certain amount of what might be called hard anatomy and concrete nouns, although again I must have used the word 'thing' a good deal and talked about Dad planting a seed. Well, what would you? I have never loved and admired them more than for the unruffled calm and seriousness with which they heard me out. I knew they knew, they knew I knew they knew and so on to the end but never mind. They left in a silence that they courteously prolonged until they were out of all hearing. It was a couple of years before Philip confided to me that he had muttered, 'Hold on to your hat – he's going to tell us the big one' as the two made their way to my 'study'. But we did it. In no sphere is it truer that it is necessary to say what it is unnecessary to say.

Rupert Hart-Davis (1907–1999), publisher, man of letters and father of three children, writes to George Lyttelton (1883–1962). Lyttelton had been a master at Eton when Hart-Davis was a pupil there; they corresponded on a weekly basis from October 1955 until Lyttelton's death.

## 22nd January, 1956

Last week I took my twelve-year-old to *Charley's Aunt*: it wasn't very good, but his agonised laughter made my evening.

◦❖◦

Laurie Lee's wife Kathy writes to Celia Goodman about Laurie's reactions to his new daughter.

## 1963

Laurie is so sweet with her. I always thought he would be much more detached. He feeds her with music when she cries – lovely trios, duets, quartets, I do hope she'll be musical.

◦❖◦

Frances Partridge epitomises the thoughtful, devoted grandmother. Her only son, Burgo, had died suddenly, at the age of twenty-eight, a few weeks after the birth of his daughter Sophie.

## 26th September, 1967

I took Sophie [aged four] out from school and brought her back here last Thursday. She is such a darling little girl, so full of rare qualities, sweetness, sense and fun, that I find it unbearable to contemplate any possible unhappiness for her. This is, and always was (perhaps disastrously for Burgo) my besetting failing, leading to self-torment and guilt, but perhaps not to the beloved creature's happiness. Sophie has grown up enormously through her holiday with Quentin and his family and her mind has leapt ahead, stimulated no doubt by his older children. There is nothing she seems unable to take in – except perhaps death, of which she is frightened. When someone was mentioned (not Burgo) who was dead, she gave a noisy shudder and said, '*I* shan't get dead, shall I?' And I loved the way she sat at the piano, not vaguely banging, but picking out notes in a really musical way with curled fingers like hammers, singing as well, often trying to and succeeding in singing the note she was striking, or if she failed, saying 'No, that's not right.' Always perfectly in tune, and often to fanciful, imaginary words.

ॐ

Corin Redgrave (b.1939), actor, observes his small son while considering his motives for writing a biography of his father, the actor Michael Redgrave.

. . . is it like pressing my face against the railings of the school playground watching my son at play? He is quite oblivious of my presence watching him. He is wearing the clothes I put on him this morning, but he wears them somehow differently. I can see him trying to make friends with a bigger boy who just ignores him. I see him being pushed or falling over and I want to intervene. But the playground is for learning about life, and I mustn't intervene because it won't help him. 'He has to fight his own battles.'

ॐ

Maureen Lipman (b.1946), actor, columnist and comedian, is the self-aware mother of two children, Amy and Adam.

Still, when I think of every stage and its accompanying worry – 'Will they ever walk, will they ever sleep through the night, ever socialize, stop clinging to me, learn to read, learn to share, go to school by bus, ever go out, ever stay *in*?' – I have to smile and shake my head in a way only American moms in movies ever seem to do. Everything in its own time, Maureen, the instincts are all there – all that's required of you is to be there and be consistent.

There is a tribe in the Kalahari Desert . . . which builds complex sand sculptures to teach their babies to stand, to crawl and, finally, to walk. The children do these things, ultimately, at exactly the same growth stage as do any other babies in the world, but the parents feel as though *they've* done it for them. And the children let them take the credit. For a while anyway.

Charlotte Moore (b.1959) is a writer and journalist. She has three sons: the
two eldest, George and Sam, are severely autistic. In her memoir, this extract
comes under the heading 'Wear and Tear'.

I'm making a visitor a cup of coffee. 'Sugar?' I ask, silently willing the
answer to be 'No'. 'Yes, please,' comes the reply. I fish my tangle of keys
out of my pocket, move quickly to the cupboard and unlock it, trying not
to attract the attention of George and Sam. I fail. They leap down from
their vantage point on top of the Aga and bound across the kitchen. I
reach for the sugar, keep the boys at bay with swift jabbing movements
of my elbows, spoon the sugar into the coffee, and return the bowl to the
cupboard as if I were a wild dog protecting a zebra haunch from a swarm
of hungry rivals. In an autistic household, the physical and emotional
effort involved in performing the simple acts of everyday life can be
considerable.

What would happen if I do what normal people do – leave the sugar
bowl on the table, or on a shelf, or in an unlocked cupboard? Well, the
boys would help themselves to it, sometimes with spoons, sometimes
with their hands, sometimes sticking their tongues straight in. What they
didn't eat would be scattered far and wide, so there'd be a patina of
stickiness to clear up, as well as no sugar left for anyone else, and a pair of
buzzing, hyperactive boys. My hypothetical visitor may be startled by my
defensive elbow action, but he'd be even more startled, and disgusted, by
the sight of the boys licking spilled sugar direct from table or floor. . . .

. . . Given their poor diet and the difficulty of inserting a toothbrush
between their gritted lips, I'm surprised they haven't had more decay.
The last extraction was about eighteen months ago. George was at the
height of his food-refusing phase and perhaps pain from the bad tooth
contributed to it, though he never mentioned it. This was also a time at
which he was reluctant to leave the house at all. I had to get him to the
(unfamiliar) hospital for the operation. His quasi-anorexia worked in my
favour in carrying out the nil-by-mouth instructions, but coaxing him into
the car was no easy matter. I allowed two hours for the twenty-minute
journey, and we needed it. Once in the car, we drove round and round
Bexhill listening to Bach. This had a soothing effect; eventually George,
wearing Wellingtons, agreed to enter the hospital. He sat in the waiting
room, shrieking and refusing to be weighed. In the end I had to stand on
the scales with George in my arms, and have my weight subtracted from

the total. Again, his self-imposed starvation came in useful. It's not every mother who can easily scoop up her gangly twelve-year-old son.

He wouldn't tolerate the pre-med. I could see that no amount of plea-bargaining was going to work; the gentle approach was only prolonging the agony. I asked the hospital staff to hold him down and administer the anaesthetic by mask, not by needle. Brutal as that may look, it's quicker and therefore kinder. Six adults were needed. The struggle wasn't pleasant, but the tooth had to come out.

In the waiting room, the other parents and children had been staring at us, horrified. In the recovery room, roles were reversed. The other children moaned and groaned, and extorted huge promises from their parents about game cubes and PlayStation Twos. George sat up, spat out some blood, drank some water and said, 'Let's go home now, Mum.' No fuss, no whingeing. The only thing he insisted on was taking his bloodstained hospital blanket home. The nurse gave us his vast diseased molar, blackened and craggy like a citadel torched by barbarians. She presented it in a sweet little bag decorated with a pink fairy and blue elf, perched on a crescent moon.

Perhaps this life would be hellish if I riled against it. Hell – my definition, anyway – is a place where you don't want to be, and from which you can't get out. When you have autistic children, there is no respite, either for them or for you. When they were a bit younger, I used to watch them sometimes, and ask them, silently, look, couldn't you stop being autistic for a bit? Just for one day? I mean, a joke's a joke, lads, but this one's gone far enough . . . But I've long since settled into a fairly calm acceptance. They are what they are. That's all there is to it.

༺༻

John Mortimer (1923–2009), barrister, writer and playwright, describes an incident on holiday with his family in Italy.

For a long time the children have been preparing a play. We heard them whispering. They locked themselves away from the Italian sunshine. We found our clothes vanishing, hats and sunglasses went missing, make-up was depleted. After dinner, we go down to . . . the coolest and most comfortable room in the house. . . . At one end of the room there is a platform, a grand piano, music-stands and piles of sheet music, a place where the true owners of the house play string quartets. We, the grown-ups, the old and the not so completely young, sit in darkness. After we have told each other how excited we are, we fall silent. And then the stage is bathed in light, performing as sunlight. Some people are having lunch, no doubt on the terrace, and then we see that the people are the children and the children are us.

Rosie is wearing her mother's shirt, her mother's earrings, her mother's skirt, and between her fingers rests one of her mother's fags, and she is gazing dreamily at a glass of wine. When Tom introduces her, in the manner of a gossip columnist, she pushes away her glass and says wearily, 'Piss off, Tom!' Claire Boxer, aged twelve, is wearing my hat, my glasses, my shirt, with a cushion acting as my stomach. Other children play other parents. They are us, in a new, fresh, well-lit and entertaining version, while we sit tongue-tied in the shadows, trying to put the best possible face on it.

'All women become their mothers,' Oscar Wilde said. 'That's their tragedy.' It may not be tragic, but it's inevitable, just as men turn into their fathers. We may wear different clothes and dance to different music, but we take over the same parts, the same loves, the same loyalties and the same old quarrels and unforgivable wrongs. Your mum and dad don't necessarily fuck you up, they just step into the darkness and invite you to take their place.

# THE ADOLESCENT YEARS

*. . . my dearest old Fat you mustn't hanker after a penniless
young clergyman with one lung.*
*William Thackeray to his daughter Anne, 1855*

Many parents nowadays seem so frightened of losing their children's affection or damaging their mental health that they hesitate to enforce any rules – unlike Agnes Paston in 1458, who writes to tell her son's tutor that if the boy (aged sixteen) has not done well or improved in his work he should be beaten till he does so, which is what his last tutor did and he was the best one he ever had. This is an extreme example from a particularly harsh mother who is also described as beating her adult daughter, sometimes twice in one day, until her head is broken in several places.

But a mother's role could be very different: in the fifteenth and sixteenth centuries, autocratic fathers dominated their families, a situation that encouraged mothers to act as mediators and interpreters between fathers and children. It was a comforting role for a mother, and one that endeared her to her children, both sons and daughters. Things hadn't changed much by the seventeenth century when Lady Brilliana Harley writes to her beloved son Ned, encouraging him to dress according to his father's wishes. Ned is fourteen years old and has just arrived at Oxford University; she also draws his attention to the fact that both she and his father are determined that his tutor should accompany him wherever he goes. At the end of her letter she puts a postscript: 'Your father dous not knowe I send. Thearefore take no notis of it, to him, nor to any. Nobody in the howes knowes I send to you.' Mothers were partisan, but secretly.

By the eighteenth century, fathers were still in control of family life but both parents had considerably more freedom to indulge and understand their sons. Lady Sarah Lennox explains that she has been the kind of mother who 'studied to become [her children's] friend'. Lord Chesterfield's advice to his son is superficial and hypocritical, but it is always revealing of the time and often amusing.

Concerns over education are central to this time in a parent's life, as are the same teenage problems across the centuries: children's debts, bad behaviour, love affairs and marriages. Not very many people seem to have been as lucky as I am in their relationship to their stepchildren. Often they are complications: Charlotte Schreiber, in 1856, regrets how badly her daughter gets on with her new stepfather and, just over a hundred years later, Elizabeth Jane Howard finally succeeds in building a good relationship with her stepsons.

ॐ

Elisabeth Clere writes to John Paston (1421–1466), urging him to find a husband for his sister Elizabeth (1429–1488), so that she can escape from her cruel mother, Agnes. She begins her letter by explaining that John's sister has a suitor called Scrope. The problem is that he is unable to bequeath any money or land to their future children, unless they have a boy, because he already has a daughter by an earlier marriage. Elizabeth thinks he would be better than no one unless John can find her an alternative.

### 29th June, (?)1449

. . . meseemeth he were good for my cousin your sister with[out] that ye might get her a better. And if ye can get a better, I would advise you to labour it in as short time as ye may goodly, for she was never in so great sorrow as she is nowadays; for she may not speak with no man, whosoever come, ne not may see ne speak with my man, ne with servants of her mother's, but that she beareth her on hand otherwise than she meaneth [unless she deceives her]. And she hath sin Eastern the most part be beaten once in the week or twice, and sometime twice on o day, and her head broken in two or three places.

Wherefore, cousin, she hath sent to me . . . and prayeth me that I would send to you a letter of her heaviness, and pray you to be her good brother, as her trust is in you. And she saith, if ye may see by his evidences that his children and her may inheriten, and she to have reasonable jointure, she hath heard so much of his birth and his conditions that, an ye will, she will have him, whether that her mother will or will not, notwithstanding it is told her his person is simple; for she saith men shall have the more dainty of her if she rule her to him as she ought to do.

Elisabeth Clere goes on, with kind good sense, to suggest that John should keep trying to find another husband because women often make this kind of decision out of present unhappiness and Elisabeth would not want that to happen to her cousin.

Cousin, it is told me there is a goodly man in your Inn of the which the father died late; and if ye think that he were better for her than Scrope, it would be laboured [try to arrange it] . . .

Wherefore, cousin, think on this matter, for sorrow oftentime causeth women to beset them otherwise than they should do; and if she were in that case I wot well ye would be sorry. Cousin, I pray you burn this letter, that your men ne none other man see it; for an my cousin your mother knew that I had sent you this letter she should never love me.

No more I write to you at this time, but Holy Ghost have you in keeping. Written in haste on Saint Peter's Day by candle-light.

By your cousin, Elisabeth Clere

The match came to nothing. Elizabeth Paston continued to live with her mother, Agnes, for five more years and eventually married in 1458.

ॐ

Agnes Paston (d.1479) was a zealous beater of her sons as well as her daughters. Clement Paston was aged about sixteen at the time.

28th January, 1458

To pray Greenfield to send me faithfully word by writing how Clement Paston hath do his devoir in learning. And if he hath not do well, nor will not amend, pray him that he will truly belash him till he will amend; and so did the last master, and the best that ever he had, at Cambridge. And say Greenfield that if he will take upon him to bring him into good rule and learning, that I may verily know he doth his devoir, I will give him 10 mark for his labour; for I had liefer he were fair buried than lost for default.

Elizabeth Grymeston (1563–1604) was the author of an advice book, written for Bernye, her only surviving son of nine children.

## 1604

My dearest sonne, there is nothing so strong as the force of loue; there is no loue so forcible as the loue of an affectionate mother to hir naturall childe: there is no mother can either more affectionately shew hir nature, or more naturally manifest hir affection, than in aduising hir children out of her owne experience, to eschue euill and encline them to do that which is good.

☙❦

When Edward Herbert (1583-1648), brother to George Herbert (1593–1633), the poet priest, went up to university his widowed mother brought her family to live in Oxford, where she seems to have proved herself an unusually good companion.

## c.1615

. . . having entered Edward into Queen's College, and provided him a fit tutor, she commended him to his care; yet she continued there with him, and still kept him in a moderate awe of herself, and so much under her own eye, as to see and converse with him daily: but she managed this power over him without any such rigid sourness, as might make her company a torment to her child, but with such a sweetness and compliance with the recreations and pleasures of youth, as did incline him willingly to spend much of his time in the company of his dear and careful mother; which was to her great content: . . . For these reasons she endeared him to her own company, and continued with him in Oxford four years; in which time her great and harmless wit, her cheerful gravity, and her obliging behaviour, gained her an acquaintance and friendship with most of any eminent worth or learning, that were at that time in or near that University; and particularly with Mr. John Donne, who then came accidentally to that place in this time of her being there.

John Donne writes to his friend Sir Henry Goodyer, seeking sympathy for the failure of his marriage plans for his daughter Constance, aged nineteen. He was obviously disappointed on his own behalf as well as hers, although, not unusually for the date, she knew nothing about it. At least, he believes that she did not, but who knows what daughters will discern from anxious fathers.

18th October, 1622

Tell both your daughters a piece of a story of my Con., which may accustom them to endure disappointments in this world: An honourable person (whose name I give you in a schedule to burn, lest this letter should be mislaid) had an intention to give her one of his sons, and had told it me, and would have been content to accept what I, by my friends, could have begged for her; but he intended that son to my profession [the Church], and had provided him already £300 a year of his own gift in church livings, and hath estated £300 more of inheritance for their children; and now the youth (who yet knows nothing of his father's intention nor mine) flies from his resolutions for that calling, and importunes his father to let him travel. The girl knows not her loss, for I never told her of it; but, truly, it is a great disappointment to me.

More than these, Sir, we must all suffer in our way to heaven, where, I hope, you and all yours shall meet your poor friend and affectionate servant,

John Donne

Lady Brilliana Harley (1598–1643) was a devout and educated Puritan who looked after her estate of Brampton Castle, in Herefordshire, while her husband was in London. Her eldest son Edward (1624–1700), has just gone up to Oxford, aged fourteen. She writes to him frequently and hopes for letters as often in return. She is one of my favourite mothers and I have included a sequence of her pious but lively letters to give a sense of her charm and her irresistible spelling. I sympathise with her predicament over the problem of the pie and admire her for her courage during the Civil War. Her son kept all her letters but none of his to her survived.

### 30th November, 1638

To my deare sonne Mr Edward Harley

Good Ned – . . . I giue God thankes that you are recouered from that indispotion you fellt, and thanke you that you did send me word of it; for I desire to knowe howe it is with you in all condistions. If you are ill, my knoweing of it stire me vp more ernestly to pray for you. I beleeue that indispotion you feelt was caused by some violent exersise: if you vse to swinge, let it not be violently; for exersise should be rather to refresch then tyer nature. . . . Deare Ned, if I could as easely conuae [convey] meself to you as my letters, I would not be so longe absent from you; . . . Deare Ned, if you would haue any thinge, send me word; or if I thought a coold pye, or such a thinge, would be of any plesure to you, I would send it you. But your father says you care not for it, and Mrs. Pirson tells me, when her sonne was at Oxford, and shee sent him such thinges, he prayed her that shee would not. I thank you for the Man in the Moune.* I had hard of the booke, but not seene it; . . . I would willingly haue the French booke you rwite me word of; but if it can be had, I desire it in French, for I had rather reade any thinge in that tounge then in Inglisch. . . .

I rwite to the last weake; send me word wheather you had my letter; I would not haue it loost.

In hast.

*The Man in the Moune was a recent book by Francis Godwin, which told the story of a man's voyage to the moon. An example of early science fiction, it proved popular and highly influential over later writers of the genre.

11th December

Your father is cheerefully well, and your brother Robert has had no fitte sence you went. Your brother Thomas cried very much the other day becaus he thought howe he was vsed to fight with you at Sheareswesbury.

*Brilliana often has unexpected remedies to offer.*

14th December

Deare Ned, be carefull to vse exersise; and for that paine in your backe, it may be caused by some indispocion of the kidnes. I would haue you drinke in the morning beare [beer] boyled with licorisch; it is a most excelent thinge for the kidnes. For the booke, if you can not have it in French, send it me in Inglisch: and I will, if pleas God, send you mony for it.

*She also supports his father's directions about what Ned should wear.*

Deare Ned, it is very well doun, that you submite to your fathers desire in your clothes; and that is a happy temper, both to be contented with plaine clothes, and in the weareing of better clothes, not to thinke one selfe the better for them, nor to be trubelled if you be in plane clothes, and see others of your rancke in better. . . . I am so vnwilling that you should goo to any place without your worthy tutor, that I send this mesenger expresly to your tutor, with a letter to intreate him, you may haue the happines of his company, wheather souer you goo; and your father by no means would haue you goo any wheather, without him. If you should goo to my brothers, I heare theare is a dangerous passage; I desire you may not goo that way, but aboute. The Lord in much mercy blles you, and presarue you from all euell, especially that of sinn: and so I rest

    Your most affectinat mother,
    Brilliana Harley

Your father dous not knowe I send. Thearefore take no notis of it, to him, nor to any.
Nobody in the howes knowes I send to you.

She has not heard from him for three weeks, which makes her anxious.

## 19th January, 1639

Deare Ned – I pray God blles you, first with thos rich grasess [graces] of his Spirit, and then with the good things of this life. I have thought it longe sence I hard from you; and I can not be very mery, tell it pleases God, to giue me that comfort; my hope is that you are well, tho I haue bine in a greate deale of feare of it. I haue thought theas three weakes a longe time; but I hope the Lord will in mercy refresch me, with good asshurance of your being well. I may well say, that my life is bounde with yours, and I hope I shall neuer haue caus to recall or repent of my loue, with which I loue you.

In this postcript to a later letter, Brilliana prevaricates somewhat about her age.

## 26th January

Deare Ned, – My agge is no secret; tho my brother Bray is something mistaken in it. When I was maried to your father, your father would haue bine asked in the church, but my lord would be no means consent; what his reason was, I know not. Then they haue a custome, that, when they fetch out the liscens [licence], the agg of the woman, must be knowne; so that, if I would haue hide my agg, then it must be knowne, and then I was betwne two or three and twenty. I was not full three and twenty, but in the liscens they rwit me three and twenty, and you knowe how longe I haue bine maried, for you know how old you are, and you weare borne when I had bine maried a yeare and 3 months.

She likes to tell Ned the gossip: on this occasion concerning the effects of bloody oysters and the local doctor's love life.

## 1st February

Good Ned, This day I received you letter by the carrier. . . . I beleeue you haue hard, that my lord of Arendell eateing of oyesters, the oyesters were bluddy, and affterwards thought he sawe a man runeing at him with a drawne sword; but none ells couled see what he thought he sawe. . . .

Doctor Deodate being so neere, came to see your father and meself; he did not forget to aske for you, with a greate deale of loue, and expreses a greate deale of desire affter your good; he is very well and merrier than ever I sawe him; his man told Pheebe, that his mistris was with chillde; if it be so, shure that is the ground of his meerth. Your ancient frinde Mrs Traford is very bigg with child, and doctor Deodate dous somethinge feare her. He tells me he was allmost in loue with her, when shee sarued [served] me, but now he can not fancy her. . . . Sence the ring I gaue you is broken, and that you esteme a peace of it, becaus I gaue it you, I will, if pleas God, by the next safe bearer send you another, that will not so easily breake: and tell [till] your father keepes his promies, in giueing you a wacth, I will let you haue mine; . . .

Several months after the previous mention of pies, the subject comes up again: either Edward told her he would like a pie or she was unable to resist sending him one.

## 10th May, 1639

A postscript – I haue made a pye to send you; it is a kide pye. I beleeue you haue not that meate ordinaryly at Oxford; on halfe of the pye is seasned with on kinde of seasening and the other with another.

She is already feeling vulnerable and aware of the threat of civil war.

## 21st June

Your father is in some doute wheather he shall goo to Loundone the next weake or noo; if nesescity so constraine him, I can not but be sorry, and if it be so, I wisch I had you with me that time your father is away. Doo not take notis of this to your father. . . . Deare Ned, theare is so much discours of wars . . .

## 1st November

My deare Ned, keepe always a wacth over your preceous soule; tye yourself to a dayly self exemnation; thinke ouer the company you haue bine in, and what your discours was, and how you found yourself affected, how in the discourses of religion; obsarue what knowledg you weare abell to expres, and with what affection to it, and wheare you finde yourself to come short, labor to repaire that want . . . My deare Ned, you are to me next my oune hart; and this is the rule I take with meself, and I thinke it is the best way to be aquanted with our owne harts, for we know not what is in vs, tell ocations and temptation drawes out that matter which layes quiet; and in a due obsaruation, we shall finde at last, in what we are proud, in what fearefull, and what will vexe and eate our harts with care and grefe.

As mothers often do, although not always to their children's satisfaction, she trusts Ned with many of her commissions.

## 29th November

Deare Ned, if theare be any good lookeing glasses in Oxford, shuse me one aboute the biggnes of that I use to drees me in, if you remember it. I put it to your choys, becaus I thinke you will chuse one, that will make a true ansure to onse face.

All my frute disches are brocken; thearefore, good Ned, if theare be any shuch blwe and white disches as I vse to haue for frute, bye me some . . .

At the end of 1640, aged sixteen, Ned goes to London to join his father.

⚜

Ralph and Mary Verney's eldest son Mun (Edmund) Verney (1636–1688) had always suffered from a crooked spine and so, at the age of seventeen, he went with his tutor, Dr Creighton, from the Hague to consult Herr Skatt in Utrecht. Dr Creighton writes a series of letters to Sir Ralph.

If they be young, the sooner they are cured, and he [Herr Skatt] selldome undertakes old people . . . If when he look upon the partie he fynd the disease curable he undertakes it, and without bargayne expects such an honest reward as the partie is or willing or able to bestow; . . .

28th January, 1653

Mun's backbone in which all the fault lies, is quyt awry, and his right shoulder half a handfull lower at least than his left. Herr Skatt hath undertaken the cure, if your sonne will stay heere three quarters of a yeare; and allreadie he is about to make harnessing for him, which your son is very willinge, for aught I can perceive, to undergo . . .

15th July

He is very well, grows apace, and of his crookedness so allmost wholly restored, that very little difference is to be seene; and when his clothes and cloak is on without his harness none at all, yet he weares his harness for the most part continuallie, and must I am afrayed till the next spring by which tyme Herr Skatt doth not doubt but to make him a perfyt man: and in the meane tyme becaus the weather is very hott in these moneths, he permitts him sum tymes for a two or 3 dayes together ease him self of his harness, and go in his single doublett, which I say he condiscends unto meerly to ease him from wearing iron bodies continuallic . . .

The iron body is lined with soft leather and worn over a linen shirt, but is tightly fitted. In the heat the shirt is always wet and it can only be changed once a week, by the doctor; even then the skin is not washed. Sir Ralph asks whether the shirt could be changed more often but his son explains that Herr Skatt would not have the time to do so because he looks after more than two thousand patients.

A year later, Edmund, now eighteen, seems to have escaped the horrible iron body, and his father writes to Dr Creighton to give his opinion about where he should study. Ralph dislikes pure scholarship, as the English are inclined to do, but he is wise about how to give advice to young men.

20th March, 1654

For Leyden, I have no fancy to it, 'tis too private for a youth of his yeares, that must see company at convenient times and studdy men as well as bookes, or else his learning may make him rather ridiculous than esteemed. A meere schollar is but a woefull creature, but if you can approve of carrying him to the Hague my good friend Dr Morley will be ready to put him into good and civill company, and advise him from his follies and perhapps that may worke more uppon him, then all that you or I can saye for I have oft observed that young men are apter to receave counsell from strangers, then such as have authority over them.

❦

William Blundell (1620–1698) writes to his sister Frances about his grandson Edmund Butler (E.B.), aged seventeen, who has smallpox.

## 9th October, 1681

On the 24th of September . . . my dear charge E.B. was seized with a pain in his back. On the 26th he raved and said and did things extremely extravagant. I removed him that night to a Doctor's house. On the 28th the smallpox appeared, which grew in six days to cover his whole face in a very horrid manner. The soles of his feet, his head, his hands were dressed in the same sort, but yet a little thinner . . . much smart he endured till they begun to die, which was 2 or 3 days since. He is now void of pain and I trust quite free from danger; yet the charge will be somewhat high! We hope his visage will suffer little, the doctor in that particular being said to be skilful and fortunate. The Patient is inwardly well and his appetite towards his victuals is now as good as ever. The Wife and Daughters of the house attend him with the greatest love and diligence, all which, and the apothecary's bill especially, is like to be somewhat. You may expect good things of this Edmund. His judgment is very sound, and his observation both of men and things is no worse than the best I have known at the entrance to the 18th year.

It is now the 13th day, and Edmund grows daily better. We hope for considerable advantages from his present distemper; that his body will be more vigorous and his face less troubled with red spots which did blemish before, but not greatly deface his visage. His hair is now cut off, and herein I do purpose to send you an unclean small lock of the same. The charge of peruques is now added to a thousand other expenses.

John Evelyn (1620–1706), the influential garden writer, designer and diarist, had eight children, four of whom died in infancy. In March 1685, John Evelyn's eldest daughter Mary died of smallpox (see page 255). Here he describes the elopement of his second daughter, Elizabeth, aged eighteen.

## 27th July, 1685

This night when we were all asleepe went my Daughter Eliz: away, to meete a young fellow . . . whom she married the next day being Tuesday; without in the least acquainting either her parents, or any soule in the house: I was the more afflicted & astonish'd at it, in reguard, we had never given this Child the least cause to be thus dissobedient, and being now my Eldest, might reasonably have expected a double Blessing: But it afterward appeared, that this Intrigue had ben transacted by letters long before, & when she was with my Lady Burton in Licester shire, and by private meetings neere my house: She of all our Children had hitherto given us least cause of suspicion; not onely for that she was yet young, but seemed the most flattering, souple, and observant; of a silent & particular humor; in no sort betraying the levity & Inclination which is commonly apparent in Children who fall into these snares; having been bred-up with the uttmost Circumspection, as to principles of severest honour & Piety: But so far it seemes, had her passion for this Young fellow made her forget her duty, and all that most Indulgent Parents expected from her, as not to consider the Consequence of her folly & dissobedience, 'til it was too late: This Affliction went very neere me & my Wife, neither of us yet well compos'd for the untimely losse of that incomparable & excellent Child, which it pleased God to take from us by the small pox a few moneths before: But this farther Chastizement was to be humbly submitted to, as a part of the burden God was pleased to lay farther upon us; in this yet the lesse afflictive, That we had not ben wanting in giving her an Education every way becoming us: We were most of all astonish'd at the suddainesse of this action, & the privatenesse of its manegement; the Circumstances also Consider'd & quality, how it was possible she should be flattered so to her dissadvantage: He being in no condition sortable to hers, & the Blessing we intended her: The thing has given us much disquiet, I pray God direct us, how to govern our Resentments of her dissobedience; and if it be his will, bring good out of all this Ill:

Not long after this elopement, on 29th August, Elizabeth died of smallpox.

Mary Evelyn (1635–1709), wife of John Evelyn, writes to her son John, aged about eighteen. He was one of five sons and the only one who lived beyond the age of six.

## 1685

I haue received your letter, and request for a supply of mony; but none of those you mention which were bare effects of your duty. If you were so desirous to answer our expectations as you pretend to be, you would give those tutors and overseers you think so exact over you lesse trouble then I feare they have with you. Much is to be wished in your behalfe: that your temper were humble and tractable, your inclinations virtuous, and that from choice not compulsion you make an honnest man. Whateuer object of vice comes before you, should haue the same effect in your mind of dislike and aversion that drunkenesse had in the youth of Sparta when their slaves were presented to them in that brutish condition, not only from the deformity of such a sight, but from a motive beyond theirs, the hopes of a future happinesse, which those rigorous heathens in morall virtue had little prospect of, finding no reward for virtue but in virtue itselfe. You are not too young to know that lying, defrauding, swearing, disobedience to parents and persons in authority, are offences to God and man: that debauchery is injurious to growth, health, life, and indeed to the pleasures of life: therefore now that you are turning from child to man endeavour to follow the best precepts, and chuse such wayes as may render you worthy of praise and love. You are assured of your Fathers care and my tendernesse: no mark of it shall be wanting at any time to confirme it to you, with this reserve only, that you strive to deserve kindnesse by a sincere honest proceeding, and not flatter your selfe that you are good whilst you only appear to be so. Fallacies will only passe in schools. When you thoroughly weigh these considerations, I hope you will apply them to your owne advantage, as well as to our infinite satisfaction. I pray dayly God would inspire you with his grace, and blesse you.

I am,
Your louing mother,
M. Evelyn.

John Evelyn doesn't think much of Sir Gilbert Gerrard's son as a possible suitor for his daughter Susanna, aged sixteen.

## 1st March, 1686

Came Sir Gilb: Gerrard to treat with me about his sonns marying my Daughter *Susanna*; The father being obnoxious, & in some suspicion and displeasure of the King, I would receive no proposal, 'til his Majestie had given me leave, which he was pleas'd to do: but after severall meetings, we brake off, upon his not being willing to secure any thing competant for my daughters Children: besides that I found his estate to be most of it in the Coale-pits as far as N. Castle, & leases from the *Bishop* of Durrham, who had power to make concurrent Leases with other difficulties, so as we did not procccede to any conclusion:

◈

William Blundell succumbs, in the end, to a request for help from his grandson Nicholas (1669–1737), aged seventeen and at school in France.

## 7th July, 1686

I have yours of June 28th which, as to the sense thereof I find to be humble and loving, but I am very sorry to perceive that the characters of your letters do still grow worse and worse. I may say the same of your spelling and of your leaving out of words. Your sister Mary is 4 years younger than you and yet she writes a very laudable hand. Now as to your small progress in school, though your memory may be very bad, you must not also pretend (as you do in your letter to me) an excuse from your want of wit. I think there is no such want, and that, if your memory and genius being defective, your wit being sufficient and your diligence as much as you please, it will be in your own power to come off with credit. To comply with your request to me I have sent to Mr. Beaugrand for your use ten shillings in money, and a book for the Flageolet. I have given your father notice that you tell me your money is spent and I hope, though his charges are very great and his fortune small, he will send you a further supply before the ten shillings is spent.

Hannah Woolley (1622–1674) was one of the first women to earn her living by writing. She is scornful about the education of sons compared to their sisters. Her comments ring true for another three hundred years.

### 1673/5

Most in this depraved age, think a Woman learned and wise enough if she can distinguish her Husband's bed from another's.

The great negligence of parents, in letting the fertile ground of their Daughters lie fallow, yet send the barren Noodles of their sons to University, where they stay for no other purpose than to fill their empty Sconces with idle Notions to make a noise in the Countrye.

❧

Mary Woodforde (b. 1638) describes in her diary the trouble her son Jack is in at school in Winchester (Winton). Schools could be places of extreme violence: as late as 1818, two companies of troops with fixed bayonets had to be sent to Winchester College to suppress an uprising among the boys.

### 6th March, 1687

This evening I had the cutting news that my second boy was in rebellion at the College at Winton, where he and all his Companions resolved not to make any verses, and being called to be whipped for it several of them refused to be punished, mine amongst the rest. Some of them did submit, . . . and if the others do not, they must be expelled. God I beseech thee subdue their stubborn hearts, and give them grace to repent and accept of their punishment due to their fault, and let them not run on to ruin, for Christ's sake.

### 8th March

Yesterday my dear Husband went to Winton about Jack, and I have received this afternoon a letter from him which gives me hopes he has now humbled himself . . .

13th March

This morning we had a letter from Sam [her eldest son, aged nineteen] wherein he expresses a great deal of dullness and indisposition to his studies, and a desire to change the air if his Father think fit to see if it would do him good. Now we are in a strait which way to incline. We beg direction of thee, O All wise and Almighty God what to do, and beseech thee to satisfy our Child to submit to which ever shall be presently concluded on for him.

Sam was admitted as a scholar to St John's College, Cambridge in June.

❦

George Savile, 1st Marquess of Halifax (1633–1695), was an English statesman and writer. He addressed his treatise *The Lady's New Year's Gift* to his daughter, Elizabeth (1677–1708), a highly intelligent and educated woman who was the mother of the 4th Earl of Chesterfield, famous for his letters to his son. Halifax reminds us just how difficult married life might be for many young women.

### 1688

It is one of the disadvantages belonging to your sex, that young women are seldom permitted to make their own choice; their friends' care and experience are thought safer guides to them than their own fancies, and their modesty often forbiddeth them to refuse when their parents recommend, though their inward consent may not entirely go along with it. In this case there remaineth nothing for them to do but to endeavour to make that easy which falleth to their lot, and by a wise use of everything they may dislike in a husband, turn that by degrees to be very supportable, which, if neglected, might in time beget an aversion.

You must first lay it down for a foundation in general, that there is inequality in the sexes, and that for the better economy of the world, the men, who were to be the law givers, had the larger share of reason bestowed upon them, by which means your sex is the better prepared for the compliance that is necessary for the better performance of those duties which seem to be most properly assigned to it. This looks a little uncourtly at the first appearance, but upon examination it will be found that Nature is so far from being unjust to you that she is partial on your side. She hath made you such large amends by other advantages, for the seeming injustice of the first distribution, that the right of complaining is come over to our sex; you have it in your power not only to free yourselves, but to subdue your masters, and without violence throw both their natural and legal authority at your feet.

◦╬◦

Nicholas Blundell (1669–1737), a Lancashire landowner, writes to his friend the Revd Thomas Roydon on the subject of his daughters' marriage prospects. Blundell goes to a great deal of trouble and expense to find husbands for his two daughters, but he does not then oblige them to marry against their will. In this case, Roydon has proposed Thomas Strickland as a suitor for Mally, Blundell's eldest daughter, aged twenty.

## 10th January, 1724

The caracture you give of Mr Strickland is very good and I question not but he deserves it, and as to his estate and what I should have settled on my daughter, I question not but we could have adjusted matters so as to make all things easy and both sides and the young Cupple Happy. I did not think proper to acquaint my daughter with what I was about until I was resolved where to fix, but upon my arrivall home I told her, haveing severall in choyce (without nameing the person,) that I hoped I had heard of a gentleman with whom she might be happy, his caracture being without exception. But she told me me she was not the least disposed to marry as yet, so beged I would not urge her to it, which I was really sorry for. I should have been truly glad of an Allyance to so worthy a Famoly and so deserving a Gentleman and do sincerely wish him well settled to his Content and Satisfaction. You may be assured that I shall never mention anything that this affaire was ever in agitation, neather shall I ever forget your readiness in endeavouring to procure me a good husband for my daughter.

To his brother Joseph:

16th May, 1724

. . . I do not find my doughters are desirous to marry nor I to settle any of my estates upon them whilst there is the least prospect of a son, all I shall do is to settle conditionally and, in case I have a son, then such a portion certain, but as for a present fortune and the estate at last, 'tis what no one can reasonably expect. I have had severall proposed but will not fix of any only such as I am pretty well assured my doughters may live comfortably with, for I assure you they are deserving of good husbands and when I think I can light of such a one I shall not slip ye opportunity. But to tell me he is a Barronet's son and will have £1500 per annum will not tempt me, I have already refused a Barronet of a better estate. I vallew the persun, parts and humours of the man (for that must make a woman happy) more than quallity. When I know who the Barronet's son is, and have enquired sufficiently of his Person, Parts and Humour, I shall think of fixing upon Preliminaries . . .

Three months later, he writes to Mr Eccleston, who has proposed another candidate.

I have had some Persons of good familys and others of good estates proposed, but none so well qualified in all respects as to think deserving of my daughters for I will do the part of a good and kind father as far as in me lyes to settle where I think they may be truly happy.

To Mr Roydon, after another approach on behalf of Thomas Strickland:

6th April, 1725

I do not find my daughter any more inclineable to marry than she was, yet am entirely of opinion that she is not so averse to it that an accomplished gentleman with whom she may be happy may obtain her favour. However I thought it would be rude to let any one come to court her, and then for her to declair she would not marry. That would look like an imposition upon a Gentleman and he might really take it as an affront put upon him. But if Mr Strickland or any other deserving gentleman think it worth while to try if he can gain her affections I am not against his coming. . . . I long since told her I would not compel her to marry, much less to marry one she could not love and so to make her miserable as long as she lives, so leave her entirely to pleas herself, all I require is that he be a Gentleman of a cumpotent Estate, one of a good caracture, and a Catholick.

To Mr Roydon again:

30th April

You are pleased to say I have a Full Purs, but if I can stretch so far as to pay £1000 in hand tis the utmost I can reach to, and £1000 more at my death if I have a Son (which tis 20 to 1 I have not), and if no son then £400 per annum and a very good Hous; this I hope, with a good wife, may make Mr Strickland or anyone elce happy who is not hard-pushed for Money; but as I have said before tis my chief aime to settle my daughters to lickeing and that they may make choyce of a man they can love, and I'll doe my endeavours to propose such to them whose Sarcomsteenses may make them happy, . . .

To his cousin Mr Gillibrand, who has been successfully promoting an alternative suitor, Mr Standish:

24th November

. . . [Mally] imparts not her Mind freely to me, elce would not have told a Confidant that she was desirous to have the Treaty brock off; this was told me, but whether by Mally's orders or noe I know not. My Answer was that I expected to heare it from her own Mouth, and if she would tell me herself that she was desirous to be Religious, or that she thought she could not be happy with Mr Standish, I would by no meanes oblige her to Marry him, to which she answered, as I was told, that I knew her mind and she would not speak to me any more about that affaire.

25th November

Mally discoursed seriously and told me her mind.

To his cousin Mr Gillibrand:

26th November

. . . she has seriously imparted her Mind to me, and says she thinks she cannot be happy with Mr Standish if he be of that suspicious Gellous Humour she takes him to be and if ever it be her fate to marry him, as she hopes it never will, 'twill be entirely by your persuasion and becaus she finds I desire it, but not in the least according to her own desire or inclination. If this really be her Thought (which I as well as yourself have but too much reason to believe) tis full time to put a Stop to proceedings for you know 'twas always my promis to her that I would not oblige her to marry against her Will and 'tis much better to break off than to preceed and make not only the young Cupple unhappy, but the whole family with which they were to live, so I hope you'l acquaint Mr Standish herewith, for I find twill be to noe purpose for the young gentleman to come againe, 'tis but to entangle him more and more and I hope he will light of one who will have a greater love for him than I feare my Daughter ever will, . . .

'Tis but reason Mally should be entirely left to her own Choyce, and if I be reflected upon for not compelling her, I would rather be taxed with that than give any occasion of being esteemed a harsh or unkind Parent . . .

❧

The Duke of Somerset (1662–1748) had two daughters: Lady Frances Seymour (b. 1728) and Lady Charlotte (b. 1730). Some fathers were unbearable.

His two youngest daughters were alternately obliged to stand and watch him during his afternoon siesta. On one occasion, Lady Charlotte, being fatigued, sat down, when the Duke awaking unexpectedly, expressed his surprise at her disobedience, and declared he should remember her want of decorum in his will. He left this daughter 20000 pounds less than the other.

Lord Chesterfield gives his son Philip, aged fifteen, cynical if skilful advice on how to praise famous men. Women are always to be praised for their beauty except when famously beautiful, and then they must be praised for their understanding.

## 16th October, 1747

Dear Boy,

The art of pleasing is a very necessary one to possess; but a very difficult one to acquire. It can hardly be reduced to rules; and your own good sense and observation will teach you more of it than I can. Do as you would be done by, is the surest method that I know of pleasing. Observe carefully what pleases you in others, and probably the same things in you will please others. . . .

Do not tell stories in company; there is nothing more tedious and disagreeable: if by chance you know a very short story, and exceedingly applicable to the present subject of conversation, tell it in as few words as possible; and even then, throw out that you do not love to tell stories; but that the shortness of it tempted you. Of all things, banish the egotism out of your conversation, and never think of entertaining people with your own personal concerns or private affairs; though they are interesting to you, they are tedious and impertinent to everybody else; besides that, one cannot keep one's own private affairs too secret. . . . Never maintain an argument with heat and clamour, though you think or know yourself to be in the right; but give your opinion modestly and coolly, which is the only way to convince; and, if that does not do, try to change the conversation, by saying, with good-humour, 'We shall hardly convince one another; nor is it necessary that we should, so let us talk of something else.' . . .

If you would particularly gain the affection and friendship of particular people, whether men or women, endeavour to find out their predominant excellency, if they have one, and their prevailing weakness, which everybody has; and do justice to the one, and something more than justice to the other. Men have various objects in which they may excel, or at least would be thought to excel; and, though they love to hear justice done to them, where they know that they excel, yet they are most and best flattered upon those points where they wish to excel, and yet are doubtful whether they do or not. As, for example: Cardinal Richelieu, who was undoubtedly the ablest statesman of his time, or perhaps of any other, had the idle vanity of being thought the best poet too: he envied the great Corneille his reputation, and ordered a criticism to be written upon the *Cid*. Those, therefore, who flattered skilfully, said little to him of his abilities in state affairs, or at least but *en passant,* and as it might naturally occur. But the incense which they gave him – the smoke of which they knew would turn his head in their favour – was as a *bel esprit* and a poet. Why? – Because he was sure of one excellency, and distrustful as to the other. You will easily discover every man's prevailing vanity, by observing his favourite topic of conversation; for every man talks most of what he has most a mind to be thought to excel in. Touch him but there, and you touch him to the quick. . . .

Women have, in general, but one object, which is their beauty; upon which, scarce any flattery is too gross for them to swallow. Nature has hardly formed a woman ugly enough to be insensible to flattery upon her person; if her face is so shocking, that she must, in some degree be conscious of it, her figure and air, she trusts, make ample amends for it. If her figure is deformed, her face, she thinks, counterbalances it. If they are both bad, she comforts herself that she has graces; a certain manner; a *je ne sais quoi* still more engaging than beauty. This truth is evident, from the studied and elaborate dress of the ugliest woman in the world. An undoubted, uncontested, conscious beauty is, of all women, the least sensible of flattery upon that head; she knows it is her due, and is therefore obliged to nobody for giving it her. She must be flattered upon her understanding; which, though she may possibly not doubt of herself, yet she suspects that men may distrust. . . .

There are little attentions, . . . which are infinitely engaging, and which sensibly affect that degree of pride and self-love, which is inseparable from human nature; . . . As, for example, to observe the little habits, the likings, the antipathies, and the tastes of those whom we would gain; . . . giving them, genteelly, to understand, that you had observed they liked such a dish, or such a room; for which reason you had prepared it: or, on the contrary, that having observed they had an aversion to such a dish, a dislike to such a person, etc., you had taken care to avoid presenting them. Such attention to such trifles flatters self-love much more than greater things, as it makes people think themselves almost the only objects of your thoughts and care.

These are some of the *arcana* necessary for your initiation in the great society of the world. I wish I had known them better at your age; . . .

*A year later, he warns him against practical jokes or even laughing out loud.*

9th March, 1748

Having mentioned laughing, I must particularly warn you against it: and I could heartily wish that you may often be seen to smile, but never heard to laugh while you live. Frequent and loud laughter is the characteristic of folly and ill manners: it is the manner in which the mob express their silly joy at silly things; and they call it being merry. . . . But it is low buffoonery, or silly accidents, that always excite laughter; and that is what people of sense and breeding should show themselves above. A man's going to sit down, in the supposition that he has a chair behind him, and falling down upon his breech for want of one, sets a whole company a laughing, when all the wit in the world would not do it; a plain proof, in my mind, how low and unbecoming a thing laughter is. Not to mention the disagreeable noise that it makes, and the shocking distortion of the face that it occasions. . . . I am neither of a melancholy, nor a cynical disposition; and am as willing, and as apt, to be pleased as anybody; but I am sure that, since I have had the full use of my reason, nobody has ever heard me laugh. Many people, at first from awkwardness and *mauvaise honte,* have got a very disagreeable and silly trick of laughing whenever they speak: . . .

This, and many other very disagreeable habits, are owing to *mauvaise honte* at their first setting out in the world. They are ashamed in company, and so disconcerted that they do not know what they do, and try a thousand tricks to keep themselves in countenance; which tricks afterwards grow habitual to them. Some put their fingers in their nose, others scratch their head, others twirl their hats; in short, every awkward, ill-bred body has his trick. . . . Remember that to please is almost to prevail, or at least a necessary previous step to it. You, who have your fortune to make, should more particularly study this art.

Nearly three hundred years after they were written, these are opinions with which we can all agree.

## 2nd August, 1748

Dear Boy,

[Duvall the Jeweller] tells me that you are pretty fat for one of your age: this you should attend to in a proper way; for if, while very young, you should grow fat, it would be troublesome, unwholesome, and ungraceful: you should therefore, when you have time, take very strong exercise, and in your diet avoid fattening things. All malt liquors fatten, or at least bloat; and I hope you do not deal much in them. I look upon wine and water to be, in every respect, much wholesomer.

❦

Lady Caernarvon is described as an unkind, irresponsible and alcoholic mother.

## 1749

'Tis said that Lady Carnarvon has given her [daughter Jane] cruel usage some time: and not long agoe, when Lady Jane was drest to go to Mrs. Holmon's Assembly with her Mother's leave [but] when the time drew near she told Lady Jane she should not goe. Lady Jane . . . begged her pardon if she resolved to go without her leave: accordingly she went, and came home in a Chair at ten o'Clock.

When her footman knocked at the door there was no entrance, and a Servant of Lady Carnarvon called from the Area That his Lady was got in to Bed, and ordered the Street Door should not be opened. Lady Jane bid him carry a Message to her Mother, presenting her duty, and that she begged she would be so good to give her Admittance, for she sat in the Street and did not know where to goe: Answer was brought That she might go where she pleased, but she should not come there. Lady Jane cryed and sent once more to intreat admittance and if that was not granted begged an order where she should go she believed her sister Lyons would not be agreeable to her Ladyship, and she knew of no other place she could go to at that time of night. Her answer was from her Mother, that she did not care where she went; she should not enter her house.

So Lady Jane went to Mr. Lyons, and the next Morning sent Mr. Lyons to her Mother to know if she would receive her, and if not, to desire her Cloths might be sent her. When Mr. Lyons came to Lady Carnarvon's he found the House shut up and her Ladyship gone out of Town.

So Lady Jane went to Colonel Inwood's, whose Wife is a Relation, and staid there. Lady Carnarvon returned in two or three days and drove to the Duke of Chandois. Asked if Lady Jane was there, the Porter said No: at which she put herself in a passion, and said she would have her. The Duke was at home and went down to the Coach. . . . She then abused the Duke, and swore so terribly, That his Grace left her and ordered the Street Door to be shut. She got out of her Coach, and knocked at the door like a Bedlam. Ten minutes cursing and swearing all the while with a Mob gathered about. A Servant of the Duke came to her, desired she would forbear, lest the Hubbub should fright Lady Dutchess, who was with Child. 'My Lady Dutchess,' says she, 'D—m her Dutchesship, I will have my Child.'

At last she went to Colonel Inwood's, and sent for her Daughter down. Lady Jane sent her duty and came directly. Lady Carnarvon bid the Footman open the door of the Coach, saying to Lady Jane in a haughty tone, 'Come in, Madam.' Says Lady Jane, 'I come to know your Ladyship's Commands, but must begg to be excused coming into your Coach, or going with you. The usage you have given me has made me resolve the contrary.' Accordingly Lady Carnarvon was obliged to go away without her.

Lady Jane's friends are going to place her in a house by herself. Lady Carnarvon's behaviour is not to be wondered at, I think, for I hear she drinks very hard, and seldom sober, not even in a morning, and some think she has quarrelled with her daughter from a design of marrying some mean Fellow.

⚘

Henry Fox writes to his son Stephen (b.1745), known as Ste., at school. He and his wife, Caroline, were notoriously indulgent parents, so this seems to be an unusually clear request. Stephen grew up to be an irresponsible gambler.

10th June, 1758

One thing, you know I much wanted to see – your hair cut to a reasonable length and gentlemanlike shortness. You and some Eton boys wear it as no other people in the world do. It is effeminate; it is ugly; and it must be inconvenient. You gave me hopes that if I desir'd it, you would cut it. I will, dear Ste., be much obliged if you will.

Many years later, Lady Susan Strangways, Henry Fox's niece, recorded in her journal a conversation she had with Lady Sarah Lennox (1745–1826), his much younger sister-in-law, about the effect Henry Fox had on them. The two women were friends from childhood.

March 1818

His excessive praises and flattery excited our vanity, made us many enemies, and unfitted us for any society that was not superfine. His maxim that young people were always in the right and old ones in the wrong could not and did not fail to give us a contempt for those to whom all deference was due; and when these maxims operated, his anger and displeasure was heightened by the disappointment of our not succeeding in the schemes he had laid for us.

❦

George Box writes to Lord Verney, begging for help for his son, who is in prison for fraudulently trying to pay off his gambling debts. A capital offence meant death.

22nd August, 1782

My Lord, – My melancholy situation I hope will excuse this application to your lordship – my son whom your lordship knows and who is but little more than sixteen years of age has been seduced to the E.O. Tables where having lost some money, which he was entrusted to receive for me, for fear of a Rebuke has been induced to write the names of several Persons not in being, to receipts on certificates as having provided Substitutes in the militia by means of which he has received upwards of £400, which is a Capital Offence if prosecuted with vigour.

... My Infirmities your lordship is not unacquainted with – my Distresses I daresay you feel for, but it is impossible that anyone unless he was in my situation could be a judge of what I feel – his Mother very ill of a nervous Disorder and a Depression of Spirits – she knows he is in Prison but does not know how capital the offence is, which I am afraid to acquaint her with for fear of distraction – as he is an only son and she most tenderly fond of him. Three sisters who are passionately fond of him almost bursting with grief ... I am hardly able to support myself under so great a Burthen. Tis impossible for me to settle this affair ... without the humane assistance of my friends, amongst a number of whom I hope I may take the liberty of ranking your lordship as one in such a case of Pungent Distress. I humbly entreat your lordship directly with £40 or £50 ... for goodness sake my lord assist me, you can't form any idea of my distress.

ও৳ও

Mary Wollstonecraft (1759–1797) writes against young women marrying too young. She died giving birth to her daughter Mary, who eloped, aged sixteen, with Percy Bysshe Shelley.

1787

Early marriages are, in my opinion, a stop to improvement. .... In youth a woman endeavours to please the other sex, in order, generally speaking, to get married, and this endeavour calls forth all her powers. If she has had a tolerable education, the foundation only is laid, for the mind does not soon arrive at maturity, and should not be engrossed by domestic cares before any habits are fixed. The passions also have too much influence over the judgment to suffer it to direct her in this most important affair; and many women, I am persuaded, marry a man before they are twenty, whom they would have rejected some years after. Very frequently, when the education has been neglected, the mind improves itself, if it has leisure for reflection, and experience to reflect on; but how can this happen when they are forced to act before they have had time to think, or find that they are unhappily married? Nay, should they be so fortunate as to get a good husband, they will not set a proper value on him; he will be found much inferior to the lovers described in novels, and their want of knowledge makes them frequently disgusted with the man, when the fault is in human nature. ....

Matthew Boulton writes to his son Matt, aged seventeen. Without the bellows, I expect the advice still holds good.

### 19th December, 1787

A man will never make a good Chymist unless he acquires a dexterity, & neatness in making expts, even down to the pulverising in a Morter, or blowing the Bellows, distinctness, order, regularity, neatness, exactness and Cleanliness are necessary in the Laboratory, in the Manufactory, & in the Counting house.

❦

Not long after the death of his wife, James Boswell admits his difficulties in making living arrangements that will ensure the sophistication of his daughters.

### 3rd July, 1789

Honest David is perpetually pressing my confining my family to Scotland. But alas, my dear friend, should I or could I now be satisfied with narrow provinciality, which was formerly so irksome and must now be much more so? I have agreed that my second daughter shall pass the winter at Edinburgh, as she has desired it, in order to finish her education. But were my daughters to be *Edinburgh-mannered girls*, I could have no satisfaction in their company.

❦

Erasmus Darwin (1731–1802), grandfather of Charles, writes about the financial provision he intends making for his two illegitimate daughters (by his housekeeper, Mary Parker), who had been brought up within his family of legitimate children. At the time of writing, the girls were aged seventeen and eighteen; Erasmus did do as he suggests, and set them up as teachers in their own school.

### 30th March, 1791

By this sum and some employment as Lady's Maid or teacher of work they may be happier than my other girls who will have not much more than double or treble that sum, and brought up in more genteel life, for I think happiness consists much in being *well* in one's situation in life – and not in that situation being higher or lower.

❦

Sarah Siddons (1755–1831), the greatest tragic actress of her time, writes to a friend, Mrs Pennington, about the marriage prospects of her daughter Sally, aged nineteen, who had asthma and intermittent chest infections. Mrs Siddons was a friend of Dr Johnson.

### 9th August, 1798

How vainly did I flatter myself that [Sally] had acquired the strength of constitution to throw off this cruel disorder! Instead of that, it returns with increasing velocity and violence. What a sad prospect is this for her in marriage? For I am now convinc'd it is constitutional, and will pursue her thro' life! Will a husband's tenderness keep pace with and compensate for the loss of a mother's, her unremitting cares and soothings? Will he not grow sick of these repeated attacks, and think it vastly inconvenient to have his domestic comforts, his pleasures, or his business interfered with by the necessary and habitual attentions which they will call for from himself and from his servants? Dr. Johnson says the man must be almost a prodigy of virtue who is not soon tir'd of an ailing wife; and sad experience has taught even *me*, who might have hop'd to have assured that attention which *common gratitude* for a life of labour in the service of my family shou'd have offered, that illness, often repeated, or long continued, soon tires a man. To say the truth, a sick wife *must* be a *great misfortune*. . . .

### S. Siddons

I am in hopes of getting a frank for this letter, for tho' I know not why, or what end it answers to write so often, yet I somehow feel easier when writing to you; certainly it is the next thing to *talking* to you.

William Godwin (1756–1836), the social philosopher, writes to his brother to tell him of his daughter Mary's marriage to Percy Bysshe Shelley. Godwin contrives to ignore the reality of the situation: the pair had run away together in 1814, when Shelley was still married to his first wife, Harriet, and Mary was only sixteen. The wedding was able to take place only because Harriet had committed suicide. It will be a long time before Mary is considered respectable.

## 1817

Were it not that you have a family of your own, and can see by them how little shrubs grow into tall trees, you would hardly imagine that my boy, born the other day, is now fourteen, and that my daughter is between nineteen and twenty. The piece of news I have to tell, however, is that I went to church with this tall girl some little time ago to be married.

Her husband is the eldest son of Sir Timothy Shelley, of Field Place, in the County of Sussex, Baronet. So that, according to the vulgar ideas of the world, she is well married, and I have great hopes the young man will make her a good husband. You will wonder, I daresay, how a girl without a penny of fortune should meet with so good a match. But such are the ups and downs of the world. For my part, I care but little, comparatively, about wealth, so that it be her destiny in life to be respectable, virtuous, and contented.

๑๖

In her old age, Lady Sarah Lennox was asked by one of her daughters-in-law about her excellent relationships with her children.

… the great and primary source certainly was seeing me from their infancy the object of their father's tender love and care, seeing me at the same time holding a high place in his estimation as his friend and companion. This taught them that I was to be loved, to be greatly considered, and to be respected …

As they rose out of infancy, I left them to their father's management, and studied to become the friend, not the tutoress of my sons. They knew that my influence never would be made use of improperly towards their father, nor had they any idea of mollifying him or changing his views by their applications to me, but they knew that their confidence in me delighted him, that it pleased him when they went to me in their little difficulties, or to make their confessions, and in me they trusted to find sympathy, kindness, my opinion or advice if they sought it, knowing at the same time that it was unaccompanied by the necessity of adopting it . . .

. . . then left to decide for themselves, their actions (probably even unknown to themselves) were somewhat of the hue of what they had just heard.

❦

William Wilberforce (1759–1833), politician and philanthropist who was prominent in the struggle to abolish the slave trade, writes to his daughter Lizzy, aged seventeen, about her relationship with her mother.

## 1818

It has often given me no little pain my dearest Lizzy, to witness little altercations between you and your mother, little rather in the occasions on which they arise, than in the real intrinsic importance of them. For I should not deal honestly with you if I did not state to you my real opinion, that they ought to be regarded as very serious blemishes in a religious character. Granting that there may be faults on both sides, I cannot forget a saying common among them, that it is the second blow that makes the battle. This applies full as accurately to the contest of the tongue as to any others. And you will not I am sure deny that the Obligation to abstain from any language that may tend to augment, or rather to keep up the irritation must press more strongly on you than on your Mother. I have often been strongly impressed by the Consideration that if any fellow creature happens to be present before whom you would be sorry to exhibit anything of the kind I allude to, you can abstain from it without any apparent difficulty; and therefore – but I need not draw an inference which I am sure will readily suggest itself to your own mind. Neither need I enlarge on the various motives which should prompt you to strive against an infirmity which you cannot but know to be wrong.

Sydney Smith writes to Francis Horner about the education of his son Douglas, aged eleven. Once he has sent the boy to boarding school he acknowledges the beastliness of the system but, like thousands of parents over the centuries, he regards it as a preparation for life.

25th November, 1816

I went in quest of schools for Douglas. At Ripon I found an insignificant man, in melancholy premises, and boys two in a bed. At Richmond I was extremely pleased with Mr. Tate, who takes thirty boys, and appears to be a very enlightened man. Westminster costs about £150 or £200 per annum. I have little to do, and am extremely poor. Why not keep Douglas at home till he is sixteen, send him for three years to Mr. Tate, then to Cambridge? I cannot think that his moral or literary improvement will be less; at the same time, if it were my duty to make the sacrifice, of course, I *would* make it, but, after all the attention I can give to it, I cannot discover a better plan, even if I had £10,000 per annum; of course it is taken for granted that I am able to teach him well, and that I shall stick to my duty.

A few years later, Sydney Smith has sent his son to Westminster. He writes to Mrs Meynell:

January 1820

Douglas is gone to school; not with a light heart, for the first year of Westminster in college is severe: – an intense system of tyranny, of which the English are very fond, and think it fits a boy for the world; but the world, bad as it is, has nothing half so bad. . . .

I hope your children are all well; if they are not, I am sure you are not; and if you are not, I shall not be so.

He writes to advise Douglas, now a King's Scholar.

Summer 1820

My Dear Douglas,

Concerning this Mr. –, I would not have you put any trust in him, for he is not trustworthy; but so live with him as if one day or other he were to be your enemy. With such a character as his, this is a necessary precaution.

In the time you can give to English reading you should consider what it is most needful to have, what it is most shameful to want, – shirts and stockings, before frills and collars. Such is the history of your own country, to be studied in Hume, then in Rapin's *History of England*, with Tindal's *Continuation*. Hume takes you to the end of James II, Rapin and Tindal will carry you to the end of Anne. Then, Coxe's 'Life of Sir Robert Walpole,' and the 'Duke of Marlborough;' and these read with attention to dates and geography. Then, the history of the other three or four enlightened nations in Europe. For the English poets, I will let you off at present with Milton, Dryden, Pope, and Shakspeare; and remember, always in books keep the best company. Don't read a line of Ovid till you have mastered Virgil; nor a line of Thomson till you have exhausted Pope; nor of Massinger, till you are familiar with Shakspeare.

I am glad you liked your box and its contents. Think of us as we think of you; and send us the most acceptable of all presents, – the information that you are improving in all particulars.

The greatest of all human mysteries are the Westminster holidays. If you can get a peep behind the curtain, pray let us know immediately the day of your coming home.

We have had about three or four ounces of rain here, that is all. I heard of your being wet through in London, and envied you very much. The whole of this parish is pulverized from long and excessive drought. Our whole property depends upon the tranquillity of the winds: if it blow before it rains, we shall all be up in the air in the shape of dust, and shall be *transparished* we know not where.

God bless you, my dear boy! I hope we shall soon meet at Lydiard

> Your affectionate father,
> Sydney Smith.

In his diary of the time, he wrote.

My son writes me word he is unhappy at school. This makes me unhappy; but, Firstly, There is much unhappiness in human life: how can school be exempt? Secondly, Boys are apt to take a particular moment of depression for a general feeling, and they are in fact rarely unhappy; at the moment I write, perhaps he is playing about in the highest spirits. Thirdly, When he comes to state his grievance, it will probably have vanished, or be so trifling, that it will yield to argument or expostulation. Fourthly, At all events, if it is a real evil which makes him unhappy, I must find out what it is, and proceed to act upon it; but I must wait till I can, either by person or by letter, find out what it is.

❦

John Constable (1776–1837), the artist, tells his friend Charles Leslie that he took two of his sons, John, aged sixteen, and Charles, aged twelve, to East Bergholt on holiday.

16th August, 1833

We ranged the woods and fields, and searched the crag-pits for shells, and the bones and teeth of fossil animals for John; and Charles made drawings, and I did nothing at all . . .

Later in the same year he writes again.

. . . dear Charley – . . . my son is transported. He has sold his first picture – a drawing (God knows what it is) is bought by the Curate of Folkestone for one shilling – ready money, I dare say.

Constable writes to a friend after Charley, now aged fifteen, goes off to sea with the East India Company; Charley had always determined to be a sailor, but the Navy offered few prospects of advancement at that time.

12th October, 1835

I have done all for the best, and I regret all that I have done, when I consider that it was to bereave me of this delightfully clever boy, who would have shone in my own profession, and who is now doomed to be driven about on the ruthless sea. It is a sad and melancholy life, but he seems made for a sailor. Should he please the officers and stick to the ship, it will be more to his advantage than being in the navy, – a hateful tyranny, with starvation into the bargain.

Margaret Ruskin (1781–1871), the mother of John (1819–1900), painter and critic, writes to her husband, John James Ruskin (1785–1864). Mrs Ruskin was an evangelical Protestant who took lodgings in Oxford to be near her son; her letters to her husband, a wine merchant living in London, describe in obsessive, claustrophobic detail, exactly what John did each day. However odd, her preoccupation with her son may not be so different from that of today's mothers, constantly at the end of a mobile telephone.

8th February, 1837

My Dearest John

Let me in the first place with deepest gratitude of heart for the blessing congratulate you and myself that our child has entered his nineteenth year without having by his conduct occasioned a moments serious uneasiness to either of us, and as we have the Divine assurance following the commandment, train up a child in the way he should go, & when he is old he will not depart from it, so I think I may venture to prophesy that his future conduct will not differ from the past. I did not see him till eleven this morning, very long service in chapel and waiting for lectures – he is thank God quite well . . . his desk arrived before he went to Chapel this morning . . . it is quite what he likes & will be very convenient . . .

I hope with you he will have little to do with uproarious meetings. I have no fear of his drinking but in these scuffles he might meet with injury tho' not at all taking part in them . . .

You could not desire to see John more attentive to all his studies – These two mornings he has been up at half past six but he goes to bed at ten and generally has some relaxation in calls or walks in the forenoon so I hope he will not be hurt and I am persuaded his quiet pursuits will come to have more charm for him than boisterous ones . . . he refused several invitations to wine parties last week two very tempting . . .

27th April, 1837

I think I must give you an account of Johns proceedings in journal fashion tuesday as I said he was to go to Concert . . . when he went home to dress, he found a note left by Mr. Donken inviting him to breakfast at nine on thursday – he could not go having a lecture at nine, called on Mr. Donken yesterday, found him at home, thinks him a most agreeable fellow, was at home with him in a minute, asked him Mr. Donken to Breakfast with him tomorrow, friday, which he agreed to do . . . – to return to Concert having tired of Mathematics (he had worked very hard at the questions given by Mr. Hill, he had done five all right and all the rest of the class only two & one of them wrong) he dressed and went to Ld. Carews, found only Mr. Denison, brother to the bishop, with him, they went to Concert together, heard some very pleasing singing and instrumental music, almost all gentleman performers – came away a little after 10, went home with Ld. Carew and drank tea, was in bed a little before eleven.

Later in his life, Ruskin wrote, unconvincingly, that his mother had come to Oxford with him 'that she might be at hand in case of accident or sudden illness'.

❧

Maria Josepha, Lady Stanley of Alderley (1771–1863), writes to her daughter-in-law, Henrietta Stanley. They write to each other often and, obviously, Lady Stanley doesn't hesitate to say what she thinks. (Henry (1827–1903) is Henrietta's oldest child; Gerald, her brother, is only four years older; Lady Dillon is Henrietta and Gerald's mother.)

### 8th June, 1843

Surely you do not send Henry alone to the play with Gerald unless you think it high time to initiate him into the knowledge of London. I should fancy, but it may be only fancy, he is not a very good companion for Henry – however you should know your own brother best, only sometimes peoples own relations do *not* know them best. I hear the thunder rumbling, very vexatious.

### 28th January, 1844

Henry will not like London & London is certainly not a good place for him to be in, with much of every afternoon disengaged – & you must not think me very prejudiced & wrong if I say I fear his Uncle Gerald's company for him. I do hope you will see & feel the necessity of their not going about together more than cannot be avoided especially to evening amusements. I *believe* it *was* Gerald who figured so unpleasantly last year in a Police Office tho' you thought it was not. No doubt the knowledge was kept from Ly. Dillon if it could be – & I would not force it upon you if I did not think it so important just now that you should watch over Henry & guard him from learning life in London as long as possible.

ଡ଼ୀଡ଼

Henrietta Stanley writes to her husband Edward to defend her daughter Alice (1828–1910) from his charge that she has no social graces. Henrietta had twelve children of whom nine survived. After her husband's death she devoted her life to women's rights and education.

## 17th December, 1846

I wrote a letter to you this morning . . . but have put it in the fire & will only say that I wish you may for the future let your own daughter share in the advantages you see the good of to others. Emily de Burgh [a girl much praised by Edward] has been constantly put forward in every way & *her* father would not have proposed that she should be sent upstairs when there was company to dinner & she has therefore become agreeable & conversible which it is impossible for a girl to be who is only allowed to appear at balls & interdited from all places where she is likely to hear any rational conversation.

Lady Stanley, writing to Henrietta, continues to show perspicacity and good sense.

## 14th February, 1847

I am sorry for Alice's, or rather *your* disappointment but I do not think you could expect a second season to be so successful as the first. There is a great deal in novelty & the wish of friends to introduce a débutante. I never expected A. would make her way like many & I doubt if one dance in Grosvenor Crescent would make much difference. I am afraid you will be obliged to bring her again out of Town without a husband which I *guess* you expected the first season. You had better make up your mind quickly, expect nothing – neither husbands or partners but let her enjoy her dances as well as she *can* & as she *will* if she does not see you *too* anxious – for depend upon it she knows well all that passes in your mind, & very few girls dance a great deal at every ball they go to.

A horrid fog Adieu

⚭

Baroness Bunsen (née Waddington) (1791–1876) was the mother of twelve children and a great letter writer. While staying with Queen Victoria at Windsor, she writes to her youngest daughter, Matilda, aged sixteen, to encourage her to learn to draw and read aloud.

### 13th January, 1853

I do wish my children would believe me, how well worth while it is to acquire the dexterity of hand and accuracy of perception requisite for drawing, in those early years when they have leisure, and also capability, as far as strength of body and of eyes goes. The power of drawing has been such a source of pleasure to me through life, such a refreshment, such a diversion of thought from care or anxiety – that I wish I could persuade those I love to provide themselves there-with, as a help on life's journey. . . . I hope you take pains with your reading aloud. . . . Will you try, my own child, to perfect and polish yourself? – 'Let our daughters be as the polished corners of the temple,' is a verse of a Psalm that always gives me an image equally just and pleasing. The corners of the temple are of good firm stone or marble; the firmer the substance, the finer is the polish they bear; but the polish which renders them beautiful to look upon, lessens nothing of their power of supporting the edifice, and connecting its parts into a solid structure.

William Thackeray writes to his daughter Anne, now aged eighteen, warning her that she cannot afford to fall in love with a young man who has no prospects.

### Boston, 18th December, 1855

Sally Baxter's marriage went off very smartly on the 12th and I hope she will get over *her* passion for an old fogey who shall be nameless [Thackeray himself] – It began to be a newsance at last to the old party, & very likely to the young one. My girls I suppose must undergo the common lot; but I hope they wont Sallify – Indulge in *amours de tête* I mean. Indeed I dont like to think of their entering into that business at all unless upon good reasonable steady grounds – with a Tomkins who is likely to make them happy and has enough to keep them – and who above all falls in love with them first – for say he is the best of young fellows but cannot keep himself – who is to do it? the old father to keep the family? that wouldn't be generous nor fair. No my dearest old Fat you mustnt hanker after a penniless young clergyman with one lung. It is as much as I can do to scrape together enough to keep my 3 daughters (your mother being one): and you must no more think about a penniless husband, than I can think about striking work – these luxuries do not belong to our station. Besides has he ever thought about you? Girls are romantic, visionary, love beautiful whiskers & so forth – but every time a girl permits herself to *think* an advance of this sort she hurts herself – loses somewhat of her dignity, rubs off a little of her maiden-bloom. Keep yours on your cheeks till 50 if necessary. Creyke has nothing – an incurable illness – & all the habits of a rich man – his illness prevents him from earning (I'm very fond of him you know & think him a fine fellow) – but you might as well ask me to give you a diamond necklace as to accommodate you with this luxury of a husband, of little darlings, of bills to pay, house to keep &c &c – You must marry a man that can keep you – and you've just pitched precisely on the gentleman that cannot. I dont say banish him from your mind – perhaps it is a fatal pashn ravaging your young bussom – perhaps only a fancy wh. has left already a head that has taken in a deal of novels – but settle it in your mind that it would be just as right for you to marry Charles Pearman (what do I say? Charles is healthy & can make his 40£ a year) as poor Creyke – and so despair & peridge, or resume your victuals and be jolly – determining that this thing never can be. Don't you suppose everybody in life wants something he cant get? Sorry we can't give you this Tomkins – Good bye Tomkins – God bless my dearest old Fat.

*To Anne, aged nineteen, and Harriet, aged sixteen:*

18th–21st November, 1856

Am not in love with Miss Block any more since Mrs. Brown told me she is here under a rubbing Doctor, and is rubbed every day for 2 hours with lard – dont like the idea of a young lady rubbed with lard – of course she has a female rubber – but still . . .

๑๑๑

*After the death of her first husband, Charlotte Guest married her son's tutor, Charles Schreiber (Charley). Her concerns focus first on her son, Ivor, and then on her daughter, Maria, as she portrays the archetypal tensions that can arise between children and their stepfathers or mothers. She had ten children, so it is no surprise to discover that she and her husband spent most of their life together travelling abroad.*

20th March, 1856

Had a letter from Ivor telling me he is gone to Paris with some friends for a few days. God grant he come out safe from that hotbed of iniquity. But I must not encourage a mother's anxieties. All young men must go and see the world, and all mothers must bear it, or ought to do so, in silence and prayer. He is as steady as, or steadier than most youths, and that reflection is a very comforting one, God bless him.

22nd March, 1856

Walked on the terrace awhile [with a friend, Mr Ponsonby]. Talked over family matters. Sometimes these dispirit me a good deal. I have now been married nearly a year. Charley has been unvaryingly kind and considerate. It is impossible for two people to be happier together or, I believe, to love each other more. He has had great forbearance with the children, but Maria has been unable to accommodate herself to the present state of affairs. . . . All this has been very trying. His great desire has been peace, and to do everything in his power to please them and make them happy. . . . Just now matters have relaxed a little, and things are more agreeable but Maria's temper is so capricious that I never know how long it will last. As far as I am myself concerned I see very little of her. I believe she shuns me. Often for days together I can get no answer from her but monosyllables, and I am sure it is months since she has said one kind word, though I have several times tried to soften her demeanour towards me, and tried to lead her to be open and friendly. . . . All this is no fancy of mine, others remark it even more than I do.

❧

Like many loving mothers, Caroline Chaplin sends a mixed message to her son Henry (1841–1923), who is being educated away from home in the house of a private tutor.

## 1857

I send you a sad batch of bills to look over, and I am sure you will feel sorry when you see how much they amount to, particularly when you remember that almost the whole of this large sum was spent in less than three months. . . . It seems very dreadful to think of throwing away so much money upon eating and drinking when so many are starving! But I won't say any more about it now, my darling boy, as I hope and trust it will be a lesson to you for the future, and that you will ever remember how wrong it is to buy what you have not the money ready to pay for. You cannot think the mischief and miseries it leads to, or the good which must arise from exercising a little self denial.

I have no doubt they cheat very much at these eating shops, and I do not at all like to pay their bills, but it must be done.

Samuel Palmer (1805–1881) writes to his eldest son, Thomas More Palmer, aged seventeen, at school.

### June 1859

If you come across any one who talks very freely about other people and laughs at them, *do* remember, if only from prudential motives, that to one who has his way to hew through the world, such a habit is absolute *suicide*. Such a habit is both hateful and treacherous; treacherous because the material of ridicule and scandal is often filched from its very victims in the confidence of social intercourse – perhaps under their very roof! While we listen to such tattle we are ourselves, perhaps, furnishing material for amusement at our expense. Nasty things are sometimes done by otherwise very nice people. Hence the danger. We should try to embody in ourselves a portion of each *good* thing we see among our friends, and so, as we roam, collect honey everywhere. The fly, unlike the bee, settles with satisfaction on every little heap of filth and refuse. Sometimes there is a good deal of drollery and even wit mixed up with what is wrong, and that makes it the more dangerous.

A year later he gives further good advice.

Influence in school and skill in music and at cricket will not in the least avail you in a college examination – indeed my experience among people of all professions has been that the *plodding* students who plodded on until they had really mastered the elements – beat out of the field the generally clever people who had in the width of their aim never really mastered the very things which were necessary to their future support. When the *heart* is set upon a thing *there* is success – and more is done in a week than in a year without it. 'Art is jealous,' said Michael Angelo 'and REQUIRES THE WHOLE MAN'. So with Letters.

Thomas More died aged nineteen; see page 273.

Six years later he writes in a more lighthearted tone to his second son, Herbert.

14th October, 1866

When we meet (D.V.), remind me about the occasional growth of our English rats to the bigness of a good-sized cat.

All facts are worth having, and should be investigated with patient accuracy; though a mountain of facts will never make even a mole-hill of truth.

ॐ

Edward Burne-Jones (1833–1898), the Pre-Raphaelite painter who described his art as a ' beautiful, romantic dream of something that never was, never will be', writes to his son Philip (1861–1926) during the latter's first unhappy term at Marlborough.

At any rate don't yield at all to them, but take your own way and never change it – only in that way will you win either now or afterwards in life. . . . there will be always people telling you how you shall think and act and dress, and what you are to say and how you are to live, down to the tiniest trifle, meaning that you are to think and act and dress as they do; and some sort of penalty you must pay all your life for differing from them, and their tyranny is excessive and relentless, and they would mostly like to destroy what they cannot convert to their own likeness.

According to David Cecil's account, Burne-Jones later told a friend never to send his son to boarding school: the son would suffer from lack of love and the parent from the loss of an irreplaceable companion.

Henry Irving (1838–1905), the most celebrated of all nineteenth-century actors, writes a tough but realistic letter to his son Harry, aged seventeen, an aspiring actor at Marlborough College.

1887

My dear Harry,

In seeking my advice concerning what you say is your determination to be an actor, you have given me a puzzle, and a grave one.

Knowing the difficulties which beset an actor's career, I had rather you had chosen another walk of life – some calling where there was more certainty of success and where a sedate application to work would ensure an ultimate reward.

This is a very hard time for young actors. There is no school where they can learn their art – where they can get the practice which is absolutely necessary. It is nearly impossible in the present day to get the training that a young man should have who may ever hope to gain distinction upon the stage.

Of course, you aim at the highest, and, unless you reach it, better not have been an actor.

Supposing, now, you were at the Lyceum, and I anxious to push you on. What could I do? How could you begin? By playing a small part in London? – a bad beginning. You must learn the A.B.C. of your work first.

By travelling around the country in some travelling company playing some one part month after month? What could you learn by that?

In my early days, I sometimes played 18 parts in a week – your Romeos, Claude Melnottes . . . and sitting up all night with a wet towel round my head, trying to master the words; and if I had not, as a lad, studied hundreds of the parts I was called suddenly upon to play, I must have broken down.

But I got practice. I learnt my art – for I studied it – the most difficult of all arts to master, and now I am an exceptionally successful actor, whose career it would be dangerous to take as an ordinary example.

And I am obliged to tell you this – and also I am sorry – that my name will be a hindrance to you and not a help, and that it will make your road more thorny.

This *has been ever* the experience of all fathers' sons.

Just for a start-off, perhaps for a month or two, my name might be of a little service. Curiosity would take many to see one – but what's that? A flash in the pan – nothing to weigh against the hard, exacting work of a life-time, when your efforts will be judged solely by your power – your power to satisfy and please the public, an exacting master.

Do not think that my name will help you – believe me, it will not. Nothing can help you but your own, your talent, perseverance and conduct in life.

Now I am not writing this to try and alter your decision, far from that. I know the more I tried to do that, the more resolute you would probably become. But I want you to realize the serious side of your undertaking, and it is indeed momentous – the future career of any young man.

Now to business! You propose as a preliminary to go to Germany and France. For what – for schooling, for the study of languages or what? Do you think you are sufficiently educated in English to start into the world, where every day and in every walk of life education becomes more necessary?

I am curious to know what your real reason for leaving Marlborough is, and would it not be better to stay another year, and show by your industry a promise of a successful future? Education is as beneficial to an artist as to a scholar. . . .

Now what I would advise you to do would be to stay at Marlborough another year. Work earnestly with your heart and soul – then perhaps a year in France under an actor like Got, who would impart to you a serious idea of the task you have before you. Then a course of *English* with a competent master, to speak your language properly and without a cockney accent which provokes upon the stage nothing but ridicule, to read Shakespeare and Milton and the English classics.

During that training of your mind you should also train your body by fencing, drilling, the practice of pantomime and so on.

Then, still almost hopeless of the chance of obtaining the necessary training, supposing you had the necessary gifts to make a fine actor, you might enter your new career with at all events a knowledge of the rudiments necessary to the practice of the art to which you had chosen to devote your life.

Vita Sackville-West (1892–1962) writes to Ben (1914–1978), her eldest son, when he fails his prelims (the first-year exams at Oxford).

### 1934

My dear Ben! really! What *do* you imagine life is made of? I curse you for being lazy, wasteful (time, not money) and *without guts*. I curse you for thinking a veneer of culture acquired principally from the conversations of people older, better educated, and above all more hard-working than yourself, is an adequate substitute for real knowledge, real application, real mental muscles. . . .

Veneereal disease, that's what's the matter with you. . . . Don't think I'm cross: I'm not: only firm. And determined that you shouldn't go soft and squelchy. I have had too many temptations in that direction myself, not to know the danger they offer. I haven't overcome them successfully myself.

❧

Marie Belloc Lowndes (d.1947), a French woman by birth, and a writer and journalist, writes to her daughter Elizabeth Iddesleigh, who had taken her son to Eton for the first time. (Her cousin Charles Lowry, or Charlie, was the housemaster, and was married to Frances, her sister-in-law.)

### Lisbon, Boxing Day, 1946

My precious darling

How very *very* well I recall my first visit to Eton. Frances filled with fears at the thought of a 'Journalist' [Lowndes herself]. I only guessed that *much* later. Dear Charlie loved me from first second. She a good many seconds later – what interested her was my sympathy with the unfortunate and unhappy. Not much of that in England, *unless* the misery is on orthodox lines. Lack of imagination is a *great* asset. The greatest asset of the British people. 'God was at Eton, so we can't be beaten', might well be Eton's *real* motto.

The floods at Eton were terrible. Amazing they kept the school there in the old days. When I was young a lot of the boys used to die. It is a most unhealthy place, now I suppose they do drain it. Boats used to paddle in the High Street. I remember the playing fields constantly under water. Queen Victoria used to drive there to see the fun.

The boys were supposed to exist for the benefit of the Masters. This was not realised by the fond parents, who were treated with distant, cold courtesy. The 4th of June was *their* day, their only day. Eton was indeed an eye opener to me when I first went there. First 'the Castle' then 'the masters' then a long way after, 'the boys'. In most of the houses the boys did not have enough to eat, hence the Tuck Shops. The Lowrys were one of the very few who gave their boys enough to eat and were regarded as Blacklegs in consequence by the other Housemasters. The boys used to queue up outside the Tuck Shops. I learnt a great deal, as I took the group of Catholics to Church, then in a slum in Windsor. It was very wrong of Catholics to send their boys to Eton. Of course almost always when the father was an old Etonian. So strong was the anti-Catholic feeling that very few parents would have their sons in a house where Catholic boys were accepted. I think Charles Lowry had 3 or 4, all sons of old Etonians who had been at Eton with him.

❧

Evelyn Waugh (1903–1966), the novelist, could be scathing about his children, but in this letter he writes lovingly and jokingly to his eldest son Auberon (1939–2001), aged sixteen.

14th June, 1955

My Dear Bron

I congratulate you with all my heart on your success with your story. You do not name the discerning magazine – *Everybody's* perhaps? Anyway it is an agreeable thing to see ones work professionally recognized. I look forward greatly to seeing the issue. They won't pay you until the end of the month in which it appears. That is the usual practice.

Your hairless uncle Alec Waugh has also had a success at last. His latest book has been taken by the American 'Book of the Month', serialized, filmed – in fact the jack-pot. It is very nice for him after so many years of disappointment & obscurity. He has not drawn a sober breath since he heard the news.

Your Uncle Auberon's hopes are less rosy, but your mother, grandmother, aunts and pig-walloper [Alick Dru, married to his mother's sister] have had and are still having a highly enjoyable time in Sunderland. Your mother still believes she has been in Sutherland.

I am glad the Headmaster is paying attention to you. His aim, I think, is to find whether it is better to continue your education or to send you with a changed name and £5 to Australia.

I trust your Empire League is not under the auspices of Sir Oswald Mosley? If it is you will end in prison like my old friend Diana Mitford.

Think of all lonely schoolboys on Ascension Day in memory of your father in 1916

Your affec. papa
E.W.

*Eight months later he writes again in a letter with which many fathers might sympathise.*

11th February, 1956

Dear Bron

I have written to enquire at what age apprentices are taken in the hotel-trade. I think you are still too young but I don't know.

Meanwhile think & *pray* about your future. This is an occasion that will affect your entire life.

I have much sympathy with your restlessness with school life. I felt as you do at your age, asked my father to remove me, was resentful at the time when he refused. Now I am grateful to him.

If there was anything you ardently wished to do – go to sea, learn a skilled trade etc – because you felt a real vocation for it, I would not stand in your way. I believe you think of hotel-keeping simply as a means of leaving school. That is a very poor motive for taking a job and hotel-keeping is not a craft which fits you for anything else. If you fail in that, you will be further from starting anything else. 'Previous experience: two years as kitchen-boy, waiter, liftman, book-keeper' is not a high recommendation for any other appointment.

If you leave school now you will not get a commission in a good regiment. Perhaps you will not get a commission at all.

Most of the interest and amusement of life comes from ones friends. All my friends are those I made at Oxford and in the army. You are condemning yourself either to a lonely manhood or one among second-rate associates. All because you lack the will-power and self-control to make a success of the next eighteen months by cooperating with those who have only your own best interests at heart, throwing yourself into the life of the school & doing your work and obeying the rules. At your age, wherever you go, you will find yourself under discipline much less humane & benevolent than that of the monks.

You have a sense of humour and a good gift of self expression. On the other hand you are singularly imprudent and you have a defective sense of honour. These bad qualities can lead to disaster.

My financial interests have no bearing on my wish for your welfare. I am sorry you should suggest that they might.

> Your affectionate papa
> E. Waugh

☙

John Betjeman (1906–1984), poet and journalist, writes to his daughter Candida (b.1942) in Italy, where she had been sent at the age of eighteen. Paul was Candida's brother, and MT a friend of his with whom she had been in love.

### 8th January, 1960

Last night we drove back in thick fog wondering where you were in the train. I have had hundreds of letters lately. I open them without looking. Paul has been helping me open some. This morning he is sad. He tells me you have broken up with MT – a quarrel or permanent? Time will tell. The one thing to do is to bear no ill will. That empty feeling that comes when one is cut off soon fills. I beg you, however, consider well and give not your heart away until you are quite sure. Sudden clicks must go on for a year before they can be certain of being the real love for life.

William Segrave (1908–1974) writes to the headmistress of the Catholic convent to which he had sent his daughter Elisa, the novelist and journalist. Elisa was thirteen at the time.

Sussex, 5th November, 1962

To Mother Shanley at The Convent of the Sacred Heart, Woldingham, Surrey, from Commander William Segrave D.S.C.

Dear Mother Shanley,

I am disturbed at Elisa's continued bad conduct. I have no doubt that you are justified in stopping her going out, but it does not seem to have much effect. She writes that she is to be fined £5 for climbing on a roof. I really don't see the point of this punishment: it means that her parents will have to pay, and in my view it is the responsibility of the Convent to devise a suitable punishment to deter the child from breaking the rules.

She appears to be taking her religious duties in a very flippant manner, and my wife (a communicating member of the Church of England) is even more worried about it than I am.

On the other hand, the child is obviously happy and particularly enjoys the Literature and French lessons.

My wife is away on a cruise in Cretan waters at the moment but returns on the 15th of this month. She was much impressed with Rhodes and the old auberges of the Knights of Malta.

> Yours sincerely,
> Willy Segrave.

 date

Elizabeth Jane Howard (b.1923) was already a successful novelist when she and Kingsley Amis (1922–1995) began to live together, after he left his wife Hilary. Not very much later, his adolescent sons arrive unexpectedly in the middle of the night.

1963

A few weeks after we'd been in Basil Street, it was past midnight and we were reading peacefully in bed, when the doorbell rang. . . . Kingsley said he'd go, but I got up as well and followed him. Ours was a flat where all the rooms led off a long passage with the front door at one end. Kingsley was now walking back from it followed by two blond-headed boys. 'This is Philip and this is Martin,' he said, 'and this is Jane.' They looked at me, impassive, too weary even for the blink of hostility, and I looked warily back. We were all trying to conceal our shock – they hadn't known I'd be there, and we'd had no warning of their arrival. I cooked bacon and eggs and left them with their father while I made up beds.

There followed a week of grandiose treats, punctuated by long and often tearful sessions spent by the boys alone with Kingsley while he attempted to explain the situation to them. But you can't do that, really. They didn't want their loyalties to be torn and any efforts to explain why he'd left their mother to live with me could only do that. Emotional protocol dictated that they should distrust and even dislike me. They were in their early teens: they'd lost their home in Cambridge and now, they feared, their father. In this situation everyone behaves in a younger manner than his or her age, reverts to an earlier period of childhood. The boys wanted scenes that would hopefully lead to Kingsley recanting, possibly returning with them when they went back to Majorca. Kingsley wanted them to love him, to forgive him – even to love me, whom they'd known for barely a week. And I wanted us all to be happy and understanding and kind to one another. One can see at once that none of these reactions could ever have been appropriate or, at least, if any of them were to be achieved it would take time.

Some months after the first visit:

. . . we realized that all wasn't well with Philip and Martin. They were at schools in South London where they were miserable and truanting. I suggested to Kingsley that perhaps they'd be better off with us, and after some consultation with Hilly, it was decided that they would.

And so I embarked upon the extraordinarily difficult business of being a stepmother. I'd had experience of this already, having had my father's second wife ranged against me, but I hadn't been ultimately vulnerable. My daughter had a stepmother who'd always behaved impeccably, being direct, supportive and friendly to me. You might have thought that these different experiences would have taught me enough. They hadn't.

The boys arrived, but hostility was very apparent. They were pleased to be with their father, but it was clear that they felt I was the cause of their parents' break-up. I decided that all I could do to begin with was to feed them well, and regularly, and to be in every other practical way as reliable as I could manage. I thought that even if they continued to dislike me, some kind of trust might come about. What I didn't do was make any attempt to form any kind of relationship with Hilly. Our feelings then for each other were of mutual fear and dislike, but it might have been possible to lay these aside and put the boys first. Kingsley was no help in this.

A salient characteristic in the Amis family was passivity. They weren't initiators; they let things happen and resented or regretted them; they didn't acknowledge that the consequences were their responsibility. I think Kingsley, when he thought about it, was assailed by guilt. He distanced himself from Hilly, and he gave the boys money to appease them. He simply wanted everybody to settle down so that he could write his books in peace and enjoy himself when he wasn't working.

The trouble about bringing up children is that it doesn't begin and end by making things nice for them. Some sort of moral direction has to be given. It wasn't long before I found myself in the unenviable position of being the irritating killjoy, the tiresome prig. We acquired, for example, a second-hand bar-billiards table for the conservatory, the kind where we had to put a shilling in a slot to play a game. I suggested this money should be for a charity, and everyone agreed, but quite soon I found that there never seemed to be any money in it. Of course the boys had found a way to take it. Not important, but they had to stop. When I approached Kingsley about it, he simply said, 'Well, it isn't very much money,' as though the amount was the point. This was in front of the boys, so they *knew* I was a prig, and their father was a good sort.

These sorts of things kept hostility flourishing. They sulked with me, were nasty behind my back, and I minded very much. Fortunately, both the boys really liked Monkey [her brother who lived with them], who was very good with them and, indeed, became a kind of uncle. They teased him with affection, and he taught them to play games. They both had their father's sense of humour – Phil, particularly, was a brilliant mimic – and these things lightened the atmosphere.

They had been, by then, to so many different schools that it was decided a crammer might be the best way to ensure they passed the statutory exams. So they went to Davis, Laing and Dick in Holland Park. It was a long time before I realized that they weren't actually *going*. It was the time of Mods and Rockers, and the boys were mods – winkle-pickers and all.

On Saturdays they used to go out on the town in search of girls. Once, having got stuck with a couple they didn't like, they gave us an insight to their world. 'What did you do?' I asked, and Phil answered casually, 'Oh, we threw water at them down some stairs.' I made a sitting room for them with their hi-fi in a room adjoining our kitchen-dining room. There was a lot of pop music and it smelt of hot socks.

Things came to a head one Christmas, their first with us, and I'd tried to make it a good one. I'd bought them each a gold wristwatch with their initials on the back, and they also had money from Dad and stockings. Black faces. 'All we want are the presents,' Phil said. I lost my nerve and went away to cry.

When I came back, Phil said, 'We've been rotten to you,' and Mart said, 'Yes, we have.' I think this time Kingsley *had* talked to them, and it showed me how much talking was needed between us.

Occasionally things worked. We were going to the film of *Othello*, and I discovered that neither of the boys knew the play. I suggested we should all read it aloud together first. Kingsley was keen, so they agreed.

This was about the time when, finding Martin lounging in a disaffected way, boredom seeping from every pore, I asked him what he wanted to do when he was older. 'Be a writer,' he said.

'You – a *writer*? But you never read anything. If you're so interested in writing, why don't you read?'

He looked at me and said, 'Give me a book to read then.' I gave him *Pride and Prejudice*. A little later he came to me and said, 'Jane, you've got to tell me how it ends.'

'Of course I won't. You find out for yourself.' He argued with persuasive charm, but I felt on firm ground: he was obviously enjoying it. That was when he started to read properly – a very good moment for me.

⚭

Jan Morris (b.1926), Welsh travel writer and historian, was James Morris, married with four children, when he chose to undergo a sex-change operation in 1972.

. . . my instinct to have children was profound. If I were not a writer, or an artist, I would certainly like to have been a plain mother, for I cannot think of a more fascinating profession than the raising of children, maddening though the little beasts can be. Indeed my children and my books, which

I was now beginning to write, seemed to me oddly of a kind. With a sad pang I used to watch the aircraft flying overhead, when I had recently delivered a manuscript to my agents, for I imagined that in one of them my book was leaving for America – so long a friend, so quickly mashed into print and book reviews. Conversely my children I regarded rather as works of art. I am ashamed to think I might have loved them less if they had been plain or stupid, and perhaps the truth is that if they *had* been, I would not have known it: they seemed beautiful to me, anyway, slim in physique, nimble in mind, and I watched them developing with the pleasure I might derive from a very well-plotted novel.

Fortunately, though they had their problems like everyone else, they were clearly not the same problems as my own: whatever the causes of my conundrum, they were evidently not hereditary. Nor so far as I could tell did so odd a parentage harm them psychologically. That I was their father in a physical sense was undeniable – they looked very like me, and escaped by the skins of their teeth some of the worse aspects of my temperament. But I was scarcely paternal in any other sense. I was anything but a father-figure, except in that I lived a fairly adventurous life. Nor were my attitudes exactly maternal, either, for even with them I was inhibited by circumstance, my body and the fear that I might in some way harm them by revealing the truth too soon. Besides, they had a marvellous mother already. No, I stood towards them in my own mind, as in my chemistry, almost as a patron. I had been the instrument of their creation, quite deliberately. I had consciously sparked the fire by which Elizabeth had forged and shaped their being. . . .

And I hope I made another contribution to the fashioning of those *objets d'art*. I hope I gave them, if nothing else, an understanding of love. It was my speciality. I believed it to be not just a fortuitous abstraction, but a positive energy, even a craft, which could be trained and encouraged. . . . If you love something hotly enough, consciously, with care, it becomes yours by symbiosis, irrevocably. I love Wales like this, . . . and the greatest pleasure I get from my Abyssinian cat Menelik is the feeling that I have, by the very magnetism of my affection, summoned him from some wild place, some forest or moorland, temporarily to sharpen his claws purring upon my knee.

I loved my children in the same fierce and calculated way, even when they were far away, and I hope they caught the habit in return. Certainly I have received from them always an affectionate if amused attitude of possession. They have looked at me rather as I have looked at Menelik, as some free spirit from somewhere else whom they have enticed and made their own. I have sidled among them, arching my back and trembling my tail, from destinations that must have seemed in their childhood as remote as any Abyssinian heath. ('Where is Africa d'you think?' I asked Tom one day, returning from a visit to Sierra Leone. 'It is the capital of Paris,' he solemnly replied.) I must have seemed as different in kind from other children's fathers as Menelik seems, hare-like and tufted, when one sees him consorting with stalwart British tabbies from the farm. But they have known for sure that I was theirs, once and for all in their ownership, and I think they learnt from me as I learnt from Elizabeth, the colossal constructive force of love, which can bridge chasms and reconcile opposites.

It was not until the eldest boys were in their late teens, they tell me, that they began to realize in what way I was different: for fifteen years at least our marriage looked from the outside not merely successful, but perfectly orthodox, and when I told the first of my friends the unlikely truth about myself, they often thought I was joking.

❧

Kenneth Tynan grew no less self-centred as his children grew older.

22nd October, 1976

I invite Willie Donaldson round for a drink. He says he'd love to come, but his son has just been expelled from Eton and the day of my invitation will be his first day home. (He's sixteen.) I urge Willie to bring him along, but he sounds doubtful, so I tell him not to worry: no orgy is planned, and no bad influences will be there to corupt the young shaver. 'It isn't that,' Willie says, 'I'm more worried about him being a bad influence on you. You see, he's a sort of walking super-market of illicit substances.' He's been expelled, it seems, in the hope that exposure to Willie's paternal example will be beneficial to his moral health. I am not clear whether the authorities at Eton are aware that Willie is a pimp.

In passing Willie asks me whether I ever take my eldest daughter out to parties. I say, 'Of course, and people are always mistaking us for brother and sister. It's very flattering.'

Ted Hughes (1930–1998), the poet, writes to his brother with great pride, describing the fishing triumph of his fifteen-year-old son, Nick.

## 28th November, 1977

Nick is becoming a pretty good scholar – took his 0 level maths a year early and got an A. Very high marks in everything. He's still a fanatic cyclist – moreso than ever. And his mania for pike-fishing had its reward. We went to Ireland, & this pal of mine over there – angling fanatic – went with us onto some beautiful lakes in Clare. This is 3 weeks ago. Nick had talked everybody sick about the 25 pounder he was going to catch. Going over, he couldn't sleep for excitement, but dozed just enough to dream of catching mighty pike. First day, we caught a few smallish ones. So that night, he re-prepared & replanned his tactics & dreamed again about mighty pike. Next day, we caught a few more small to medium. So that night, he regrouped & planned a fresh approach, then dreamed about mighty pike. Next day – beautiful day on a spectacular lake – he fished with the old greenheart rod you bought me long ago, and a 19th Century reel (a classic, I picked it up in a heap of junk) and hooked a huge fish. It took him 15 minutes to get it to the surface. The handles bent on his reel. He burst all the blisters on his hands (from 2 days rowing). Finally we got it out. Exactly 25 lbs. Biggest pike alive I've ever seen. Our Irish pal had only ever seen one bigger, & he'd caught thousands. We put it back, after war-dances & celebrations on a lovely green island in the middle of the lake. Nick is now hooked on Ireland. We had a marvellous time.

❧

Laurie Lee writes about his sixteen-year-old daughter, Jessy.

## May, 1980

My daughter, I must confess is a self-indulgence . . . she has taught me more about women than I have ever learnt in a lifetime of devoted interest in the subject. Perhaps because I have had to order, placate, reassure and understand this one more intensely than any other.

# ADULT CHILDREN

This is not the way for peace, to embroil the whole
christian world in wars and then to declare it for religion . . .
*Countess of Buckingham to her son, 1627*

Once again, it is a foreign traveller (writing in the eighteenth century) who describes with ironic dismay the coldness that exists between parents and their adult children. In contrast to this, there are many examples of parents who continue to be fully involved with their sons and daughters, however grown up or independent, and who go on giving advice or support even though they may end up holding opposing opinions on any number of subjects including, inevitably, religious beliefs or political allegiances: in the early 1600s, the Countess of Buckingham admonishes her son for making war in the name of religion and, later in the century, the Verney family, like many others, finds parents and children divided in the Civil War.

Disagreements over marriages and money can become long-term predicaments. Some parents, like Daniel Defoe in 1730, claim that their adult children abandon them in the worst of circumstances; William Wilberforce, by contrast, chooses to impoverish himself in order to rescue his son from debt.

Of course, the relationship between parents and their children grows more equal; they enjoy gossip and jokes, while they help or interfere in the upbringing of their grandchildren. Children change as they grow up, but parents often do not; those who have always shown themselves to be egocentric or selfish continue to do so, although, as in Antonia White's case, reconciliation between a parent and a child often happens after the birth of grandchildren.

Isabella of Angoulême (1187–1246) was probably betrothed to Hugh of Lusignan Le Brun before she married King John of England in 1200, when she was only thirteen years old. She gave birth to five children, all of whom grew to adulthood. When John died in 1216, Isabella was in her early twenties. Hugh had by now arranged to marry Isabella's eldest daughter Joan (1210–1238), who was still a child; but when Hugh inherited, in 1220, Isabella went to France where she proceeded to marry him herself.

In a letter to her son, Henry III, she explains her reasons for marrying the man betrothed to her daughter (Joan aged ten). All good reasons but perhaps not quite the whole story. In her second marriage she gave birth to a further nine children. All of them survived to adulthood: she must have been a remarkable woman and mother.

## 1220

We hereby signify to you that when the Earls of March and Eu [father and uncle of Hugh] departed this life, the lord Hugh de Lusignan remained alone and without heirs in Poictou, and his friends would not permit that our daughter should be united to him in marriage, because her age is so tender, but counselled him to take a wife from whom he might speedily hope for an heir; and it was proposed that he should take a wife in France, which if he had done, all your land in Poictou and Gascony would be lost. We, therefore, seeing the great peril that might accrue if that marriage should take place, when our counsellors could give us no advice, ourselves married the said Hugh Earl of March; and God knows that we did this rather for your benefit than for our own. Wherefore we entreat you, as our dear son, seeing it conduces greatly to the profit of you and yours; and we earnestly pray you that you will restore to him his lawful right, that is Niort, the castles of Exeter and Rockingham, and 3500 marks, which your father, our former husband, bequeathed to us; and so, if it please you, deal with him, who is so powerful, that he may not remain against you, since he can serve you well – for he is well-disposed to serve you faithfully with all his power; and we are certain and undertake that he shall serve you well if you will restore to him his rights, and, therefore, we advise that you take opportune counsel on these matters; and, when it shall please you, you may send for our daughter [who had been sent to Hugh some years ago], your sister, by

a trusty messenger and your letters patent, and we will send her to you.
   *(translated from the Latin)*

⚛

Eleanor, Queen Dowager of England (1223–1291), writes to her son, Edward I. In the letter she pleads on behalf of a friend, a mother longing to see her child who had been given into another's care.

## 4th March, after 1285

Sweetest son, we know well how great is the desire that a mother has to see her child when she has been long away from him, and that dame Margaret de Nevile, companion of Master John Giffard, has not seen for a long time past her child, who is in the keeping of dame Margaret de Weyland, and has a great desire to see him. We pray you, sweetest son, that you will command and pray the aforesaid Margaret de Weyland, that she will suffer that the mother may have the solace of her child for some time, after her desire. Dearest son, we commend you to God. Given at Amesbury, the 4th day of March.
   *(translated from the French)*

⚛

Margaret Paston writes to her son John (1442–1479), who had returned home from Court but then left again in a hurry after a disagreement with his father. The anxieties she writes about are familiar to us all: her son left without warning but his father believes she agreed to his going, which has upset her. She urges John to try to make it up with his father, to be dutiful and helpful to him, to write to him but not to ask for more money; if he does all those things it will 'cause your father to be better father to you'.

## 15th November, 1463

. . . I conceive that ye think ye did not well that ye departed hence without my knowledge. Wherefore I let you wit I was right evil paid with you. Your father thought, and thinketh yet, that I was assented to your departing, and that hath caused me to have great heaviness. I hope he will be your good father hereafter, if ye demean you well and do as ye owe to do to him; and I charge you upon my blessing that in anything touching your father that should be his worship, profit, or avail, that ye do your devoir and diligent labour to the furtherance therein, as ye will have my good will; and that shall cause your father to be better father to you.

It was told me ye sent him a letter to London. What the intent thereof was I wot not, but though he took it but lightly, I would ye should not spare to write to him again as lowly as ye can, beseeching him to be your good father, and send him such tidings as beth in the country there ye beth in; and that ye beware of your expense better (than) ye have be before this time, and be your own purse-bearer. I trow ye shall find it most profitable to you.

I would ye should send me word how ye do, and how ye have chevished for yourself sin ye departed hence, by some trusty man, and that your father have no knowledge thereof. I durst not let him know of the last letter that ye wrote to me, because he was so sore displeased with me at that time.

In the middle of the letter she changes subject for a moment to urge her son to let her know if a young man named Wykes is going to propose to Jane Walsham, a girl in whom she has an interest. She is concerned about the girl, who claims to have lost her heart to Wykes, and is trying to protect her.

Item, I would ye should speak with Wykes and know his disposition to Jane Walsham. She hath said, sin he departed hence, but she might have him she would never [be] married; her heart is sore set on him. She told me that he said to her that there was no woman in the world he loved so well. I would not he should jape her, for she meaneth good faith; and if he will not have her let me weet in haste, and I shall purvey for her in other wise.

The rest of the letter is full of the practical problems that her son has left unresolved. Whereas today's belongings might be sports stuff, bikes or a car, in the fifteenth century they were his armour, harness and his horse.

As for your harness and gear that ye left here, it is in Daubeney's keeping. It was never removed sin your departing, because that he had not the keys. I trow it shall apair but if it be take heed at betimes. Your father knoweth not where it is. I sent your grey horse to Ruston to the farrier, and he saith he shall never be naught to road, neither right good to plough nor to cart. He saith he was splayed, and his shoulder rent from the body. I wot not what to do with him.

Your grandam would fain hear some tidings from you. It were well do that ye sent a letter to her how ye do, as hastily as ye may. And God have you in his keeping, and make you a good man, and give you grace to do as well as I would ye should do. Written at Caister the Tuesday next before Saint Edmund the King.

Your mother, M. Paston

I would ye should make much of the parson [of] Filby, the bearer hereof, and make him good cheer if ye may.

❦

Agnes Paston writes to her adult son, John Paston (husband of Margaret, above). Although very tough with her children, as previous letters have shown, she shows a gloomy gentleness in this letter.

29th October, 1465

By my counsel, dispose yourself as much as ye may, to have less to do in the world. Your father said, 'In little business lieth much rest.' This world is but a thoroughfare, and full of woe; and when we depart therefro, right naught [we] bear with us but our good deeds and ill. And there knoweth no man how soon God will clepe him, and therefore it is good for every creature to be ready. Whom God visiteth, him he loveth.

❦

Thomas Mull, agent and servant to Thomas Stonor (d.1474), writes to his employer about Stonor's relationship with his son William (d.1494), aged about twenty-two. Mull tries to encourage Thomas to be closer to his son, a young man of whom Mull seems to have a fond understanding.

1472

Syr, as for my Cosen Willyam, for God is sake callyth hym forth with you when he is at home with you, and let him walke with you, and gevyth wordes of good comforte, and beth good ffader unto hym, as I certenly knowe ye be, and so letyth hym veryly understond and know. For, Syr, he is disposid to be a musyr and a studyer, which remembreth and breketh that as much as ye may.

❧

John Aubrey (1626–1697), antiquarian and biographer, writes about Sir Walter Raleigh's relationship with his son, who shows wit and humour in his dealings with his father.

. . . Sir Walter being invited to dinner to some great person where his son was to go with him, he sayd to his son 'Thou art expected today at dinner to goe along with me, but thou art such a quarrelsome, affronting . . . that I am ashamed to have such a beare in my company.' Mr Walter humbled himself to his father, and promised he would behave himself mighty mannerly. . . . He sate next to his father and was very demure at least halfe dinner time. Then sayed he, 'I, this morning, not having the feare of God before my eies but by the instigation of the devil, went to a whore. I was very eager of her, kissed and embraced her . . . and went to enjoy her, but she thrust me from her and vowed I should not, "For your Father lay with me but an hour ago".' Sir Walt, being strangely surprised and put out of his countenance at so great a table, gives his son a damned blow over the face. His son, as rude as he was, would not strike his father, but strikes over the face the gentleman that sat next to him and said 'Box about: 'twill come to my father anon.' 'Tis now a common-used proverb.

Aubrey also recalls the submission of grown children towards their parents, unlike the behaviour of the Raleigh family.

Gentlemen of thirty and forty years old were to stand like mutes and fools bareheaded before their parents; and the daughters (grown women) were to stand at the cupboard-side during the whole time of their proud mother's visit, unless (as the fashion was) leave was desired, forsooth, that a cushion should be given to them to kneel upon after they had done sufficient penance in standing.

Mary, Countess of Buckingham (1570–1632) writes to her son the Duke. In June, Buckingham was preparing to lead an expedition against the French at La Rochelle on behalf of the Protestant Huguenots. In September his mother writes to him about his warlike intentions: words that still have significance today.

## 1627

At your departure from me you told me you went to make peace, but it was not from your heart. This is not the way for peace, to embroil the whole christian world in wars and then to declare it for religion and make God a party to these woeful affairs as far from God as light and darkness; . . . You know the worthy King [Charles I] your worthy master never liked that way, and as far as I can perceive there is none that cries not out on it. . . . And do not think it out of fear and timorousness of a woman I persuade you to do this. No, no, it is that I scorn. I would have you leave this bloody way in which you are crept into, I am sure contrary to your nature and disposition.

Four years later she is writing to her grandson, Basil Feilding (c.1608–1675) about the dangers of travelling in Italy and how he should occupy his time. She has written to her contacts in different parts of the country to tell them of his arrival, so that they will welcome him and thereby protect him from any dangers. Her letter is not so very different from one that a grandmother might write nowadays.

## July 1631

. . . I hope that Almighty God will . . . help you to make the best profit of your travels and withall, to foresee and avoid all that may endanger your life and health. If Padua be so good a place and so advantageous as you write I shall be glad if you would spend your time here till near winter rather than by removing to endanger yourself. I have heard that the chief thing that Padua is commended for is the study of physics but if you find in some other thing you can profit yourself I shall be glad that you stay there this summer. I suppose that you will, towards winter, if you can without danger of sickness, see some other more famous places in that country, to the chief of which I have procured letters to be sent beforehand by which you shall not only be protected from danger, but also made very welcome you making it known how near you are in blood to me.

☙❧

Sir Edmund Verney (1590–1642) writes to his daughter-in-law Mary (known as Mischief), aged nineteen and married to his eldest son Ralph (1613–1696). Edmund and Ralph are in Bath to take the waters.

## Bath, August 1635

I cannott prevaile with yr Husband to leave mee without a quarrell, therefore good heart, forgive us boath, since his absence is against boath our wills, hee is every day in the bathe, I praye God it may doe him goode; for my parte, I am suer I find none in it, but since I am come heere, I will try the uttermost of it, that I may not be reproacht att my returne for doeing things by halves; att our first coming the towne was empty, butt now itt is full of very good company, and we pass our time awaye as merrily as paine will give us leave . . . and soe deare heart, farewell, yor lovinge father and faithfull frend.

A year later, Ralph is at home, looking after the Claydon estate, under his father's minute directions.

## 1636

The Gardner shall pleach noe Hedge this yeare. . . . if you fiend him fidle about his woarke, agree with him by the great [to be paid by the quantity he does rather than by the day] for trewly I will noe longer indure his daye woarke; it is intollerable to beare with his knavery. . . .

I am not sorry the gray nagge is sould, though I should have been glad to have had more for him, but I will not part with the white geldenge, unless I may have £35 for him. . . .

I am sorry to heare your horses thrive as ill as myne.

Occasionally Edmund enjoys a joke.

## 19th January, 1636

A merchant of lundon wrote to a factor of his beyoand sea, desired him
by the next shipp to send him 2 or 3 Apes; he forgot the r, and then it
was 203 Apes. His factor has sent him fower scoare, and sayes hee shall
have the rest by the next shipp, conceiving the merchant had sent for tow
hundred and three apes; if yor self or frends will buy any to breede on, you
could never have had such a chance as now. In earnest this is very true.

Edmund was a demanding father, as we have already seen. He also shows a
harsh, unforgiving side in his dealings with his third son, Edmund (1616–
1649), who is at Oxford. According to his tutor, young Edmund has been
absenting himself from lectures and prayers.

## April 1637

Sonne, . . . my griefes grow high uppon mee; for you were a sonne in
whom I tooke delight; a sonne that I had a p'ticular affection for above
some others, and above most of my children. But God has in you punisht
mee for that partiallity. For your former offenses, though they were great
and of a base nature, yet when I had your many faithful promises for a
reformation, my love to you was such that I was not only content but
desirous to remitt them . . . that indulgence has wrought no other effects
than to encourage you to bee more wicked; you are now growen soe
lewd and false that I blush to thinke you mine. You have not only beene
content to forfeit your owne credit, but you have, as much as in you lyes,
suffered mee and my reputation to fall in the opinion of friends.

Edmund was also in debt. As is often the case with parents, his father claims
that Edmund's mother has intervened on his son's side, but to no good effect.

I find by [your mother's] importunity that if I would pay these debts you
have now promist a greate amendment and I find you have foold her, as
heretofore you did me, into a beleefe of it. But Sir let mee tell you . . . as
you have been so unnaturally base as to follow your drunken, lyinge, false
humor, and as you have left yourselfe and mee for your meane company,

soe I can leave you to them without any farther care of you. I will say noe more, but that by beinge my unworthy sonne, I am made your unhappy father.

Sir Edmund, now aged forty-nine, writes to Ralph from York, where he has gone with Charles I in the campaign against the Scots.

## 30th March, 1639

Good Raphe since Prince Henry's death, I never knew soe much griefe as to part from you, and trewly because I saw you equally afflicted with it my sorrow was greater: but Raph wee cannott live always together. It cannott bee longe ere by cource of nature we must be severd; and if that time be prevented by accident yett wee must resolve to beare it with that patience and courage as becomes men and cristians; and soe the great god of Heaven send uss well to meete againe eyther in this world or in the next.

In an unusual reversal of roles, Ralph writes to his father begging him not to go on to the Borders to fight beside Lord Holland.

## May 1639

I find . . . that you meane (voluntarily) to attend my Lord Holland to the Borders (though many others stay with the Kinge, that have farr lesse reason) for Sr you know your yeares, your charge, your distracted fortune, your former life, were priviledge enough to keepe you Back, without the least staine to your reputation; you may easily guesse how this afflicts mee, for if you goe, (knowinge your forwardness) I shall never think to see you more, but with griefe confesse that never man did more wilfully cast away himselfe. – Till now I never had the least reason to suspect your affection. But when I see you thus hastily run to your owne ruine, and as it were purposely to loose that life that is soe much dearer to mee than my owne, how can I thinke you love mee? hath the vaine hope of a little fadinge Honour swallowed up all your good nature? are your compassions quite shut up? will neither the numberlesse sighs of your dearest friends, nor the uncessant cries of your forlorne widdow, nor the mournfull groanes of your fatherlesse brood prevaile to stay you?

are you absolutely resolved by this one act . . . (by needlesse hazardinge your selfe) [to] expose your wife, and children to perpetuall misery and intaile afflictions upon your whole posterity. I beseech you consider it and bee not soe egere to make your selfe & us (your unhappy children) the very objects of pitty it selfe, pardon my boldnesse, it concerns mee neerly; should I now bee silent, perhapps heerafter 'twould bee too late to speake, . . .

His father replies:

My designe of goeing to the Borders with my lord of Holland had only matter of kindness, none of danger in it. yette because it might seeme soe to my frends I was desirous they might not know it, but that designe was putt off and now wee are all goeing theather wher I desire you to putt soe much trust in mee as to beleeve I will not willfully thrust myself in danger, nor will I thinck you could wish mee to leave any thing undone when it falls to my turne to bee in Action. Raphe I thanck you for your good advice; it has boath exprest yor Judgment & affection . . . but trewly I thinck wee are not in much danger of fighting.

To his father's great distress, once the Civil War began, Ralph chose to support Parliament against the King. In 1642 his father was killed at the Battle of Edgehill.

❦

Shortly before the Battle of Edgehill, Susan, Countess of Denbigh (1583–1652) writes to her son, Basil Feilding, a Roundhead who had been given an appointment in the Parliamentary army. His father, the Earl of Denbigh, was a Royalist fighting for Charles I.

### 1642

My dear Son,

I have so often written to you to alter your course that I am out of all hope of persuading, yet my tender and motherly care cannot abstain from soliciting of you to go to the King before it be too late. All that party will be able to make their peace, when you will be left out to your ruin and my sorrow. I have not language to express my grief that daily comes more and more into my thoughts, your overthrow presents itself so apparently before my eyes, have pity upon me your poor mother. . . . You cannot be so void of reason but to see the unjust and valiant actions of that part of the Parliament which are against the King. All the world sees it plainly, the mask is taken off their faces. They can no longer cosen the world with their pretensions of making the King happy . . . I cannot forget what a son I had once and I hope to see him so again and with that hope I take my leave. Our Lord bless you and my daughter, your loving mother, Su Denbigh

She writes again after her husband, Basil's father and a Royalist, has been killed fighting the Parliamentary army in Birmingham.

## 1643

My dear Son, – I am much comforted with receiving of your kind letter in this time of my great sorrow for the loss of my dear husband, your dear father, whose memory I shall ever keep with sorrow and a most tender affection, as he did deserve from me and all the whole world . . . I beg of you my first born to give me the comfort of that son I do so dearly love, that satisfaction which you owe me now, which is to leave those that murdered your dear father, for what can it be called, but so? which when he received his death wounds but with the saying he was for the King, there was no mercy to his grey hairs but wounds and shots, a horror to me to think of. O my dear Jesus, put it into my dear son's heart to leave that merciless way that was the death of his father, for now I think of it with horror, before with sorrow. Now is the time that God and nature claims it from you. Before you were carried away with error, but now it is hideous and monstrous. The last words your dear father spoke of you was to desire God to forgive you and to touch your heart. Let your dying father and unfortunate mother make your heart relent; . . . You may allege you cannot sleep in quiet as long as you stay with them, and sure it is true. I do believe that you are not so much respected by that party as you think you are, for they do many things and make many offers to save themselves. I believe it is so, but you know nothing of it, I think. . . . So with my blessing, I take my leave, your loving mother, Su Denbigh

Basil remained on the side of Parliament.

Lady Brilliana Harley writes to her eldest son, Edward, who has just left Oxford and gone to London with his father, the statesman Sir Robert Harley (1579–1666). Although it was the convention for boys to be sent away to other great households as servants, Brilliana points out the disadvantages for Edward of employing a single boy as his servant.

## 22nd May, 1641

Deare Ned, take my counsell, I belieeue you will not finde it beest to take Gorges his brother; it is a most teadious thinge to be sarued by a chillde, without you had other saruants that might healp out his defects; they want witt and discretion, and haue theair pastions unbrideled, wich all togeeather makes them teadious saruants; and I consider when you are at the ends of court, and nobody about you but a child, if you should not be well, you would finde it a trubell; and so you would being well; when you imploye him in any saruis you would tast his childrischness in all he did. I speake from experience. I haue had chillderen sarue me; and I finde very yonge men and women no good saruants; . . . Pleas yourself in your choyce, and I shall be pleased; but take my word; boys are trubellsome saruants.

Her letters continue to be sent as regularly as ever while the threat of war grows stronger.

## 17th February, 1642

I mise you very much; and deare Ned, sometimes thinke of me, tho you cannot mise me. Your brother Robine seemes to be extremely discontented. I wisch your father would rwite to him, to take his minde of it.

As she had realised three years earlier, she and the rest of her family are in danger in her castle at Brampton, because Herefordshire is a fervently Royalist part of the country.

## 4th June

At Loudlow they seet vp a May pole, and a thinge like a head vpon it, . . . and gathered a greate many about it, and shot at it in derision of roundheads. . . . I acknowledg I doo not thinke meself safe wheare I am. I loos the comfort of your fathers company, and am in but littell safety, but that my trust is in God; . . . I wisch meselfe, with all my hart, at Loundoun, . . . but if your father thinke it beest for me to be in the cuntry, I am every well pleased with what he shall thinke beest. I haue sent you by this carryer, in a box, 3 shirts; theare is another, but it was not quite made; on of them is not wasched; I will, and pleas God, send you another the next weake, and some handchersher.

## 20th June

My deare Ned – If you beleaue how glad I am to haue this paper discours with you, you will read it as willingly as I rwite it. Since your father thinkes Hearefordsheare as safe as any other country, I will thinke so too; but when I considered how long I had bine from him, and how this country was affected, my desire to see your father, and my care to be in a place of safety, made me ernestly desire to come vp to Loundoun; but since it is not your father's will, I will lay aside that desire.

## 2nd July

My deare Ned, at first when I sawe how outrageously this cuntry carried themselfes against your father, my anger was so vp, and my sorrow, that I had hardly patience to stay; but now, I haue well considered, if I goo away I shall leaue all that your father has to the pray of our enimys, which they would be glad of; so that, and pleas God, I purpos to stay as long as it is poscibell, if I liue; and this is my resolution, without your father contradict it.

I cannot make a better use of my life, next to saruing my God, than doo what good I can for you.

## 15th July

I haue offten toold you, I thought you would see trubellsome times; but, my deare Ned, keepe your hart aboue the world, and then you will not be trubelled at the changes in it . . .

As the Civil War begins, Edward, aged eighteen, joins the Parliamentary army and her husband remains in London.

## 13th December

My deare Ned – My hart has bine in no rest sence you went. I confes I was neuer so full of sorrow. I feare the prouicion of corne and malt will not hoold out, if this continue; and they say they will burne my barnns; and my feare is that they will place soulders so neare me that theare will be no gooing out. My comfort is that you are not with me, least they should take you; but I doo most dearly miss you. I wisch, if it pleased God, that I weare with your father. I would haue rwite to him, but I durst not rwite upon papaper. Deare Ned, rwite to me, though you rwite upon a peace of clothe, as this is.

## 11th June, 1643

O! my deare Ned – that I could but see you! I liue in hope that the Lord will giue me that comfort, which I confes, I am not worthy of. I heare from a good hand that you are ready to come out of Loundoun. . . . deare Ned, belieeue my hart and soule is with you.

## 11th July

I am sorry you haue lost so many hors out of your trope; but I hope they will be made up againe. I knowe not what they will doo heareafter, but, as yet, I can get but very little towards the byeing of a hors; what it is, I haue sent you inclosed. If you want any thing I can possibilly healp you to, let me knowe it, and I will . . .

She stayed to defend their home, Brampton Castle, which was under siege for six weeks from August until the end of September. This is the last letter she wrote to Edward, proudly addressing him as Colonel.

9th October

For my deare sonne Colonell Harley

My deare Ned – Your short but wellcome letter I receaued by Prosser, and as it has pleased God to intrust you with a greater charge, as to change your trope into a regiment, so the Lord in mercy blles you with a dubell measure of abillitys, and the Lord of Hosts be your protector and make you victorious. My deare Ned, how much I longe to see you I cannot expres, and if it be possibell, in parte meete my desires in desireing, in some measure as I doo, to see me; and if pleased the Lord, I wisch you weare at Brompton. I am now againe threatned; there are some souldiers come to Lemster . . . and they say they meane to viset Brompton again; but I hope the Lord will deleuer me. My trust is only in my God, whoo neuer yet failled me. . . .

I haue taken a very greate coold, which has made me very ill thees 2 or 3 days, but I hope the Lord will be mercifull to me, in giuing me my health, for it is an ill time to be sike in.

My deare Ned, I pray God blles you and giue me the comfort of seeing you, for you are the comfort of

Your most affectinat mother, Brilliana Harley

She died a few days later and Brampton fell into the hands of the Royalists. It was destroyed and the remaining family were imprisoned but they all survived. Edward became a powerful Member of Parliament after the Restoration. He died in 1700.

Lord Mountgarret (1595–1679), an Irish Royalist in dire financial straits, writes threateningly to his eldest son, Richard (d.1706), who wants to marry Emilia Blundell, aged nineteen, daughter of William Blundell, another Catholic landowner. Richard and William had met when they were imprisoned as Catholic recusants after the Irish wars.

3rd November, 1658

Son,

I am informed that you are so miserably blinded as to incline to marry and so with one wretched act to undo both the gentlewoman and yourself, and (as much as in you lieth) to dash all my designs, which concern myself and house. Son, I charge you by the bond of nature and duty which you owe me, that you presume not to proceed in so desperate a purpose as a thing which I detest and abhor. And therefore lay these words close in to your heart, and read in them as high indignation of mine, as if they were far more sharper. In me an entire fatherly love and just care of you hath never been wanting; be not you wanting in the obedience of a son in a matter of so great importance as this to me and my family: but let this in brief suffice to keep you from plunging yourself into ruin. If it do, I shall be heartily satisfied; if it do not, I shall take order that the blow smart there where in justice it should. And Son, be assured that this is the final and unalterable resolution of

> Your very loving father,
> Mountgarret.

Richard and Emilia married three years later.

Lady Gardiner (1626–1704) writes to her brother Sir Ralph Verney, describing the exasperating behaviour of her stepdaughter Ursula. Her husband, John Stewkeley, is in London.

## 4th May, 1674

I wish he had stayed at home, Bot yr sex will follow yr Enclynations which is not for women's convenincys. I should bee more contented if his daughter Ursula ware not heare, who after 8 months plesure came homb unsatisfied, declaring Preshaw [their home] was never so irksome to her, & now hath bin at all the Salsbury rasis, dancing like wild with Mr. Clarks whom Jack can give you a carictor of, & came home of a Saturday night just before our Winton [Winchester] rasis, at neer 12 a clok when my famyly was a bed, with Mr. Charls Torner (a man I know not, Judg Torner's son, who was tryed for his life last November for killing a man, one of the numbar that stils themselves Tiburn Club), And Mr. Clark's brother, who sat up 2 nights till neer 3 a Clok, & said, shee had never bin in bed sinc shee went a way till 4 in the morning, & danced some nights till 7 in the Morning. Then shee borrowed a coach and went to our rasis, & wod have got dancars if shee could, then brought homb this crue with her a gaine, & sat up the same time. All this has sophytiently vexed me. her father was 6 days of this time from home, and lay out 3 nights of it, & fryday shee was brought home & brought with her Mr. Torner's linin to be mended & washed heare & sent after him to London, where he went on Saturday, to see how his brother Mun is come of his tryall for killing a man just before the last sircut, And sinc these ware gone I reflccting on thes actions, & shee declaring she could not be pleased without dancing 12 hours in the 24, and takeing it ill I denied in my husband's absenc to have 7 ranting fellows come to Preshaw & bring musick, was very angry & had ordered wher they should all ly, shee designed mee to ly with Peg G, & I scaring her, and contrydicting her, we had a great quarill.

James II (1633–1701), the last Catholic king of England, writes to his daughter Mary (1662–1694). In 1677 Mary had married Prince William of Orange, a Protestant prince. Eleven years later they were invited to claim the English throne in the bloodless revolution of 1688. James fled to France and William and Mary were crowned king and queen.

### 28th September, 1688

This evening I had yours of the 4th. . . . I suppose it is to inform you of his [Prince William's] design of coming to England, which he has been so long contriving. I hope it will have been as great a surprise to you as it was to me, when I first heard it, being sure that it is not in your nature to approve of so unjust an undertaking. I have been all this day so busy, to endeavour to be in some condition to defend myself from so unjust and unexpected an attempt, that I am almost tired, and so I shall say no more but that I shall always have as much kindness for you as you will give me leave to have.

### 2nd October

. . . since I came back, I have been so very busy to prepare things for the invasion intended, that I could not write till now, that 'tis near midnight, so that you might not wonder if my letter be short. For news, you will hear it from others, for really I am very weary; so shall end, which I do, assuring you of my continuing as kind to you as you can desire.

### 9th October

I had no letter from you by this post, which you see does not hinder me from writing to you now, not knowing, certainly, what may have hindered you from doing it. I easily believe you may be embarrassed how to write to me, now that the unjust design of the prince of Orange invading me is so public. And though I know you are a good wife, and ought to be so, yet for the same reason I must believe you will still be as good a daughter to a father that has always loved you so tenderly, and that has never done the least thing to make you doubt it. I shall say no more, and believe you very uneasy all this time, for the concern you must have for a husband and a father. You shall still find me kind to you, if you desire it.

John Milton (1608–1674) married a second time. This marriage caused a rift with his children by his first wife, reflected in his Will.

The portion due to me from Mr. Powell, my former wife's father, I leave to the unkind children I had by her, having received no part of it, but my meaning is, they shall have no other benefit of my estate than the said portion and what I have besides done for them, they having been very undutiful to me. All the residue of my estate I leave to the disposal of Elizabeth, my loving wife.

❧

Lady Wentworth writes to her son about the lottery for cash and wives in the eighteenth century.

4th August, 1710

Its a very sickly time hear, and at London aboundenc dyse of feavours, but the smallpox is the raening diseas. . . .

[P.S.] The Million Lottry is drawing, and som very ordenary creeture has gott 400*l.* a year.

22nd August

Pray my dear why will you let Lady Mary Thin goe, she is yoang, ritch, and not unhandsome, som sey she is pretty; and a vertious lady, and of the nobillety, and why will you not trye to gett her. Its said Lord Villors Lady was worth fower scoar thousand pd; you might have gott her as wel as Lord Villors.

In trouble from creditors, Daniel Defoe (1659/71–1731) had made over all his property to his son Daniel, who subsequently refused to support his mother and unmarried sister – the kind of situation satirised by Jane Austen in *Sense and Sensibility*. Daniel Defoe writes to his son-in-law, Henry Baker, married to Sophia Defoe.

### 12th August, 1730

. . . it would be a greater comfort to me than any I now enjoy, that I could have your agreeable Visits with Safety, and could see both you and my dearest Sophia, could it be without giving her the Grief of seeing her Father *in tenebris* [in prison], and under the Load of insupportable Sorrows. I am sorry I must open my Griefs so far as to tell her, it is not the Blow I recd from a wicked, perjur'd, and contemptible Enemy, that has broken in upon my Spirit; which as she well knows, has carryed me on thro' greater Disasters than these. But it has been the injustice, unkindness, and, I must say, inhuman dealings of my own Son, which has both ruin'd my Family, and, in a Word, has broken my Heart; and as I am at this Time under a weight of very heavy Illness, which I think will be a Fever, I take this Occasion to vent my Grief in the Breasts who I know will make a prudent use of it, and tell you, that nothing but this has conquered or could conquer me. *Et tu! Brute.* I depended upon him, I trusted him, I gave up my two dear unprovided Children into his Hands; but he has no Compassion, but suffers them and their poor, dying Mother to beg their Bread at his Door, and to crave, as if it were an Alms, what he is bound under Hand and Seal, besides the most sacred promises, to supply them with; himself, at the same Time, living in a profusion of Plenty. It is too much for me. Excuse my Infirmity, I can say no more; my Heart is too full.

Lord Hervey (1696–1743) reports the reaction of Queen Charlotte, wife of George II, on the marriage of her daughter Anne, the Princess Royal, aged twenty-five, to William, Prince of Orange, aged twenty-three. The couple are being put to bed after their wedding.

## 1734

. . . when he was undressed and came in his nightgown and nightcap into the room to go to bed, the appearance he made was as indescribable as the astonished countenances of everybody who beheld him. From the make of his brocaded gown, and the make of his back, he looked behind as if he had no head, and before as if he had no neck and legs. The Queen, in speaking of the whole ceremony next morning alone with Lord Hervey, when she came to mention this part of it, said, 'Ah! mon Dieu! Quand je voyois entrer ce monstre, pour coucher avec ma fille, j'ai pensé m'évanouir; je chancelois auparavant, mais ce coup là m'a assommée. Dites-moi, Lord Hervey, avez-vous bien remarqué et considéré ce monstre dans ce moment? et n'aviez vous pas bien pitié de la pauvre Anne? Bon Dieu! C'est trop sotte en moi, mais j'en pleure encore.'

Anne and William had five children.

⚜

Lady Mary Wortley Montagu writes to her daughter, Mary, aged thirty-one, who has just given birth to her fourth daughter. Lady Mary was living in Italy and had not been aware that Mary was pregnant again.

## 7th May, 1749

I don't know whither I shall make my Court to you in saying it, but I own I can't help thinking that your Family is numerous enough, and that the Education and disposal of 4 Girls is employment for a whole Life.

* 'Oh, Lord! When I saw the monster who was about to sleep with my daughter I thought I was going to faint. I was frail already – but such a blow – it might be the death of me! Tell me, Lord Hervey, have you really thought how monstrous he looks? And don't you feel sorry for my poor Anne? Good Lord! I know it's silly but the very thought of it reduces me to tears.'

A few years later, she writes a long letter filled with rather bossy instructions about her granddaughter's education.

28th January, 1753

. . . every Woman endeavors to breed her Daughter a fine Lady, qualifying her for a station in which she will never appear, and at the same time incapacitating her for that retirement to which she is destin'd. Learning (if she has a real taste for it) will not only make her contented but happy in it. No Entertainment is so cheap as reading, nor any pleasure so lasting. She will not want new Fashions nor regret the loss of expensive Diversions or variety of company if she can be amus'd with an Author in her closet. To render this amusement extensive, she should be permitted to learn the Languages. I have heard it lamented that Boys lose so many years in meer learning of Words. This is no Objection to a Girl, whose time is not so precious. She cannot advance her selfe in any proffession, and has therefore more hours to spare; and as you say her memory is good, she will be very agreably employ'd this way.

There are two cautions to be given on this subject: first, not to think her selfe Learned when she can read Latin or even Greek. . . . True knowledge consists in knowing things, not words. . . .

The second caution to be given her (and which is most absolutely necessary) is to conceal whatever Learning she attains, with as much solicitude as she would hide crookedness or lameness. The parade of it can only serve to draw on her the envy, and consequently the most inveterate Hatred, of all he and she Fools, which will certainly be at least three parts in four of all her Acquaintance. . . .

. . . The ultimate end of your Education was to make you a good Wife (and I have the comfort to hear that you are one); hers ought to be, to make her Happy in a Virgin state. I will not say it is happier, but it is undoubtedly safer than any Marriage. In a Lottery where there is (at the lowest computation) ten thousand blanks to a prize, it is the most prudent choice not to venture.

I have alwaies been so thoroughly persuaded of this Truth that notwithstanding the flattering views I had for you, (as I never intended you a sacrifice to my Vanity) I thought I would ow'd you the Justice to lay before you all the hazards attending Matrimony. You may recollect I did so in the strongest manner.

But then she loses her nerve and worries about the reaction of her son-in-law, Lord Bute.

## 6th March, 1753

I cannot help writeing a sort of Apology for my last letter, foreseeing that you will think it wrong, or at least Lord Bute will be extremely shock'd at the proposal of a learned Education for Daughters, which the generality of Men beleive as great a prophanation as the Clergy would do if the Laity should presume to exercise the functions of the priesthood. I desire you would take notice I would not have Learning enjoin'd them as a Task, but permitted as a pleasure if their Genius leads them naturally to it. I look upon my Grand daughters as a sort of Lay Nuns. Destiny may have laid up other things for them, but they have no reason to expect to pass their time otherwise than their Aunts do at present, and I know by Experience it is in the power of Study not only to make solitude tolerable but agreeable.

✥

Lord Chesterfield at his most sophisticated and witty:

I repeat it again and again to you, let the great book of the world be your principal study. *Nocturna versate manu, versate diurnal*; which may be rendered thus in English: Turn over men by day, and women by night. I mean only the best editions.

✥

Thomas Gainsborough (1727–1788), the artist, writes to his sister Mary Gibbon. He has discovered that his eldest daughter, Mary (Molly), aged twenty-five, is secretly involved with Johann Christian Fischer, a man Gainsborough does not want as his son-in-law. His younger daughter, Margaret (Peggy), aged twenty-four, is also attracted to Fischer.

## 26th December, 1775

If I complain that Peggy is a sensible good Girl, but Insolent and proud in her behaviour to me at times, can you make your arm long enough to box her ears for me whilst you live at Bath? And (what has hurt me most of late) were I to unfold a secret and tell you that I have detected a sly trick in Molly by a sight I got of one of her Letters, forsooth, to Mr. Fischer, what could all your cleverness do for me there? . . . I have never suffered that worthy Gentleman ever to be in their company since I came to London; and behold while I had my eye upon Peggy, the other Slyboots, I suppose, has all along been the Object. Oh, d—n him, he must take care how he trips me off the foot of all happiness.

I desire, my Dear Sister, you will not impart a syllable of what you have here, and believe me ever yours most affectionately,

Thos. Gainsborough

P.S. She does not suspect I saw the letter.

Mary and Johann were married five years later, on 21st February, 1780.

23rd February, 1780

Dear Sister,

I imagine you are by this time no stranger to the alteration which has taken place in my family. The notice I had of it was very sudden, as I had not the least suspicion of the attachment being so long and deeply settled; and as it was too late for me to alter anything, without being the cause of total unhappiness on both sides, my *consent*, which was a mere compliment to affect to ask, I needs must give, whether such a match was agreeable to me or not, I would not have the cause of unhappiness lay upon my conscience; and accordingly they were married last Monday, and are settled for the present in a ready furnished little house in Curzon Street, May Fair. I can't say I have any reason to doubt the man's honesty or goodness of heart, as I never heard any one speak anything amiss of him; and as to his oddities and temper, she must learn to like as she likes his person, for nothing can be altered now. I pray God she may be happy with him and have her health. Peggy has been very unhappy about it, but I endeavour to comfort her . . . We shall see how they go on . . . I hope you are all well, and with best wishes,

I remain your affectionate Bro., Thos. Gainsborough

The couple separated within a few years.

Lady Pembroke (1737–1831) writes anxiously to her son George, aged twenty-two.

### 9th January, 1781

People of a thin habit should keep themselves warm & guarded against moist, sharp, & cold air, but they should be as carefull to avoid also too free a perspiration. The custom of wearing flannell next the skin, particularly in bed, is almost as bad as a Diabetes. It enfeebles, drains, & ematiates. The moisture, & damps that flannell keeps the skin in, whenever it touches it, & its growing so readily dirty, shews what a flux of perspiration it promotes. When it is not next the skin, the warmth of it, at a proper season, is salutary; but too much heat, during rest, when the body ought to be at liberty & uncontain'd, condenses our own excrementitious atmosphere about us, stops the kind influence of the right tempered, beneficial air, & makes us liable to catch colds, etc. . . .

So says Doctor Cheyne, from whose Book the above is copied, (*so you see what a wise woman I am*), & you are accordingly earnestly desired *not* to betake yourself to flannell under waistcoats, at least not before you have fairly stated the above objections to Dr Cadogan, & heard his opinion of them. Ld P: [Pembroke] himself owns that his comely embonpoint [large stomach] is not a rule for your agreeable meagreness. He hopes you have received the hare, pheasant & brace of woodcocks safe. . . .

I do really *beg* you will not wear *any* waistcoat in bed, & wear the flannel one *over* your shirt when the weather is winter; in the day, it is particularly bad for you to wear it next your skin.

I desir'd Ly Trevor to shew you my picture when I was a girl when you came next to see her, & she has put it in the room in view on purpose, which I forgot to tell you, so pray go & look at it, & give my love to her. . . .

Dont forget your bathing, nor return often to your three o'clock in the morning suppers, tho' tempting.

Lord Pembroke writes to George in the same year. In his case, he is equally anxious to know the gossip.

## Sunday, 6th May

In the name of wonder, My dear George, what is this Mindening story of our cousin Ned Onslow, & Phelim Macarty Esq? The latter, must, of course by his name be a deflourer of Virgins; & I should hope that no kinsman of our's donne dans le sexe masculin. Pray let me know seriously about it by the return of the post.

Lord Pembroke writes again that year, about a girl in whom George is interested.

## 20th September

I have heard, & believe her good tempered, & all you say & wish. Upon honor, I have allways heard so; & if she is not so, I will be the first to advise you against it. Ye can know nothing of her but through yourself, by getting acquainted with her, & that ye may easily do sans vous compromettre du tout, . . . ; but if ye wait for the information of others, & lay by for it, she will certainly be snapped up before ye know any thing of the matter. I really believe *they* [the girl's family] have thoughts about *you*. Ralpho can do nothing but perhaps give ye an opportunity of seeing her; for he is hardly deep enough to be entrusted with a negotiation. Possibly by making Weston your way to town, ye may see her. Pray try; if that fails, be bold in town. Speak, attack, spada in mano pronta a ferir! Believe me, I would rather have ye marry a beggar & be happy, than to see ye sacrificed for the Bank of England; but this, I own, by *all* I have heard, would, I verily believe, answer *all* ends.

Many letters passed between them about George's dissatisfaction with army life, a profession chosen for him by his father.

## 4th September, 1783

I can be no stranger to your situation in life; my own was similar to it, with the difference only, that my father died when I was fifteen. I need not be told neither, that country quarters are disagreeable Séjour; but I could not, & I can not help recommending patience, as others have had, unless I turn hypocrite to court you. To quit a profession, & have none, I have allways held a very silly thing, but every line of life carries some constraint with it, & so it ought to do; none so little, I sincerely believe however, upon my honor, as the military one in England.

❧

Sarah Siddons describes acting with her eldest son, Henry, aged twenty-six; he had determined to become an actor against his mother's advice.

### 2nd June, 1801

My dear Harry is with me, and how you wou'd laugh to see him personating in turn my Son, my Lover, and my Husband; oh, how I wish you cou'd see it, and know *him*, for he's a fine, honorable, but alas! melancholy character. He is not well indeed, and that may make him appear sad – I hope 'tis only accidental sadness.

To another friend she writes:

My son Harry's success has been a very great comfort to me. I do think, if I can divest myself of partiality, that it is a very respectable attempt.

❧

The Earl of Uxbridge (1744–1812) writes to his son Arthur Paget (1771–1840), a diplomat serving abroad. Uxbridge includes an affectionate reference to Arthur's illegitimate daughter, adopted by her aunt, Arthur's sister Louisa Erskine. The baby was also called Louisa.

### 6th November, 1804

Your little Lou is the most engaging, sensible, and beautiful baby I ever saw; she and the Erskines are now with us. I believe I like her the more for being so very like you. You must take care of yourself, or you may be served as Sir Thomas Rumbold has [Rumbold had been kidnapped by French troops].

The following year, Arthur's mother, the Countess of Uxbridge (1742–1817), writes to him on the same subject. The Uxbridges had a loyal family of six sons and five daughters.

### 29th April, 1805

Little Lou did not come with the Erskines, . . . they have set their hearts so much on her bearing their Name, that I think you had better acquiesce.

The Countess is often full of alarms.

### 30th July, 1807

I have a more shocking story than any of yours to relate; poor Lady Frederick Campbell was found burnt to death a few days ago, and great part of the House consumed, owing, it's said, to reading in bed. Remember this, my dearest Arthur, and I beseech you, take warning from it.

### 22nd February, 1815

What a Tragedy is this of the poor Duke of Dorset [killed out hunting, aged twenty-one]. My heart aches for his wretched Mother. It is very remarkable the number of Heads of great families that have fallen victims to Hunting.

☙❧

Dora Jordan had been the comic actress of the age, but by 1816 she was living in France, poor and cut off from her thirteen children. She had been utterly abandoned by her former lover, the Duke of Clarence and future William IV.

It is not, believe me, the feelings of pride, avarice, or the absence of those comforts I have all my life been accustomed to, that is killing me by inches; it is the loss of my only remaining comfort, *the hope I used to live on from time to time, of seeing my children.*

She died the same year.

Richard Lovell Edgeworth (1744–1817), father of twenty children by four wives, speaks to his much-loved daughter Maria (1767–1849), on his deathbed. She was to inherit a large estate.

## 1817

On my dying bed I entreat you not to squander away your property on whoever at the moment you may think may want it. Never have the meanness to give any of your relations the hope that you will leave them anything.

❧

Prince Hermann Pückler-Muskau (1785–1871) landscape designer and traveller, writes to his wife, Lucie; they had gone through a divorce of convenience for financial reasons. He had been hoping to catch an heiress during his travels in Europe, but it was the publication of the letters he wrote every day to Lucie that made his fortune. This particular letter has sometimes been used as evidence for the apparent lack of intimate family life among the English.

## 8th July, 1828

Grown-up children and parents soon become almost strangers; and what we call domestic life is therefore applicable only to husband, wife and little children living in immediate dependence on their father: as soon as they grow up, a republican coldness and estrangement takes place between them and their parents. An English poet maintains, that the love of a grandfather to his grandchildren arises from this – that in his grown-up sons he sees only greedy and hostile heirs, – in his grandchildren, the future enemies of his enemies. The very *thought* could never have arisen but in an English brain!

William Wilberforce (1759–1833) is a father who goes to extreme lengths to rescue his son, William, from the failure of his business setting up a dairy farm.

To Henry Thornton:

29th December, 1828

I cannot recollect that I ever explained to you the circumstances which led me to acquiesce in my son's wish to take a great dairy farm near London. It is due to him to say that his having given up the law was a case of absolute necessity. He would have been in his grave ere now had he continued in it. . . . While he was in law, both Mr. Kindersley and Mr. Colman declared he was one of their most diligent pupils. As it is . . . he has only of late recovered his health. When forced to abandon the law, he tried to get into several modes of occupation . . . but all in vain. I have not time I find to explain matters fully. Suffice it to say that his present occupation seems likely to be a source of augmenting emolument to him. But I could not spare him all the capital necessary – a considerable part of it has been borrowed on mortgage. He stated to me a few days ago that owing to the staying abroad of a gentleman who had agreed to lend him £6,000, he was like to be put to extreme difficulties or inconveniences. Of this £6,000, I found £2,000 was to repay what your house had lent him till January. I myself have hoped to be able to supply him, having intended to sell some land near Beverley and Hull. . . . Indeed the house, in which I first drew my breath, though I cannot part with it without emotion, must with the premises be sold, and I am assured that I may hope to get from £5,000 to £6,000 for the whole. As much more I may expect from the land I intend to dispose of. I therefore request you to do me the real kindness of lending me the £6,000 for him (in truth £4,000, new loan, as two thousand of it are for yourselves) with the more confidence because I shall ere long be able to repay it. I assure you I shall consider *myself as* your creditor and you know enough of my property to know that the money is perfectly safe. I can truly assure you that I don't believe I have lessened my inheritance through the good providence of God which supplied me for many years with an increase of income from the Hull business. And though not a rich man as times go now, yet I have enough thank God to enable me to live in comfort. . . . If you wish William to converse with you on the business he would answer the summons I am persuaded. His manager is a man of tried integrity – have known him above 20 years.

By 1829 William's losses were so heavy that recovery was impossible, and in November 1830 he had to go abroad to escape his creditors. Wilberforce writes to another friend, Thomas Babington.

14th March, 1831

I must allow William £600 per annum more when I am able.

And finally:

After much Consideration of Accounts, Mrs. W. and I become convinced that it is absolutely necessary to leave Highwood Hill – We could not go on here in any way without a greater Establishment and more Company than we can now maintain.

In a postscript, he adds:

William's loss is full fifty or fifty [an indecipherable figure] thousand pounds.

Because Wilberforce could not bear to let his son take the loss and become an exile, he made arrangements to cover the debt himself. He refused any help from his friends but owing to the size of the debt (more than a million pounds in today's money) he was obliged to sell his house and let all his servants go. He was aged seventy-three, and in very poor health.

What I shall miss most will be my books and my garden, though I own I do feel a little the not being able to ask my friends to take a dinner or a bed with me, under my own roof.

He died two years later.

On his birthday, Sydney Smith writes to his daughter Saba (1802–1866), who was married to Dr Henry Holland.

3rd June, 1835

Dearest daughter,

Sixty-four years old to-day. If H— and F— [her stepchildren], in the estimation of the doctor, are better out of town, we shall be happy to receive them here before your rural holidays begin; your children are my children. . . .

We are going through our usual course of jokes and dinners; one advantage of the country is, that a joke once established is good for ever; it is like the stuff which is denominated *everlasting*, and used as pantaloons by careful parents for their children. In London you expect a change of pleasantry; but M. and N. laugh more at my six-years-old jokes than they did when the jokes were in their infancy.

Sydney Smith writes to the Revd Dr Wordsworth, pleading for his son Wyndham not to be sent down from Cambridge University for betting.

9th July, 1835

Revd Sr

I only heard yesterday of the unfortunate affair in which my Son Wyndham Smith of your College is implicated, and I set off immediately for Cambridge. I humbly and respectfully submit to you the following considerations.

To lay Betts is an offence, but the habit, and the magnitude of course is to be considered. The amount here is extremely trifling, and there is no evidence of such being the young man's habit.

. . . The whole knowledge of this offence of making a Bett only came to Light in a very painful and unusual method; for which I do not blame Mr. Fleming, but I submit that your judicial powers would be called for to an alarming extent and the *apparent* Characters of young men be not a little changed, if all the Letters they write to each other were to be opened, and the improprieties they would bring to Light were to be discussed and punished by you; and I use this argument not to abolish punishment but to mitigate it, as the Criminal has hardly had fair play –

I am sure Mr. Fleming did not know Wyndham Smith was my Son, or he would have written to me and not to you. He is a very amiable and good natured man and (as well as many of the branches of his family) is a very old acquaintance of mine and I am sure he would be the first to deplore the Severity to which he has subjected my Son.

I have written to Mr. Fleming by this post begging he would write to you, and undertaking that my Son should write to him a most ample apology. –

To remove the young man from your College would amount to his entire ruin. No other College will receive him without such testimonials as would make his removal an act of great inconsistency; or if they did receive him he remains with a mark of infamy upon him, which I could not ask him to bear, and under which any young man's moral Character would sink. I earnestly beg of you to commute his removal for a formal Notice of immediate Expulsion for the next Offence, or if this be not sufficient to satisfy the justice of the College let him be rusticated. . . .

I hope I have said nothing in this Letter to offend, and that the expression of a father pleading for his Son will be favorably construed – I lost my other Son by death a year or two since, and this is my only Son, – the only child remaining in my house. I earnestly beg of the College that he may not be doomed to ruin and disgrace, for such an act of mere juvenile indiscretion.

Sydney Smith

May I beg the favor of you to lay this before the College?

William Wordsworth (1770–1850) writes to his daughter Dora (1804–1847), who has told her father she wants to marry his friend Edward Quillinan (1791–1851), a poor poet whom she had known for many years.

## c.5th April, 1838

I take no notice of the conclusion of your Letter; indeed part of it I could not make out. It turns upon a subject which I shall never touch more either by pen or voice. Whether I look back or forward it is depressing and distressing to me, and will for the remainder of my life, continue to be so.

The following year he gives in, as many fathers do, although not very graciously.

## c.24 April, 1839

. . . I believe Mr Q. to be a most honourable and upright man, and further that he is most strongly and faithfully attached to you – this I must solemnly declare in justice to you both; and to this I add *my blessing upon you and him*; more I cannot do . . .

He writes to his wife, Mary.

## 8th June

Yesterday I had a long interview with Mr Quillinan; tell dearest Dora. – I fear it was not satisfactory to either party. He seems wretched at the thought of the marriage being put off; and, as I told him, I could not look at [it] with that chearfulness and complacency and hopefulness, which ought to accompany such a transaction. As the event was inevitable, I told him I felt it my duty to try to make the best of it; but how I should succeed I could not tell. But said I blame no-one; I only do regret that the affair should have pressed on this way in my absence, this was [? sad] of all, only I must add that I felt easier for having seen him and that our interview was perfectly friendly. – Now my dearest Mary read as much of this to Dora as you like.

The next day he writes to Dora.

9th June

My dearest Dora,

I am looking for Mr Quillinan every moment. I hope to revive the conversation of yesterday. The sum is: I make no opposition to this marriage. I have no resentment connected with it toward any one: you know how much friendship I have always felt towards Mr Q, and how much I respect him. I do not doubt the strength of his love and affection towards you; this, as far as I am concerned, is the fair side of the case. On the other hand, I cannot think of parting with you with that complacency, that satisfaction, that hopefulness which I could wish to feel; there is too much of necessity in the case for my wishes. But I must submit, and do submit; and God Almighty bless you, my dear child, and him who is the object of your long and long-tried preference and choice.

> Ever your affectionate father,
> Wm Wordsworth

The couple were eventually married on 11th May, 1841.

ষ৳৯

Sydney Smith writes to Lady Grey about Wyndham, his second and only surviving son, now aged thirty.

21st December, 1843

Talking of Children I have thought it expedient that my Son and I should have separate Establishments. I allow him £500 per Annum, and he lives at Southampton. Our habits were incompatible; he was tired to death of the Solitude of this place and the arrangement was as agreeable to him as to me. He is to visit us here from time to time and we have parted good friends.

Frances Trollope (1780–1863), novelist and mother of Anthony Trollope, was a popular mother-in-law, however demanding. Here she writes to her eldest son Thomas, aged thirty-nine, who had married Theodosia the year before.

Brighton, 3rd October, 1849

My dearest Tom,

The date of this letter will probably suggest to you the reason of my unusually long silence. I have been again very unwell. And the attack left so much debility that I have come hither in the hope that sea air, and the vapour baths, might do me good. I certainly feel better here. But I now write, not so much for the purpose of telling you all this, as to make a request to you and Theodosia which I must say I think you *ought* to comply with.

My health and spirits have been shaken by all the sorrow I have gone through. And I confess to you that I feel my separation from you to be almost too painful under my present circumstances. For very nearly forty years, my dear son, you and I have lived together in more perfect harmony than is often found, I believe, in any connection in life. And now, when I so very greatly need the comfort and support of your society, I am deprived of it. I should be very unwilling to put you and your dear wife to any serious inconvenience, but I feel that your coming to me for a few weeks now, might be *very* beneficial to me.

Having said this, I shall say no more. You and Theodosia must judge for yourselves. I will be honest enough to confess to you both, that London has at this time nothing to offer in the way of amusement. But you may cheer one who greatly needs cheering, and who is most affectionately

Your mother, F. Trollope.

Five years later, she is still writing with the same request.

August 1854

Your account of yourself, my dearest Tom, makes me very uneasy. Your rheumatism is evidently *climatic*, and Florence at this season is poison to you.

Dear Theodosia is so deeply incrusted with the notion that the heat of

Florence in the month of August, is as genial to an active Englishman as the breezes of the mountains which surround it, that I will not bother her, or myself, by endeavouring to convince her of the contrary. But I think that if she could see, as I have done, how *flabby babies* become firm by one week's residence here, she might catch, though reluctantly, a glimpse of the truth. Give her my most truly affectionate love, and tell her that nothing but my long experience of what your constitution requires, could induce me to combat her intense aversion to move, or be moved.

That your child should inherit this your peculiar need of bracing air, is certainly not improbable. But on this point I will not dwell, because Theo might fairly answer 'perhaps she inherits my *anti-locomobility!*' So I will quit theory, and try to drive you into something practical, and practicable.

Do you think it would be possible to persuade her to come here *bag and baggage*? There is still one very nice lodging to be had, and this I will take at my own expense, if you will consent to occupy it. In what way can I spend my money better? The keeping house here is not expensive. And Filippo and his family might sleep in your house at Florence to guard it.

*Or* should you like San Marcello better? In that case I would join you there, and what your journey hither would have cost me, shall pay your journey *there* to take lodgings for us. I should like either of these plans equally, – for the *object* of both is the same. I think the San Marcello plan would suit *you* best. If we could contrive to meet *en route*, I would pay half the *vetturino*, and in either case the lodgings would be paid by me. God bless you all three!

      Ever your own loving mother,
      F. Trollope.

Walter Savage Landor (1775–1864), poet and writer, made over his estate to his sons to avoid the consequences of a lawsuit. He was then dependent on his eldest son Arnold for his income.

### Siena, 1859

A shower, a very slight one, yesterday, reminded me that I had only a thin coat on, and not another to change. In vain I applied to my family for cloathes. . . . I have given to my son property worth thirteen or fourteen thousand scudi a year; it is hard I cannot receive from him a change of clothes . . .

☙❧

William Morris (1834–1896) writes to Georgiana Burne-Jones (1840–1920) and includes this despondent comment:

It is sad to think that our children's children will not be able to see a single genuine ancient building in Europe.

On a happier note, he writes to his daughter May (1862–1938), giving her instructions on how to reach him in Hammersmith.

### 15th September, 1879

As to Willesden station; don't try it: it is a mere trap for the unwary; everything is arranged so that you shall miss your trains there; there are scarcely any men about, & what there are refuse to answer questions; the first time I went there I got into the wrong train; the second time I was so exacerbated by the coolness of the officials, that I had to offer to fight the only one I could find: fortunately for me he refused battle: but if you try the place, you may get back to Naworth, or you may get to Aberdeen, or Truro, or Northampton, or Norwich or Boulogne but to Hammersmith you will never get, unless you walk there – carrying your luggage, which would be wearying: no, *put yourselves in a cab* at Euston & come straight to Hammersmith.

Anthony Trollope writes to his son Henry (known as Harry), aged thirty-one, on his way to Cape Town. The letter was sent from the SS Caldera.

2nd July, 1877

I dont like any one on board, but I hate two persons. There is an old man who plays the flute all afternoon and evening. I think he and I will have to fight. And there is a beastly impudent young man with a voice like a cracked horn, who will talk to me. He is almost unsnubbable, but I think I will silence him at last, as far as conversation with me goes.

We have got through the bay of Biscay without disasters, and now the water is quite as smooth as a lake. It has not yet been very hot, but I feel the heat coming. By this time tomorrow I expect to be sweltering – I have not yet put on anything specially light as I am keeping my things for the real heat.

I fancy from all I hear and the little I see that I shall find the Cape a most uninteresting place. The people who are going there on board this ship are just the people who would go to an uninteresting Colony.

Three years later he writes again to Harry, now living in Paris. Within two years Trollope has died.

21st December, 1880

Dear Harry

I ought to have written to you before, but one day has passed after another and I have not done as I ought.

I miss you most painfully. But I had expected that. I only hope that you may come back with the summer. This is the longest day of the winter and I shall begin now to look for the lengthening days. Ah, me! How I used to look for the shortening days, when I was hunting, and had the first of November as a golden day before me for which my soul could long. I have now to look for the time when the green things in the garden may begin to shew themselves. But the expectation of green things in another garden prevents me from being sad.

I finished on Thursday the novel I was writing, and on Friday I began another. Nothing really frightens me but the idea of enforced idleness. As long as I can write books, even though they be not published, I think that I can be happy.

Samuel Butler (1835–1902), writer, exposed his hatred for his father in his book *The Way of All Flesh*. In these letters, however, the Canon sounds quite reasonable.

*Canon Butler writes to his wife about his son Samuel.*

I don't want to make him a schoolmaster any more than I want to make him a clergyman, but he does not strike me as filling any place, and he is of an age to be doing so. He talks of writing; but it requires more than his powers to do this. He has not that in him that will be read. He is too bumptious and not sufficiently practical.

To Samuel:

12th May, 1859

Dear Sam,

Most fathers would I believe on the receipt of this morning's letter have been intensely angry. I am much distressed – distressed at your obliquity of vision, distressed at your opinion of myself, distressed at your seeming callousness of heart.

I will not suffer however that I should be provoked to do other than my judgment prompts me to do. I judged that it was wisest for your good that I should not encourage you in your artist's career. This is my sole motive for refusing to assist you in it. You have shown no decided genius for drawing. You are as yet at the commencing point. To all except men of a decided professional talent it is a very uphill and hopeless task and I think still I should do wrong to afford you the slightest possible encouragement to a course for which for aught I know you may be just as unfitted as for a soldier, lawyer, schoolmaster or tutor. . . .

The notion that I should disinherit you is yours not mine. I said only that I would not contribute to this career of folly. Neither do I see reason to alter this view. The notion that I will not pay you the next two quarters is yours not mine. I stated distinctly the contrary.

George Sitwell (1860–1943) writes to his son Osbert Sitwell (1892–1969) during the First World War. Osbert received the letter on his arrival in the front-line trenches. With great tolerance he described the good effect it had on him 'by the sheer fun of its contents'.

16th December, 1914

My dearest Osbert,

As I fear a line sent to Chelsea Barracks may not reach you before you leave tomorrow, I write to you, care of your regiment, B.E.F. so that you may find a letter from me waiting for you when you arrive in the trenches. But I had wanted if possible to give you a word of advice before you left. Though you will not, of course, have to encounter anywhere abroad the same weight of gunfire that your mother and I had to face here* – it has been my contention for many years that there were no guns in the world to compare for weight and range with the great German naval guns, and that our own do not come anywhere near them – yet my experience may be useful to you. Directly you hear the first shell, retire, as I did, to the Undercroft, and remain there quietly until all firing has ceased. Even then, a bombardment, especially as one grows older, is a strain upon the nervous system – but the best remedy for that, as always, is to keep warm and have plenty of plain, nourishing food at frequent but regular intervals. And, of course, plenty of rest. I find a nap in the afternoon most helpful, if not unduly prolonged, and I advise you to try it whenever possible.

Ever your loving father, George R. Sitwell.

* The Sitwell parents had been close to a bombardment in Scarborough; Osbert wrote that a 'piece of shell went through the front door' and 'many fragments penetrated into the house'. His father retreated to the basement during the bombardment.

Marie Belloc Lowndes was the sister of Hilaire Belloc (referred to as Uncle H.). The first entry comes from her journal.

## 10th April, 1917

There has been a spate of very early marriages and I heard of a lady who was asked if she was happy about her youthful son's marriage. She replied, 'I don't know what I should feel if it were not wartime, for in that case he would still be at Harrow!'

Marie writes to her son Charles, who was aged sixteen when war began. He won the M.C. and joined up again in the Second World War when he was forty-one.

## 27th August, 1918

We *long* to know how you are getting on. . . . By the way I *have* just told Granny that you have moved to some place where your Regiment is – so you can write how you like. Have you everything you want. How about soap and Keating's Powder?

I met Uncle H. today. He was wearing yellow spectacles – just like Sir Edward Grey – He does not think War likely to end before April or even *June*. A French Saint says it will end before Christmas. Oh! how I wish it would, and that I could have you, my darling boy, home again.

The war ended in November, so the French saint was right. Keating's Powder was a very popular insecticide.

৩৮৩

The following lunatic conversation between George and Osbert Sitwell took place at some time in the 1920s.

'This wicked taxation will most probably drive you out of England, in which case you must emigrate to Canada or America and build a copy of the house there: but though I shan't, I fear, still be here to help you and the architect with my advice, I can give you a few tips now. The new Renishaw [their vast family house with Italian garden] must be an exact replica of the present house and garden, except in one respect: the stones needn't be numbered and moved one by one across the

Atlantic, nor need it even be built of the same stone: but you must find a position for it with a natural resemblance to the original site.'

I was floored and stunned by the outlining of these new measures of economy.

'How am I to pay for it?' I asked.

'You must keep expenses down in every other direction. It needn't cost so much: it would be unnecessary, for instance, to make the lake at first. You could wait for that until you had settled in the house, then you could keep an eye on the work yourself.'

'But what I want to know,' I reiterated, 'is how I am to pay for the purchase of the site and for building a house?'

'As for that, there are always the Building Societies. I understand they exist, as their name implies, for the purpose of encouraging building. They'd be only too pleased to help, I imagine. It'd be a real chance for them. Now you'll see, my dear boy, why it is so important to be economical in small things. The pocket-money you have enjoyed might have come in very useful, for a shilling a week soon mounts up at compound interest.'

'It's too late to do anything about that now, I'm afraid,' I said rather unsympathetically. 'The question is, who is going to find the money for everything?'

'I have already told you – the Building Societies. You may have to draw on the resources of more than one of them, of two or three perhaps, but of course they'd jump at it. It's the sort of opportunity they don't often get.'

The building operations you suggest are not of the kind that the directors would support,' I objected.

'Then they've no right to call themselves *Building Societies*,' he replied crossly. 'It's a piece of imposture. I never heard of such a thing. But of course you're wrong. They'd jump at it. Meanwhile I can continue, as long as I am still with you, to advise you about the details which will save you money. . . . For example, when you've made the lake, you needn't plan English wild flowers round the water at once. You can take your time over it. You'll find all the arrangements ve r y enjoyable. Then, in making the lake, you can leave out the island. That'll mean a big saving, and it's not really necessary, anyhow not at present. You'll have, of course, to make a copy of the Lake Pavilion. But you can't do that until I've built the original, so you see why it's so important for me to get on with it. It ought to be started immediately. All the plans are ready. One other point:

it would pay you probably to sell the furniture and pictures in the house and to have exact copies made to furnish the new Renishaw. This is an age of copying and we ought to learn to make use of it. No one out there would know the difference, and it would mean a great saving.' . . . At this moment, those elegant cannibals, the jays, burst out from their dark castles in the trees, gave a screech and a mocking cackle of laughter, and my father, suddenly recalled to himself, said:

'I suppose it's time to start back now.'

Few parents would entirely disagree with George:

Don't argue, it stimulates the brain cells and prevents me from sleeping.

⎰⎱

Quentin Bell (1910–1996), writer and artist, remembers a visit to his grandparents' house, Seend.

My eyes were opened to the realities of life at Seend when I was about fifteen, old enough to be allowed to join the grown-ups at dinner, where I found the old Bells, my parents, my uncle Cory, his son and daughter, and Julian. Cory, always a clumsy fellow, managed to break the stopper of a decanter. 'You hog,' roared my grandfather. 'That's what you are, a hog, a hog!' Lieutenant-Colonel Cory Bell (retired), MP, DSO, Croix de Guerre, sat mute and shamefaced while his father shouted at him. It seemed to me something barbarous. Did this, I wondered, happen in other families?

⎰⎱

John Sampson (1862–1931), a philologist with a particular interest in gypsies, and grandfather of the journalist Anthony, writes to his secret, illegitimate daughter Mary, of whom he was very fond, after learning that she has achieved a second-class degree.

Dear, you have done quite well! A first would have been just a shade more delightful, but I hadn't been *building* on that.

Arthur Ransome (1884–1967), the author of *Swallows and Amazons*, writes to his daughter Tabitha Lewis, aged twenty-four. Tabitha's mother, divorced from Ransome when Tabitha was fourteen, prevented her daughter from forming a relationship with her father, encouraging her to mistrust and dislike him.

Low Ludderburn, 7th September, 1934

My dear Tabitha,

I had your letter in which you remarked 'I have married a Dock Labourer', and gave no further information except that he had blue eyes and sunburn. I have now had a postcard from you; on which you say 'My name is Lewis'.

I had supposed and perhaps hoped that your first statement was a joke, but, if your name is Lewis, I suppose there is no joke about it.

But, when you tell me as little as that, you cannot expect me to say anything except that I am very sorry for your mother.

I dare say your husband's profession is more interesting than you make it sound. Dock Labourers do not usually take their wives to Paris, or have addresses 'care of' a Bank.

In any case I can have nothing against your husband's profession, even if you have accurately described it, so long as he is good at it and you think it is your mission in life to help him to be good at it. If you really care enough for him to take his friends for your friends, his family for your family (as they will be the family to which your children will belong), if you are ready to give up your dogs and your motor car, and to fill his thermos for him and cook his meals and to scrub his doorstep and keep him a clean house to come home to . . . if all this is so, you may be doing well. If on the other hand you are merely giving him an unreal background, and keeping up yourself friendships in which he cannot share, you will ruin both yourself and him. That way, I can see no hope or self-respect for either of you.

I must also say that I cannot pretend to think highly of a man, no matter what his job, who marries you without having the ordinary decency to tell your parents (or one of them at least) what he proposes to do. But that may be your fault, not his.

You do not tell me where you are living, or where his work is, or even what his name is, or where he was educated, or what are his interests, or how old he is, or what he has done so far with his life, or at whose house you met him, or what his parents are like, or, indeed, anything about him.

Your affectionate [no signature]

❦

Winifred Keates (1880–1964), grandmother of the writer Jonathan Keates, writes a hasty but heartfelt letter to her son Basil, aged twenty-three. He has fallen in love with a Russian ballerina he met in Paris and has announced that he is planning to marry her. Perhaps because of his mother's advice, he broke off the affair.

# 1936

My dear

I went to the flat this morning & found your letter & spent a long while answering it then came to the conclusion that what I had written was no sort of an answer so I am now having another go. I shall go back to the flat on Saturday and be there till Monday so if you have any more to say on the subject, write there, will you? I just couldn't do with all Cicely's comments & you know how she always expects to read your letters if they come here.

You used to mention your Russian friends & then I made some foolish maternal remark & you slammed the door in my face so to speak but from your going to the Ballet & then to Monte Carlo I drew my own conclusions. It's very difficult my dear to advise you & you must read what I say & then make your own decision according to your feelings. Letters are tiresome & I can only read & judge on what they convey. I like the girl's letter: it might have been so different & I think she is right in saying you are young (you wont like that but you always have been a late developer) & I think she may be happier with an older man, just as Cicely would have been. I don't feel from reading your letter & hers that you really do love her – not swept off your feet. Probably what you feel now is only more or less the sort of desire you have for a thing that is definitely beyond your reach. A good deal of your attraction must have been caused by your cold Northern attitude, so different from what she generally met, but whether that same coldness wouldn't have become an annoyance and irritation later on is a question. She has behaved very decently & as she said, she could not do more than she has done without being an obvious vamp.

I don't quite gather what your intentions are but if matrimony I don't think you love her well enough, but you have made yourself such a thick protective covering for your very sensitive feelings that it is always difficult to get at the real you. You seem to have been trying to make yourself love her & that's no good at all. Love comes mostly like a flash but at any time without effort. She too was not so taken up with you that she could not bear another man to kiss her (& this is only stating a fact, not just being catty)

I think you would both be happier apart, she with someone older & more her master. Some women are only happy with cave men. So my dear you must do what you think best, but its no use pretending & making yourself believe you love a girl when you only love love. Another thing she says is wise. Don't let this set you off kissing every girl you meet. Quite a lot of girls don't like it. And when you really meet the right girl I think you will know straight away.

If however I am all wrong & life is a dreary desert & the sun gone out, try your luck once more. You can always tell her not to answer if she means no. It is so difficult & so important that to open the matter again may be very upsetting for her. I really think you would be wiser to do nothing more.

I hope this may be some help. It's a rigmarole. You may make something of it. Thank you my dear & I do wish you didn't have all this bother.

Mother.

Wednesday.

My dear,

I have been so unhappy ever since I wrote to you & I hope what I wrote was not too discouraging & after all I hardly answered your one question, whether you would help your case by writing again. I tremble to think what I may have done. Only I felt I must answer – quickly – as if you write at all you must write at once. But still, after sleeping on the matter, I feel you would be kinder to her to let it rest. You do see, don't you, how frightfully difficult this is for me to decide from just two letters. I feel so sorry because I did like her tone. This is all by way of a postscript & I hope by now you have made your decision. Anyway I could shake you for being so close & then suddenly bursting the whole subject on your poor defenceless mother, who at the same time feels very proud that you can so turn to her in this emergency. I only hope I havent failed you my dear. This is all – I wont write any more.

Mother

Whichever way you decide be sure I will help you all I can.

❧

Charles Morgan (1894–1958), novelist and critic, writes to Marie Belloc Lowndes. Susan was her daughter.

2nd September, 1938

I think you and your Susan ought to be painted together. There was a moment when she, seated in a chair higher than yours, was looking down at you while you talked. If ever my daughter listens to me with such an expression on her face I shall feel that life hasn't been wasted. Alive, tender, amused – and with the repose of a drawing by Holbein.

❧

Writing in his diary, which he kept continuously from 1st January 1930 to 4th October 1964, Harold Nicolson reflects on his relationship with his sons, Nigel, aged twenty-three, and Ben, aged twenty-one.
7th June, 1938

We have never imposed any sense of filial duty on either Ben or Nigel. They know that they can make any possible claim on us and that we shall never make any claim on them. That is the only basis for a proper relationship between one generation and another. Our love for them is really extended egoism. Vita and I are intelligent enough to realise that. They are intelligent enough to realise that it is something more than that. Thus we harmonise well. It is more difficult for me than for Vita. She is essentially a solitary soul. I try to live my own life again in those of my sons. I know that this drives them to fury, and I try to control it. I know that it is rather grotesque of me (with all my activities) loving them both so much and thinking more about their lives than about my own. But they understand it. Benzie in a gentle way. Nigel in a dutiful way. I know that they are very fond of me. But I am sometimes terrified by my adoration of them. It just isn't cricket. I try to conceal it, but they are spry enough to see that it is there. And faintly, kindly, gently they regard it as *aidoia* [*aidoia gerontos* = the shame of an old man]. In just such a way did I resent Mummy's adoration of myself. But now that I am older (or is it old?) I feel that her adoration was a sort of compass-rock in my life. Ben and Nigel have hitherto been successful in life and do not know what suffering is. Ben had a sense of it at Eton, and I think we helped him at that moment. Nigel has never really suffered, and if he did, he would rush away from us, fearing soft appreciation, gentle love. Yet if I were wretched, both of them would fly to my assistance and be of the utmost help. I never thought of that before. I cannot do much to help them, but they (if things went wrong) would sacrifice everything to help me. That is true. Hurray! I have untied one knot in our relationship.

⚜

Clementine Churchill (1885–1977) writes to her husband, Winston Churchill (1874–1965), in the middle of the Second World War, about their son Randolph, aged thirty-one, who had married Pamela Digby in October 1939.

### 11th April, 1942

My Darling,

Please don't think I am indifferent because I was silent when you told me of Randolph's cable to Pamela saying he was joining a parachute unit . . . but I grieve that he has done this because I know it will cause you harrowing anxiety, indeed, even agony of mind.

I feel this impulse of Randolph's . . . is sincere but sensational. Surely there is a half-way house between being a Staff-Officer and a Parachute Jumper. He could have quietly & sensibly rejoined his Regiment & considering he has a very young wife with a baby to say nothing of a Father who is bearing not only the burden of his own country but for the moment of an un-prepared America it would in my view have been his dignified & reasonable duty.

My Darling – Do you think it would be any use my sending an affectionate cable begging him on *your* account to re-join his Regiment and give up this scheme in which if he begins one feels he must perhaps persevere?

❦

Sacheverell Sitwell (1897–1988), author and art critic, writes to his friend the ballerina Moira Shearer, on hearing of the sudden marriage of his son Reresby to the bright and beautiful Penelope Forbes.

## 1952

We [he and his wife Georgia] were both knocked out entirely in Chicago by that news of Reresby – whom I am afraid has been so deceitful with us. . . . Poor G. was in tears for 48 hours, the blasted girl he has married is so uninteresting & 30 years old [four years older than her husband]. . . . It has been a terrible blow – and a grim prospect being landed with someone so boring. I rather liked Chicago – that apart. . . .

❦

Antonia White (1899–1980) depicts the consequences of her daughter's nervous breakdown, which happened just before Susan, aged twenty-two, took her final exams at Oxford. Writing in her journal, White's unsympathetic reaction is shockingly revealing; particularly as she had had a breakdown at precisely the same age. (Lyn is her other daughter, Lyndall; Thomas is Thomas Chitty, Susan's future husband.)

## 10th May, 1951

Since the last entry, everything bouleversé. Sue's increasingly bad state culminating in two attempts at suicide, the observation ward, the Maudsley. For three weeks I behaved with unnatural calm and efficiency. The real break did not come till last Saturday when I developed a state as bad as Sue's. The 2 of us obviously terribly tied together in this. She has this breakdown at the time most critical for her and for me: her finals:

my book. She attempts to destroy herself and, in a sense, me too. Yet neither time does she succeed (she takes precautions not to) and she also inquires anxiously even when she is very remote, how my book is going.

## 3rd August

Sue left here on Saturday. Chaos, insolence, lying . . . Six weeks since she left the Maudsley. At first, gentle, melancholy, gradually becoming apathetic, lacking all confidence. Then switched to wild high spirits, assertiveness, tremendous energy, endless starting of new and never-finished projects. Soon all attempts to help in the least at home frankly abandoned. Then a crescendo of insolence, extravagance, endless demands, crazy disorder until I said if she could not behave reasonably she had better go off on her own . . . endless trouble for me and Lyn. Incredible vanity and conceit: out to exploit everyone. Her room which was put in apple-pie order only 6 weeks ago left in more dirt and disorder than I've ever known even Sue create. Has behaved most oddly since . . . Keeps ringing up here, trying to be very grown-up and off hand . . . immensely on the make . . . She has worn me down till I am tired and trembling and can't settle down or concentrate but this time I am not going to give in to her. I am very quiet and cold: have made no scene nor written to her nor appealed to her . . . Any impulse she has to gratify *at once*. Outwardly everyone impressed by how radiant she looks . . . But any moral sense seems to have gone quite completely. There are times when it is extremely difficult to believe that the whole suicide and Maudsley episodes were not quite consciously and coldly planned and executed . . . That look of hers in St Francis [Observation Ward, Greenwich] which struck Si and me so much: the satisfied smile of a child who has brought it off.

. . . I doubt if she really believed that I could let her go off and not allow her to go on treating this place as a convenience. I think she still believes she has only got to appear with a bottle or a bunch of flowers to have me just where she wants me again. But this time . . No. And this has never happened to Sue before. I'm not impervious. Dear me, no. I've been reduced almost to pulp. But I think I am growing a protective skin . . . I find both her and Thomas [Chitty – Susan's future husband] a little repulsive at the moment: it doesn't look quite so idyllic and romantic when one knows the facts. At the moment they're busy petting each other's vanity. The interesting time will come when there is a clash between those two egoists and they want different things. Thomas sponges on Sue quite considerably . . . But what is going to happen when she becomes a liability, instead of an asset. Thomas is mild and gentle but he is, I think, every bit as selfish as she is and has more staying power . . . At the moment of course he seems absolutely hypnotised by her and *looks* fathoms deep in love. But I think she is more *dependent* on him than he is on her: I suspect, when she is not spending money or at her job, she is completely lost and simply does not know what to do with herself when he is not about. With no one to gossip with or rebel against she is going to miss her home quite considerably . . . She found Oxford bad enough – the money of course is being quite fatal to her [£400 insurance policy, maturing when Susan became 21]. But how could we have known that? As long as it lasts she will probably continue in her inflated state . . . Whenever I write about Sue, I am frightened. How much of her there is in me . . .

## 6th August

It is a queer thought that this is the first time for 22 years that Sue has not been costing me money. She has been a financial drain on me from the moment she was conceived . . . She has always caused *unnecessary* trouble all her life . . . The last four years she has been more demanding and less co-operative than ever. It will be interesting to see how long she does manage on her own. She is of course relying not on her pay but on the 21st birthday money and that of course came from the family so is indirect support from parents. She would have to manage very carefully indeed if she really lived on her £4 a week [from working as a zoo attendant at Battersea Fun Fair during the Festival of Britain], kept her £100 for dress and left her capital. But she could do it: if she and Thomas pooled their money they could have £8 a week leaving Thomas £2 a week for extras as she has. Their rent is £2.10 [shillings] and they could cater for £3.10 comfortably. Often I *have* resented this money burden: chiefly when Sue is so ungrateful and demanding . . . never even trying to see . . . that one just *can't* afford drinks, entertainments, restaurants etc. let alone holidays abroad. I think I really can have a clear conscience about Sue now. She has made her own choice, she has enough to live on and she has got to the age where she *should* be independent.

Susan refused to see her again until 1957, but White continued to write up her feelings about her daughter.

## 12th September, 1951

. . . I am envious of Sue. Why, chiefly? Her height and slimness. Her 'getting away' with things – even to eating such a lot and remaining incredibly slender! Her distinguished look . . . I'm afraid I get a bit sick of the 'beautiful daughter' stuff . . . Lyndall is just as attractive and I *don't* feel this envy about her. But envy extends to lots of people besides Sue. People who are loved, who have a husband or an intimate friend to share their lives . . .

St Cecilia's Day, 16th November, 1953: Sue is married to Tom, and pregnant.

Today I rang up Sue after getting Tom's father's letter. I heard her voice for the first time for 22 months almost to a day. She was not angry about my ringing up. She said she was going to tell me after the baby was born I said she no doubt had her reasons for telling me nothing about the baby and so on. She said yes and I could probably guess what they were. I said I couldn't . . . She said she would write to me and explain . . . speaking to her took away some of the nightmare feeling. I shan't be surprised if she doesn't write.

Susan gave birth to a son, Andrew, on 20th November, 1953.

## 20th March, 1957

A week ago last Tuesday I heard from Sue for the first time for 5 years. It is awful that I cannot even be properly thankful yet: the shock has been so great. It has affected me exactly like the fire and the libel case: a week of restlessness, bad sleeping, inertia and extreme tiredness. I have done no work: only revision and letters. I will be seeing Sue and the grandchildren on April 13th or May 4th. It will be, in a way, 'on sufferance' and, for me, rather artificial. I am told I must make no reference to the past as 'our two versions of what happened will never agree'. She does not say what her version is, of course. . . . Of course it is beyond anything I could have hoped. And I see that now I *had* at last given up hope. The restoration of it is almost more painful than what I had grown used to. They say that restoring circulation after nearly freezing or drowning is agonisingly painful. I feel *dreadfully* ungrateful to God .. but I *am* thankful underneath. It means much patience and humility on my part and I do implore grace for that. I know it is the cool, hard, casual Sue I am going to see, not the other. I need so much grace and strength for it.

## 21st March

The shock feeling persists. I don't know if it is Sue or not: tension in head and eyes; tired, dull irritable. Not a word from Sue, after a week to tell me which day! . . . Everything frightens me . . .

## 29th March

Still tired and restless. My eyes are a nuisance, giving more trouble than before the new glasses. What small beginning I made on the novel I have destroyed but I *do* think I now have the right idea for the first chapter . . . I heard from Sue yesterday that it is to be 13th April, for which I am very grateful. I begin to take it in. It has all got to be kept as light and casual as possible. I don't suppose I'll see her alone, even for a minute. But her notes, though casual, are not unfriendly . . .

They met on 13th April and were reconciled sufficiently to continue to see each other until White's death in 1980.

෴

Bertrand Russell writes to his daughter Kate, aged thirty. She had recently joined the Christian church.

## 21st October, 1954

In your letter of August 31 you speak of your 'dreadful burden of undefined guilt' and your having 'lived so long with your own shame'. I do not know why you feel this, and I think there must have been something very much amiss in your upbringing and in the way your parents treated you. You have never (so far as I know) been particularly sinful – quite the opposite, I should have thought. Anyway, what you say gives me a feeling of 'sin' and 'shame'. As a parent I have been a dismal failure.

However, I love you, my dear Kate, although you think no one but God could love you.

All good wishes to all of you.

Yours affectionately
Diddy

ॐ

Rupert Hart-Davis writes to George Lyttleton.

4th December, 1955

Last Tuesday with pride and sorrow I watched my son Duff march off towards Germany with his battalion (1st Coldstream). He looked enormous (the same size as me) and terribly young, and since tears always spring to my eyes at the first strains of a drum-and-fife band (as at a glimpse of the King or Queen), I was more moved even than I had expected to be. The band continued to play *Auld Lang Syne* on the platform until all the women were weeping. I left before the train went.

21st October, 1956

Since I saw you my life has been overwhelmed by the Box-and-Cox appearances of my elder children – the boy on leave from Germany, the girl up from Wales to see him. He lost the keys of the flat, ransacked all my drawers trying to find a black tie, borrowed my bag and brought it back full of mud and water after playing the Wall Game – but to such a patriarch as you these irritations are only too well known. In my theatrical youth I once told a dear old cockney actor that the night before I had had too much to drink and been sick. A fond, nostalgic look came over his face, and he said 'Sick after drinking; it sounds like primroses to me, boy.' I'm devoted to my errant son, and he is a very present help in the abundant apple-harvest . . .

Rebecca West reveals the bitterness of her failed relationship with her son.

20th August, 1959

Motherhood is the strangest thing, it can be like being one's own Trojan horse.

๑๛๑

Maureen Lipman (b.1946) recalls the way her daughter Amy reacted to discovering how sad her father had been when she went off to university.

. . . Amy sat in the garden reading her father's latest play which revolves around a group of parents accompanying their offspring to their Cambridge interviews. . . . I found her spilling over with the kind of sobs I dimly remember from her twelve-year-old school-days of 'best friend betrayal'.

'Poor Dad,' she sobbed. 'I feel so awful. I didn't know he felt so lost when I went off – I didn't know he felt like an old eskimo – I feel so terrible.'

# AT THE END

*. . . my sad and afflicted husband . . . cried out so terribly*
*that his cry was heard a great way . . .*
*Mary Countess of Warwick, on the death of her son, 1664*

The opening letter in this chapter is the first of two from fathers who are about to die: Thomas More's last letter to his daughter Meg, written the night before his execution in 1535, is a well-known text, but its poignancy is undiminished; Captain Scott's last letter is equally famous although he only leaves one child compared to More's children and dependents.

In other letters, broken-hearted parents write about children of all ages who are dying or have died: infants, young children and grown-up children. Sometimes most of the children in a family die. The descriptions, often written by fathers in the early period, record the circumstances that have led to the child's death in anguished detail.

The longest extract is an exchange of letters between Charles Darwin and his wife during the last days in the life of their daughter Annie. At the beginning of the twenty-first century, child mortality is far lower than it was in earlier times, so fewer British parents have to live through this terrible ordeal; and when it does happen, parents are more likely to be able to travel to be together in moments of crisis and are less likely to exchange letters at the time: this series of letters provides a unique example of scientific observation and personal suffering.

Although the culture that gave any meaning to death has vanished, and with it a little of the comfort, there are still reflections of it in Susan Hill's beautiful and hopeful description of the death of her premature daughter, Imogen. But, whatever the circumstances, the agony of a child's death extends in an unbroken line through each parent's life, an inescapable pain that lasts until their own death.

In prison and using a piece of coal, Thomas More writes his last letter to his daughter Meg, the night before his execution.

5th July, 1535

Oure Lord blesse you, good daughter, and youre good husbande, and youre little boye, and all youre and all my chyldren, and all my godde-chyldren, and all my frendes. Recommende me when you maye to my goode daughter Cicely, whome I beseeche oure Lorde to comforte. And I sende her my blessyng and to all her chiydren, and praye her to praye for me. I sende her an handkercher, and God comforte my goode sonne her husbande. My good daughter Dauncey hath the picture in parchemente that you delivered me from my Lady Coniers; her name is on the back. Shewe her that I heartelye praye her, that you may sende it in my name to her agayne, for a token from me to praye for me. I lyke special well Dorothy Colly; I pray you be good unto her. I marvel whether thys be she that you wrote me of; if not, yet I pray you be good to the t'other as you may in her affliction, and to my goode daughter Joane Alleyn too. Give her, I pray you, some kynde answer, for she send hither to me this day to pray you be good unto her. I cumber you, good Margaret, much; but I would be sorry if it should be any longer than to-morrow, for it is St. Thomas' Even, and within the (octave) of St. Peter; and therefore to-morrow long I to go to God: it were a day verye mete and convenient for me. I never liked your maner toward me better than when you kissed me laste, for I love when daughterly love and deare charity hath no leysure to loke to worldlye curtesey. Farewell, my dere chylde, and pray for me, and I shall for you and all youre frendes, that we may surely mete in heaven. I thanke you for youre gret cost. I send now to my good daughter Clement, her algorisme stone; and I send her and my good sonne and all hers God's blessing and myne. I pray you at time convenient recommend me to my good sonne John More; I liked well his natural fashion. Our Lorde blesse him and his good wyfe my loving daughter, to whom I pray him to be good, as he hath gret cause; and that if the land of myne come to his hande, he break not my will concerning his sister Dauncy. And our Lord blesse Thomas and Austin, and all that they shall have.

Sir Walter Raleigh (1552–1618), adventurer and poet, had led an unsuccessful expedition to South America during which his son, aged twenty-two, was killed in a fight with the Spaniards. He writes to his wife.

## 1616

I was loth to write, because I knew not how to comfort you: and, God knows, I never knew what sorrow meant till now. All that I can say is, that you must obey the will and providence of god; and remember, that the Queen's Majesty bore the loss of Prince Henry with a magnanimous heart, and the Lady Harrington of her only son. Comfort your heart (dearest Bess), I shall have sorrow for us both. I shall sorrow the less, because I have not long to sorrow, because not long to live. . . . I have cleansed my ship of sick men, and sent them home. . . . The Lord bless you and comfort you, that you may bear patiently the death of your valiant son.

Raleigh was executed for piracy two years later.

ॐ

Sir Simonds D'Ewes (1602–1650) was a Puritan politician whose diary includes details of his family life. Two of his infant sons had already died but when his third son was born he seemed a healthy child.

## 1631

On Friday June the 24th, some quarter of an hour after four of the clock in the morning, was my dear wife safely delivered of her first son, which brought to us, by its abortive end, much more sorrow than joy; and the rather because we feared it perished by the cursed ignorance or neglect of such as were employed about my wife during her lying-in, for it was a goodly sweet child born: but my wife having some resolution to be a nurse, it was fatally advised by such as were about her, that the child should not suck any other till her breasts were fully drawn and made fit for it, during which time it was so weakened, as it afterwards proved the cause of its ruin. . . .

We had too much rejoicing both at the birth and christening, and therefore this sad issue taught us more moderation for the time to come. Our sweet infant was a little ill, Thursday, July the 7th, but we had no suspicion or fear of his approaching end till Saturday, July the 9th, when he was surprised with a violent and little intermitting looseness or scouring; with which he having been grievously afflicted and disquieted all the day, he had some intermission about four of the clock in the afternoon, and so lay quietly breathing out his last and innocent breath till near upon six of the clock that same evening, when he rendered up his blessed soul into the hands of his eternal creator. I had attended him, fasting the greatest part of the day; and when he had given up the ghost, my dearest and myself could not refrain from many tears, sighs, and mournings. We were the more cast down with this loss, because but a little before our young and only daughter, Anne D'Ewes, fell sick on Thursday, June 23rd, in the afternoon, so dangerously, that she twice swooned away; and much ado was there to fetch life into her again.

*Three years later, his wife gives birth to their fourth son.*

## 1634

Between two and three of the clock in the afternoon of the same day, she was safely delivered of her fourth son . . . who was at this time, his three elder brothers being dead, our heir apparent. . . . We had present affliction with him upon his birth, by the failing of two nurses, one after the other, within a fortnight after my wife had been delivered; so as being in a great strait, and fearing we might lose him as we had done our first, we were fain to pitch upon a poor woman who had been much misused and almost starved by a wicked husband, being herself also naturally of a proud, fretting and wayward disposition; which together in the issue conduced to the final ruin and destruction of our most sweet and tender infant, who fell into fits of convulsions, under which, having at several times suffered extremely, it died at last of them, being near two years old, on Monday 9th day of May, in the year 1636; leaving myself and my dear wife the saddest and most disconsolate parents that ever lost so tender and sweet an infant.

Gervase Holles (1607–1675) mourns his two-year-old son, a few months after the death of his wife in childbirth. I love the last line of this little memoir.

## 1635

. . . not long after (for the progresse of my misfortunes was begunne) I lost my poore George, my only sonne. He was when he died about two yeares and two monethes olde, a strong and healthfull childe, never sicke so long as he lived untill his last sad accident surprised him, which was a bleeding at the nose. It tooke him upon a Sunday morning when I was at the church, from which I was called together with his grandfather and grandmother. He bled all that day, all applications that wee used proving ineffectuall to staunch it; at night it stopt and he was gotten to bed and slept soundly. In the morning (whilst his mayd was dressing of him) he fell on bleeding againe, and so continued untill he expired; which happened about two of the clocke in the afternoon upon Monday the 10th of August, and was buried in the same grave with my brother John at the feet of my father aº 1635.

If a fond father is to be trusted with the account of his owne childe, I may speake him of no ordinary expectation. He was as hansome and as well shaped as could be wished; at a yeare olde he spoke plainly, and had so strange a memory that (before two yeares of his life passed) he could blazon any coat of armes ever in the canting termes of the Heraldes, a thing hard to be credited but that there are so many (yet living) witnesses of it. Full of life and spirit which yet had a mixture of mildnes and gravity, and he would many times suddainly step aside from the height of his little sportes and (kneeling against the wall) would say his prayers. In short he was of so much forwardnes yt no man besides my selfe hoped for him a long life. And my cosen Barne (seeing me much afflicted after his death) tolde me he wonder'd I should greive so much because he did not thinke I ever expected to enjoy him long, for he was a miracle. I hope I shall be excused for saying so much of this little boy. He was borne my heyre, and this is all his inheritance.

Sir Edmund Verney writes to his son Ralph about Ralph's daughter Anna Maria, aged nearly four.

## 19th May, 1638

Raphe, your sweete child is going apace to a better woarld; shee has but a short time to staye with uss. I hope you have such a sence of God's blessings to you as you will not repine at his decrees; make all convenient haste to your good wife who wants your comfort, yet come not too faste for that maye heate your bludd; and that maye give an end to all our comforts; . . .

Ralph writes to his brother Henry.

## January 1639

You shall herewithal receive a ringe filled with my deare gerle's haire; shee was fond of you, and you loved her therefore I now send you this to keepe for her sake.

Mary Verney writes to Ralph, her husband, who is in exile in France with their two elder children, Edmund and Margaret (Peg). She had just given birth to her fourth child, another Ralph, who was not with her but with her family at Claydon.

## London, 21st October, 1647

I am soe weary that tis a payne to me to hold ye penn, but yet I cannot conclude, ontell I have chidd thee that thou dost nevor give me an account how thyselfe and boy and gerle have your helthes, and yett I have intreated itt of you before now: tis a duty I weekly performe to thee, and I assure you I expect ye same from you, for my deare hart there is nothing in this world soe nearly concernes mee.

Her husband has not had the courage to tell her that her daughter Peg, aged nine, has died in France and he knows that, at the same time, her new baby, Ralph, has also died. Mary adds a postscript to her next letter.

### 28th October

Since I writt this, I have receaved ye sad nues of our toe deare children's death, which afliction joyned with being absent from thee is – without god's great mercy to me, a heavier burthen than can be borne by thine owne unhappy M.

Mary to Ralph:

### 4th November

My dearest hart, I was in soe much afliction for ye losse of my deare children, when the last letters went from hence, that I was nott in a condition to wright or doe anything elce and truly att present I am soe weake that I am scarse able to goe upp and downe my chamber butt my trust is in my good God; for he gave them to me and he took them from me, and I hope, and I trust he will in his good time deliver me out of all my troubles and give my mind some quiett and bring me to thee for untell I am with thee I canott take any content in any thing in this world . . .

Ralph to Mary:

### 1st December

. . . I am soe full of greife for the Death of my poore children, that I must needes vent some part of it to thee. What shall I say? for every line, every word and sillable about this businesse, encreaseth both thy sorrows and my owne. Therefore I shall endeavour to leave deploring theire losse, for they are most unspeakeable gainers by this Change; and since tis soe (if we did not love our selves much more then them) wee should rather rejoyce at their happinesse, then by repining at the Will of Heaven, . . . Had you butt seene with what unparraleld patience poore Pegg bore all her paines, and with what discreation and affection she disposed of her wearing cloathes unto her maide that tended her, and lastly with what admirable cheerfulnesse and courage desiring prayers to bee made for her, shee peaceably resigned her soule into the hands of him that gave it, I am most confident thou wouldst have learned of this our innocent Babe to bee courageous in all thy conflicts, patient in all thy afflictions, and her example would have taught thee to submitt all things to the good pleasure of God, how nearely soever they concerne thy selfe or mee.

Mary Verney had three daughters, all of whom died. Two of her three sons survived.

❧

Ralph Josselin writes in his diary about Mary, who was his first child, aged eight.

19th May, 1650

. . . my deare Mary, wonderfull ill, and so is little Ralph, the lord in mercy sanctifie his hand, and dealing with mee, and showe mee, why he contends with mee. this day also my little Jane was taken ill, the good lord in mercy doe mee good by these rebukes. . . .

21st May

The last night Mary talked idely, shee began to sweate, god takes the feare of her death much from my heart, her fitts are violent in her head . . .

22nd May

my little Mary, very weake, wee feared shee was drawing on . . .

23rd May

. . . my Mary rested very little the night past, yett shee knew mee in the morning . . .

24th May

. . . my Mary very ill, this morning shee sleepes sweetly, soundly . . .

25th May

hopes of Maries life especially towards night, but it was onely hopes . . .

26th May

This morning all our hopes of Maries life was gone . . .

27th May

This day a quarter past two in the afternoone my Mary fell asleepe in the Lord, her soule past into that rest where the body of Jesus, and the soules of the saints are, shee was: 8 yeares and 45 dayes old when shee dyed, my soule had aboundant cause to blesse god for her, who was our first fruites, and those god would have offered to him, and this I freely resigned up to him, it was a pretious child, a bundle of myrrhe, a bundle of sweetnes, shee was a child of ten thousand, full of wisedome, woman-like gravity, knowledge, sweet expressions of god, apt in her learning, tender hearted and loving, an obedient child to us. It was free from the rudenesse of little children, it was to us as a boxe of sweet ointment, which now its broken smells more deliciously than it did before, Lord I rejoyce I had such a present for thee, it was patient in the sicknesse, thankefulle to admiracion; it lived desired and dyed lamented, thy memory is and will bee sweete unto mee.

Twenty-three years later, his son Thomas died; he was the fourth child to die.

15th June, 1673

about one a clocke in the morning my eldest sonne Thomas and my most deare child ascended early hence to keepe his everlasting Sabbath with his heavenly father, and Saviour with the church above, his end was comfortable, and his death calme, not much of pain til the Saturday afore. in my course this morning I read Josh; I: which had words of comfort, god making his word my counsellour and comfort. He was my hope. but some yeares I have feared his life, god hath taken all my first brood but Jane. lett all live in thy sight sanctified. a wett morning, the heavens for some time have mourned over us.

In 1658, John Evelyn's son Richard (Dick), aged five, dies of the Quartan Ague, now thought to be malaria.

## 27th January, 1658

After six fitts of a *Quartan Ague* it pleased God to visite my deare Child *Dick* with fitts so extreame, especiale one of his sides, that after the rigor was over & he in his hot fitt, he fell into so greate & intollerable a sweate, that being surpriz'd with the aboundance of vapours ascending to his head, he fell into such fatal Symptoms, as all the help at hand was not able to recover his spirits, so as after a long & painefull Conflict, falling to sleepe as we thought, & coverd too warme, (though in midst of a severe frosty season) and by a greate fire in the roome; he plainely expird, to our unexpressable griefe & affliction. We sent for Physitians to Lond, whilst there was yet life in him; but the river was frozen up, & the Coach brake by the way ere it got a mile from the house; so as all artificial help failing, & his natural strength exhausted, we lost the prettiest, and dearest Child, that ever parents had, being but 5 yeares & 3 days old in years but even at that tender age, a prodigie for Witt, & understanding; for beauty of body a very Angel, & for endowments of mind, of incredible & rare hopes.

᭤᭠᭤

Mary Rich, Countess of Warwick, writes of the death of her only son, aged twenty.

## 1664

. . . the eighth day of that month [May], my dear and only son fell ill, and it proved to be the small-pox, in which distemper of his, after I had removed his wife out of the house from him to her father's (for fear of her being infected) . . . , I shut myself up with him, doing all I could both for his soul and body; and though he was judged by his doctors to be in a hopeful way of recovery, yet it pleased God to take him away by death the 16th of May, to my inexpressible sorrow. He wanted about four months of being of age. . . .

I was, under this sharp trial, so enabled from above with some degree of patience, that I did endeavour to comfort my sad and afflicted husband, who, at the news of his death, when it was told him by my good friend the Earl of Manchester, cried out so terribly that his cry was heard a great way; and he was the saddest afflicted a person could possibly be. I confess I loved him at a rate that, if my heart do not deceive me, I could, with all the willingness in the world, have died either for him or with him, if God had only seen it fit . . .

❧

John and Mary Evelyn lived through the deaths of seven of their eight children. Here Evelyn records the death of their nineteen-year-old daughter Mary.

### 7th March, 1685

Newes coming to me that my Daughter Mary was falln ill of the Small Pox, I hastned home full of apprehensions, & indeede found her very ill, still coming-forth in aboundance, a wonderfull affliction to me, not onely for her beauty, which was very lovely, but for the danger of loosing one of extraordinary parts & virtue. &c: Gods holy will be don.

### 8th March

My Deare Child continuing ill, by reason of the Disseases fixing in the Lungs, it was not in the power of physick without more plentifull expectoration to recover her, insomuch as Dr. Short (the most approved & famous Physition of all his Majesties Doctors) gave us his opinion, that she could not escape, upon the Tuesday; so as on Wednesday she desired to have the B: Sacrament given her (of which yet she had participated the Weeke before) after which disposing her selfe to suffer what God should determine to inflict, she bore the remainder of her sicknesse with extraordinary patience, and piety & with more than ordinary resignation, and marks of a sanctified & blessed frame of mind, rendred up her soule to the Lord Jesus on Saturday the 14 of March, exactly at halfe-an houre after Eleeven in the fore noone, to our unspeakable sorrow & Affliction, and this not to ours (her parents) onely, but all who knew her, who were many of the best quality, greatest & most vertuous persons: . . . O deare, sweete and desireable Child, how shall I part with all this goodnesse, all this Vertue, without the bitternesse of sorrow, and reluctancy of a tender

Parent! Thy Affection, duty & love to me was that of a friend, as well as of a Child, passing even the love of Women, the Affection of a Child: nor lesse dearer to thy Mother, whose example & tender care of Thee was unparalleled; nor was Thy returnes to her lesse conspicuous: O how she mourns thy losse! o how desolate hast Thou left us, Sweete, obliging, happy Creature! To the grave shall we both carry thy memory . . .

Mary Evelyn, a highly educated and much admired woman, writes to Lady Tuke, a month later.

## April 1685

How to expresse the sorrow for parting with so deare a child is a difficult task. She was welcome to me from the first moment God gave her, acceptable through the whole course of her life by a thousand endearments, by the gifts of nature, by acquired parts, by the tender love she ever shew'd her father and me: a thred of piety accompanied all her actions, and now proves our greatest consolation. The patience, resignation, humility of her carriage in so severe and fatall a disease, discover'd more than an ordinary assistance of the Divine goodnesse, never expressing feare of death, or a desire to live, but for her friends sake. . . . What shall I say! She was too great a blessing for me, who never deserved any thing, much lesse such a jewell. . . .

. . . What shall I add! I could ever speake of her, and might I be just to her without suspition of partiality, could tell you many things. . . .I acknowledge, as a Christian, I ought not to murmur, and I should be infinitly sorry to incur God's further displeasure. There are those yet remaining that challenge my care, and for their sakes I endeavour to submitt all I can.

ৎৡৡ৵

Mrs Elizabeth James writes her diary detailing the sudden death of her son William, aged six.

## 20th April, 1750

After Dinner Dear Billy was taken with vomiting.

21st April

Mr Medhurst applied a Blister to his head . . . he was shaved all over his head

22nd April

Billy is a little better. Applied 2 blisters to his arms about half past two in ye afternoon, clap's Pigeons to his feet at 9 at night.

24th April

Mr Leigh came this morning. Carried off the last hop poles. Dear Billy died at 25 mins. past 4 in ye afternoon.

26th April

Dear Billy was interr'd in ye Vault, was carried by four old servants. . . . Mr Leigh and I went in ye coach, all ye Servants had gloves.

❧

James Boswell's wife gave birth to a son on 28th August, 1770 but the child died within two hours. The day after the death of his son Boswell writes to the Revd William Johnson Temple:

I have much need of your comfort.

Temple replies:

You ought not, you cannot feel much for what you have lost. People of reflection love their children not so much from instinct as from a knowledge and esteem of their good and amiable qualities. Think then no more of your misfortune and trust that Providence will be more favourable to you upon another occasion.

Boswell cannot agree:

The consolation of hearing from you and the prospect of seeing you soon do me more good than your philosophical consideration on the death of my child. I grant you that there is no *reason* for our having an affection for an infant which, as it is not properly a rational being, can have no qualities to engage us; yet Nature has given us such an instinctive fondness that being deprived of an infant gives us real distress. I have experienced this; and there is no arguing against it.

ᐧᕀᐧ

Queen Charlotte (1744–1818) writes to Lady Pembroke after the death of Lady Pembroke's daughter Charlotte, aged eleven.

Kew, 9th July, 1784

I hope I need not add that I have & do now very strongly feel for your loss, *twice have I felt* what you do feel, the last time without the least preparation for such a stroke, for in less than eight and forty hours was my Son Octavius, in perfect health, sick, & struck with Death immediately. Religion was my only support at that time, & I hope my dear Lady Pembroke has found it there likewise. *The Almighty* is the best & only refuge to fly to in the time of trouble for He is our Strength, our Comforter, our Friend, & our Father. He searches our hearts, knows our secret thoughts, nay, knows even before we ask, & orders us in His holy Scripture to come unto Him that He may comfort us. To Him therefore it is owing that we are innabled to go through the vicissitudes of life with chearfulness & bear our misfortunes with resignation; & I am pretty sure that though my dear Lady Pembroke's life has not hitherto proved to be very happy, there will come a time that you will be rewarded for your sufferings *both here & hereafter*, & this hope & confidence we obtain by a steady unalterable adherence to Providence. Oh! may you both *be* & *feel* happy is my sincere wish.

You expected a letter & have found a Sermon, of which I am most ashamed, but Alas! I said but what I thought & you know me to be an open character. It was my heart not my head which guided my pen for a moment, therefore you must pardon it.

The day after the death of his son Thomas William, aged six years, from measles, Wordsworth writes to Robert Southey.

2nd December, 1812

For myself dear Southey I dare not say in what state of mind I am; I loved the Boy with the utmost love of which my soul is capable, and he is taken from me – yet in the agony of my spirit in surrendering such a treasure I feel a thousand times richer than if I had never possessed it. God comfort and save you and all our friends and us all from a repetition of such trials – O Southey feel for me!

Dorothy Wordsworth writes to a friend, Catherine Clarkson, about her sister-in-law Mary.

5th January, 1813

She is as thin as it is possible to be except when the body is worn out by slow disease, and the dejection of her countenance is afflicting; insomuch that though we force ourselves into seeming chearfulness whenever we can, I feel that it knits about the heart strings and will wear her away if there is not a turn in her feelings.

❧

Sydney Smith writes to Lady Grey. His eldest son, Douglas, had died in April, aged twenty-four.

13th July, 1829

My spirits are very much improved, but I have now and then sharp pangs of grief. I did not know I had cared so much for anybody, but the habit of providing for human beings, and watching over them for so many years generates a fund of affection of the magnitude of which I was not aware.

A month later he writes to Mrs Beilby Thomson.

## 6th August

In the meantime I have from time to time bitter visitations of sorrow. I never suspected how children weave themselves about the heart.

❦

Elizabeth Gaskell writes to her friend Anne Shaen, nearly three years after the death of her only son, William, aged nine months, from scarlet fever.

## April 1848

I have just been up to our room. There is a fire in it, and a smell of baking, and oddly enough the feelings and recollections of 3 years ago came over me so strongly – when I used to sit up in the room so often in the evenings reading by the fire, and watching my darling *darling* Willie, who now sleeps sounder still in the dull, dreary chapel-yard at Warrington. That wound will never heal on earth, although hardly any one knows how it has changed me. I wish you had seen my little fellow, dearest dear Annie. I can give you no idea what a darling he was – so affectionate and *reasonable* a baby I never saw.

Five years after Willie's death she writes to another friend, Tottie Fox.

## 26th April, 1850

. . . *here* there is the precious perfume lingering of my darling's short presence in this life – I wish I were with him in that 'light, where we shall all see light', for I am often sorely puzzled here – but however I must not waste my strength or my time about the never ending sorrow; but which hallows this house. I think that is one evil of this bustling life that one has never time calmly and bravely to face a great grief, and so view it on every side as to bring the harmony out of it.

This series of letters between Charles Darwin and his wife, Emma, who was eight months pregnant with her ninth child, was written as their second daughter, Annie, aged ten, struggled against a terminal illness. Darwin is with Annie in Malvern while Emma is at home at Down House. They reveal in extraordinary detail the excruciating hope and agony known to anyone who has ever watched over a child in such circumstances.

Brodie was Annie's nurse, Catherine Thorley was her governess and Henrietta her elder sister; Fanny Wedgwood was married to the Darwins' cousin, Hensleigh Wedgwood, and Fanny Allen was Emma's aunt. Dr James Gully offered a hydrotherapy cure in a clinic in Malvern, in which Darwin believed. Parslow was their long-time manservant and friend.

Anne had had scarlet fever the year before and not really recovered. In Malvern, according to Darwin's biographer Janet Browne she may have caught typhus.

From Charles to Emma:

Malvern, 17th April, 1851

4 oclock

My dearest Emma,

I am assured that Annie is several degrees better: I have in vain tryed to see Dr Gully as yet. She looks very ill: her face lighted up & she certainly knew me. – She has not had wine, but several spoon-fulls of broth, & ordinary physic of camphor & ammonia – Dr Gully is most confident there is strong hope. – Thank God she does not suffer at all – half dozes all day long. I will write again if I can anyhow see Dr Gully before seven oclock. My own dearest support yourself – on no account *for the sake of our other children*, *I implore you*, do not think of coming here. –

> Yours my dearest,
> C. Darwin

I am assured there is great hope. – Yesterday she was a little better, & today again a little better. –

Friday, 18th April

– 4 oclock. There is no material change, but she appears much prostrated. – I will send another line before Post closes, if I see Dr Gully –

12 oclock. I have left a space above for last account. Dr Gully slept here last night & is most kind. – After I wrote her pulse ceased to intermit & that encouraged Dr Gully a little: before that, when I wrote he did not think she wd last out the night. – To day, he says she is no worse, & at present this is the best which can be said. She does not suffer thank God. – It is much bitterer & harder to bear than I expected – Your note made me cry much – but I must not give way & can avoid doing so, by not thinking about her. It is now from hour to hour a struggle between life & death. God only knows the issue. She has been very quiet all morning, but vomited badly at 6 a.m. which, however bad, shows she has more vital force than during two previous days. Sometimes Dr. G. exclaims she will get through the struggle; then, I see, he doubts. – Oh my own it is very bitter indeed. – God preserve & cherish you. – Her one good point is her pulse, now regular & not very weak, excepting for this there would be no hope. We give her spoonfuls of gruel with brandy every half hour.

1 oclock. The Dr repeats what he said, 'she is not worse': – 3 oclock, – she keeps the same, quite easy, but I grieve to say she has vomited a large quantity of bright green fluid. – Her case seems to me an exaggerated one of my Maer illness. – We must hope against hope.

My own poor dear unhappy wife
C. D.

18th April

7 oclock

Dr Gully not come.

She appears dreadfully exhausted, & I thought for some time she was sinking, but she has now rallied a little. The two symptoms Dr G. dreads most have *not* come on restlessness & coldness. – If her three awful fits of vomiting were not of the nature of a crisis, I look at the case as hopeless. – I cannot realise our position, God Help us. –

7.30. Dr Gully has been & thank God he says though the appearances are so bad, positively no one important symptom is worse, & that he yet has hopes – *positively he has Hopes.* – Oh my dear be thankful. –

Four deluges of vomiting she has had today – poor thing –

From Emma to Charles:

Down, Saturday, 19th April

My own dearest

The conclusion of your letter does leave me with some hopes, almost as much as I had yesterday. It is a blessing that our darling does not suffer, & I hope that even the vomitting does not cause much. How kind of Dr Gully to sleep in the house. & must have been a great support to you Now dear Fanny is with you, you must let her experienced eye do some of the watching, tho' I know what an effort it must be to leave her for a moment, but you will be quite exhausted. Aunt F. helps me through the long hours of suspense, & I feel quite unnatural sometimes in being able to talk of other things. Poor little sweet child I often think of the precious look she gave you the only one I suppose. No wonder she would brighten up at your sight you were always the tenderest of human beings to her & comforted her so on all occasions.

I am sadly afraid we shall not hear tomorrow The morning is the only chance Mr Acton says.

Goodbye my dearest. I shall probably send for Etty on Monday. God bless you I know you would suffer. Yours my beloved E.D.

From Charles to Emma:

19th April

11. oclock

I make *two* letters for safety. & put the second in at last minute.

First letter

My own dear. You will have received before this the Electric telegraph message, which I despatched at 9 this morning. – And it will have much comforted you. – After the second of yesterdays letters, when Dr G. maintained she was not essentially worse, she began to sleep tranquilly & continued so throughout the whole night, Dr Gully came at 11 30 to see her keeping nice & warm with no vomiting, & she took a very little gruel. This morning she is a shade too hot: but the Dr who was here at 8½ thinks her going on very well. – You must not suppose her out of great danger. –

She keeps the same; just this minute she opened her mouth quite distinctly for gruel. – & said that is enough. – You would not in the least recognize her with her poor hard, sharp pinched features; I could only bear to look at her by forgetting our former dear Annie. There is nothing in common between the two. – Fanny Henleigh is here most kind of course: she does not think badly of her looks. How truly kind of her coming – Poor Annie has just said "Papa" quite distinctly. – Etty is gone with Hannah to London by Cheltenham Coach: (Etty never dreamed of danger to Annie) on Monday she goes with the others to Leith Hill. – Hensleigh is here on way to Newport. – I cannot express how it felt to have hopes last night at 11 30 when Dr Gully came, saw her asleep & said "she is turning the corner" – I then dared picture to myself my own former Annie with her dear affectionate radiant face. – I have got your note. My dear dear Mammy let us hope & be patient over this dreadfull illness. –

2. oclock.

We expect Dr Gully every minute; but he is fearfully overworked with 88 patients. – Annie has kept just in same tranquil, too tranquil state: she takes a table-spoonful of gruel every hour, & no physic. All trace of fever is now gone. & yet she is not chilly. – She begins to drink a little more this afternoon & I think that is good. – She has no evacuations, but this is hardly wonderful, considering her . . . vomiting. – 3 oclock. – the Dr has been. He says she makes no progress, but no bad symptoms have appeared: but I am disappointed. 4 oclock We have been trying an injection with no success. But she has taken two spoonfuls of tea with evident relish, and no sickness, thank God. I find Fanny an infinite comfort – 5 oclock. just the same. I will write before late Post if Dr G. comes –

My dearest , C.D. –

From Charles to Emma:

Sunday, 20th April

My dear Emma

I had not time to send a second later letter yesterday. I do not know, but think it is best for you to know how every hour passes. It is a relief to me to tell you: for whilst writing to you, I can cry; tranquilly. I forget whether I told you that she vomited yesterday evening & *slightly* a second time. A second injection produced no sort of effect & did not relieve, but seems unimportant We then had to get Surgeon to draw her water off: this was done well & did not hurt her, but struggled with surprising strength against being uncovered &c. soon it evidently relieved her. All night she has slept tranquilly except for about 10 minutes, when she wandered in slightly excited manner. Dr G. came at 11 30 & again said not worse. She has, however, taken less gruel this night & is fearfully prostrated. Yet when Brodie sponged her face, she asked to have her hands done and then thanked Brodie. & put her arms round her neck, my poor child & kissed her –

She vomited a mouthful this morning. It is certain she suffers very little –dosing nearly all the time: occasionally she says she is very weak. I expect Dr G. immediately. Last night Dr G. said, "you must not trust me, for I can give no reason for my intuition, but yet I think she will recover" Fanny H. sat up till 2 oclock God bless her. she is most sympathetic yet encouraging. Poor dear devoted Miss Thorley thus had one entire nights rest. –

8 oclock. A.M. Dr G. has been & again he says *positively* no symptom is worse, but none better: he cares less about food than I expected: if she can weather the fortnight, he has some hopes. – Your two heart-moving notes have come. My dear dear wife. – I do not sit all the while, with her, but am constantly up & down: I *cannot* sit still. –

10 oclock. I grieve to say she has vomited rather much again: but Mr Coates has been & drawn off again *much water* & this he says is a very good symptom. Last night he seemed astonished at her "fearful illness" & he made me very low; so this morning I asked nothing & he then felt her pulse of his own accord & at once said, "I declare I almost think she will recover". Oh my dear was not this joyous to hear. – He then went on to say (& I believe him from what my Father has said) that Fever at the same period is generally either fatal to many or though appearing very bad does not kill one: & now he himself has had 6 or 7 *most severe* cases in the low country beneath Malvern & not one has died. –

She has her senses remarkably today which is very good as showing head not affected: she called Papa when I was out of room unfortunately & then added "is he out?" This & her speeches to Brodie show more clearness of mind than I have seen, & she knew what Mr Coates was going to do. – Several of Mr Coates fever patients have had their bladders paralysed the whole time. Oh I do wish for Tuesday the fortnight to be over. – But I must not hope too much. – These alternations of no hope & hope sicken one's soul: I cannot help getting so sanguine every now & then to be disappointed.

12 oclock. Again she has vomited & complains of fatigue rather more. She is very sensible; I was moving her, when she said "Dont do that please" & when I stopped "thank you". –

2 oclock, again she has vomited but again Dr G. who has just been here says her pulse is rather better, certainly not worse. – We have put mustard poultice on stomach, & that has smarted her a good deal, – which shows more sensibility than I expected. –

3 oclock; she is a little chilly & we have given her a little Brandy – & hope she is asleep & I trust will warm. – I never saw anything so pathetic as her patience & thankfulness; when I gave her some water, she said "I quite thank you". – Poor dear darling child. The Dr will come at 7 again. –

4 30 The chilliness has pretty well gone off & no more sickness, refreshing sleep.

I will write again, if I have time

Yours, C. D

From Emma to Charles:

Monday, 21st April

12 o'clock

My dearest N.

Your 2 letters are come & dear Fanny's. Your account of every hour is most precious. Poor darling she takes much more notice than I expected. I am confused now & hardly know what my impression is but I have considerable hope. I suppose a dose of opening physic has never been thought of. One must trust entirely to Dr Gully. Thank dear F. for her note. It gave me some comfort. Every word about her is precious. I have sent Bessy up to fetch Etty & she probably will find her gone to Leith Hill so it won't signify. I have sent the 30 second glass off. It is such a comfort to know that you still bear up my own. It wd be so distressing. I am quite well & have considered every thing in case I should be taken short, but I don't the least expect it. I think very likely Eliz. may come on Wed. How glad I am that the vomitting is not distressing to her. I have been living on the words of the Telegraph message till today. I am not quite so hopeful. Goodbye my own dearest. It is a dreadful period for all of us but except at post time my sufferings are nothing to yours.

yours, E. D.

By your account & Fanny's there certainly is much more vigour.

From Charles to Emma:

21st April

My dear Emma

To go on with the sick life. After Dr G. left yesterday at 7 30 (& Fanny wrote whilst he was in the room) we bathed her with vinegar & water, & it was delicious to see how it soothed her. In the night she rambled for two hours & became considerably excited, but I find the Dr does not care so much for this, as he has ceased to fear the head, which was his main fear. viz stupefaction coming on. – But to return when the Dr came at 11 30 he pronounced her decisively better. At 10 oclock the surgeon failed to draw the water; but in the dead of the night her bladder acted of itself & has again, & so have her bowels, after above a week & the action with consciousness. – I was in wonderful spirits about all this & no doubt it is very good, but I have just now been a good deal damped (8 A.M.) by the Dr. finding her pulse tremulous & his strong dislike to her bowels having acted loosely – I tell you all this, for it will prevent the too strong & ultimately wretched alternations of spirits. An hour ago I was foolish with delight & pictured her to myself making custards (whirling round) as, I think, she called them. I told her I thought she would be better & she so meekly said "thank you" Her gentleness is inexpressibly touching. – Fanny is devoting herself too much sadly, but I cannot stop her: she sat up till 4 this morning (leaving Miss Thorley a whole night to her surprise for she arranged to call her at 2 oclock:) & then Fanny lay on Brodies bed to save rousing the servants at her own adjoining house. – We are under deep obligations to Fanny never to be forgotten. Poor Annie is in a fearful mess, but we keep her sweet with Chloride of Lime; the Dr said we might change the under sheet if we could, but I dare not attempt it yet. We have again this morning sponged her, with vinegar, again with excellent effect. She asked for orange this morning, the first time she has asked for anything except water. Our poor child has been fearfully ill; as ill as a human being could be: it was dreadful that night the Dr. told me it would probably be all over before morning. If diarrhœa will but not come on, I trust in God we are nearly safe. – I have hopes that vomiting is stopped for today. –

Susan & Catty have written most kindly: the former is better. Catty offers to come here on Wednesday: upon the whole, perhaps it wd be better not, but I am perplexed what to say, & must consult Fanny. –

My own dear how it did make me cry to read of your going to Annie's garden for a flower. I wish you could see her now the perfection of gentleness, patience & gratitude, – thankful till it is truly painful to hear her. – poor dear little soul. –

12. oclock. – She has appeared rather more prostrated with knees & feet chilly & breathing laboured, but with some trouble we have got these right, & she is now asleep & breathing well. She certainly relishes her gruel flavoured with orange juice, & has taken table-spoon every hour. – No sickness, no purging: I wish there was a little less prostration. – She wanders & talks more today a good deal. –

3 oclock. She is going on very nicely & sleeping capitally with breathing quite slow – We have changed the lower sheet & cut off the tail of her Chemy [chemise] & she looks quite nice & got her bed flat & a little pillow between her two bony knees – She is certainly now going on very well.

> Yours, C. D.

*Second letter of the same day*

7.30 P.M.

Fanny gave her a spoonful of tea a little while ago, & asked her whether it was good & she cried out quite audibly "it is beautifully good." – She asked, so says Brodie, "where is poor Etty?". –

The Dr has been here everything going on as favourably as possible: but we must have the surgeon this evening again, I am sorry to say. –

She has slept most tranquilly almost all afternoon, perhaps too tranquilly – We have bathed her again with vinegar. –

*From Emma to Charles:*

Tuesday, 22nd–23rd April

My dearest

Your 2 letters of Monday are certainly better. Poor sweet little thing! I felt more wretched today than any day, but now I do think looking at the accounts of the last 4 days that there has been progressive improvement from that time. Poor dear Catherines letter is most kind but I think dear Susan will be so melancholy without her I almost hope you have not accepted. I feel greatly relieved at the bowels acting. I shall write a few lines in the afternoon but I always feel bewildered at first but my impression is considerably better. Eliz. comes today dear soul.

Goodbye I am quite well. I will ask her to get up chloroform but I don't expect to want it till the right time.

God bless you E.D.

Wednesday. I forgot to put Malvern on this yesterday so it came back, but I hope you wd not be uneasy.

Eliz is come.

From Emma to Charles:

Wednesday, 23rd April
before post time

My own dearest

I have just sent off my return note by Parslow for the chance of it reaching you sooner. The oftener I read over your letter of Monday the more hopeful it made me. Your minute accounts are such a comfort & I enjoyed the spunging our dear one with vinegar as much as you did. I have been thinking about a few slops that might suit her when she can take a little food but it is more for the pleasure of fancying I have something to do for her or think of for her. If the bowels sh'd be too loose I believe rice gruel is a very good innocent food & binding (viz rice boiled for many hours till it loses shape & the solid part drained away.) it perhaps might be flavoured with cinnamon or currant jelly. Whey from milk is another harmless drink & very digestible I believe & a good deal of the nourishment of the milk in it without the heavy part. Aunt F. says it is slightly opening so that I am doubtful about it. I should think a spoonful of raw yolk of egg beat up in hot water & a little salt might be a change when you can venture.

But your difficulty will not be in the variety but in venturing to give her any quantity of any thing. Eliz. came at 2 having slept at Southampton. She is quite hopeful from the last accounts. I try to prepare my mind for a great deal more anxiety & draw backs.

I am afraid Cath. will be mortified if she is not made use of & when Fanny goes & you are not quite so anxious I think she would be of the greatest use & comfort to you. How kind Fanny is. I have heard from Caroline. Etty very well & happy she says "I will take the greatest care of her & I think I shall be able to make her feel friendly & comfortable with me should she have any little trouble or hurt. I am deeply touched at your writing to me at such a time & I can indeed with truth say it is impossible to feel more for you than Jos & I do.!" She had rec'd Fanny's account which gave her much more hope. Willy is very eager to hear how she is every day & tho' I tell him all the changes I don't think he realizes the real fear. I was sending down the little ones in Eliz. fly yesterday as far as At S. to be out of the way, when Franky asked what the drivers name was & fell into such a fright at been driven by a stranger, tho' Parslow was going also, that I had him out & he was a long time getting to rights.

(After post. Alas my own how shall we bear it. It is very bitter but I shall not be ill. Thank dear F)

The final paragraph, written in pencil, refers to a letter from Fanny Mackintosh Wedgwood, below.

From Fanny to Emma:

## 22nd April

My dearest Emma    I am thankful that you felt there was much to fear in yr note yesterday for I grieve to write you a worse report this evening there has been a change today & signs of sinking – I tell you every thing just as it is my dearest Emma & thankful also for the mercy that is given us of there being not the least appearance of any suffering in your sweet patient darling – Charles had written you this morning – too hopefully & he will not send it & cannot write you *this* himself – he is gone to lie down & has gone through much fatigue – her night was not disturbed & less wandering than the night before but the effort of the fever throwing itself off from the bowels is more than her strength seems able to bear & she has lost strength every time – we are now giving brandy & Ammonia every qr of an hour – which she takes with no difficulty –   Dr Gully is just gone – he thinks her in imminent danger & not having gained ground – Fanny [Allen] will send us a word for all our sorrowing anxiety is for you now my Emma in this great suffering – God support & raise you for Charles sake – I need not say that if any change for the better wch is always possible with a child shd be given us – you shall have a message – But I have told you the worst – Oh that I should have to send you such sad sad news – Our only comfort will be to hear of you – I have persuaded Charles to lie down for a while Thank you for yr sweet note Your affec

FEW

From Charles to Emma:

Wednesday, 23rd April

My dear dearest Emma

I pray God Fanny's note may have prepared you. She went to her final sleep most tranquilly, most sweetly at 12 oclock today. Our poor dear dear child has had a very short life but I trust happy, & God only knows what miseries might have been in store for her. She expired without a sigh. How desolate it makes one to think of her frank cordial manners. I am so thankful for the daguerreotype. I cannot remember ever seeing the dear child naughty. God bless her. We must be more & more to each other my dear wife – Do what you can to bear up & think how invariably kind & tender you have been to her. – I am in bed not very well with my stomach. When I shall return I cannot yet say. My own poor dear dear wife.

    C. Darwin

From Emma to Charles:

Thursday, 24th April, 1851
before 12

My dearest

I know too well what receiving no message yesterday means. Till 4 o'clock I sometimes had a thought of hope, but when I went to bed I felt as if it had all happened long ago. Don't think it made any difference my being so hopeful the last day. When the blow comes it wipes out all that preceded it & I don't think it makes it any worse to bear. I hope you have not burnt your letter I shall like to see it sometime. My feeling of longing after our lost treasure makes me feel painfully indifferent to the other children but I shall get right in my feelings to them before long. You must remember that you are my prime treasure (& always have been) my only hope of consolation is to have you safe home to weep together. I feel so full of fears about you. They are not reasonable fears but my power of hoping seems gone. I hope you will let dearest Fanny or Catherine if she comes stay with you till the end. I can't bear to think of you by yourself. No doubt you will have sent Miss Th. home to recover her cheerfulness. I will write to her in a few days to fix her time of return— Your letter is just come & I feel less miserable a good deal in the hopes of seeing you sooner than I expected, but do not be in a hurry to set off. I am perfectly well. You do give me the only comfort I can take in thinking of her happy innocent life. She never concealed a thought, & so affectionate so forgiving. What a blank it is. Don't think of coming in one day. We shall be much less miserable together.

yours my dearest

Poor Willy sends his love. He takes it & cried quietly & sweetly.

Darwin was persuaded to go home to Emma before the funeral took place. He arrived within a day of Annie's death. That evening Emma wrote to Fanny.

24th April

We have done little else but cry together and talk about our darling . . . I think everybody loved her. Hers was such a transparent character, so open to kindness and a little thing made her so happy . . . From her having filled our minds so much for the last nine months it leaves such an emptiness . . . I suppose this painful longing will diminish before long. It seems as if nothing in this life could satisfy it.

❧

Samuel Palmer writes to George Richmond after the death of his son Thomas More Palmer, aged nineteen, from consumption.

July 1861

Yesterday was the *only* day a part of which I have not passed in bitter weeping. . . .

I dreamed one night that . . . I held my living son in my embrace – we went thoroughly into the subject, and found that the death and funeral at Abinger had been fictitious. For a second after waking the joy remained – then came the knell which wakes me every morning – More is dead! More is dead!

Two months later, he writes to Alexander Gilchrist.

## September 1861

How can I thank you enough for the consideration you have given to the grave stone? . . . we want something of the simplest kind . . . in good taste . . . any Red Lion Square design for those medieval body stones would be well worth seeing. I must lay by my pen for a little while for this morning my grief broke forth all afresh and my eyelids are stiff with weeping. In the night I dreamed that the dear boy was alive and about, temperately, to resume his studies – that he was in Douro Place and that I was talking with him. This has occurred twice – in the former dream I heard him sweetly singing – Who can describe the horror of awaking from such dreams to the dread reality? I have been ill in bed for two days with a sort of influenza – the stupefaction was such a luxury.

❦

Matthew Arnold (1822–1888), poet and critic, saw three of his children die in four years. In January 1868 his infant son Basil died and on 23rd November his eldest son Thomas died at Harrow School. He was sixteen years old and had always been very frail. Arnold had written to Lady de Rothschild when he was deciding whether or not to send Thomas to Harrow.

## 4th November, 1867

I think Lady Charles Russell has a boy who, like my eldest boy, is an invalid, and I daresay you will some time or other be kind enough to ascertain from her whether the school life is at all trying for him, or whether she has any difficulty in getting him excused fagging or violent exercises.

He writes again after Thomas dies.

## 30th November, 1868

My dear Lady de Rothschild,
   I was sure you would be touched by the death of my poor little boy, to whom you have so often showed kindness. I imagine every one here

thought he could not get through the winter, though they could give no special name to his complaint except to call it, with the doctors, 'failure in vital power' following upon the slight shock given to him by his fall from a pony in Westmorland. But his mother and I had watched him through so many ebbings and flowings of his scanty stock of vital power that we had always hopes for him, and till I went into his room last Monday morning an hour before the end I did not really think he would die. The astonishing self-control which he had acquired in suffering was never shown more than in the last words he said to me, when his breath grew shorter and shorter, and from this, and the grieved face of the doctor as he entered the room, he knew, I am sure, that the end was come; and he turned to me, and – his mamma, who was always with him, and whom he adored, having gone into the next room for a moment – he whispered to me, in his poor labouring voice, 'Don't let mamma come in.' At his age that seems to me heroic self-control; and it was this patience and fortitude in him, joined to his great fragility and his exquisite turn for music, which interested so many people in him, and which brings us a sort of comfort now in all the kind and tender things that are said to us of him. But to Mrs. Arnold the loss of the occupation of her life – for so the care of him really was – will for some time to come be terrible.

৵৹৵

Matthew Arnold writes to his mother on the death of his second son, Trevenen William (known as Budge), who was eighteen years old.

18th February, 1872

My dearest Mother – I do not know that I shall write much, but I must tell you what pleasure it gave us to have your letter and Fan's this morning. When I wrote last Sunday there was not even a trace of illness to be seen in Budge, though I hear now he had been much knocked up by running a mile very fast the day before; but he was entirely himself all Saturday and Sunday, and indeed particularly gay. When I came home on Monday evening Flu told me that Budge had gone to bed with a bad cold and toothache. I saw him three times that evening and found him very sick and miserable. I concluded he had a bilious attack, such as I often used to have when a boy, and that he had a cold with it. So it went on, headache taking the place of toothache, and I cannot say I was the least uneasy. But, when Victorine called to us on Friday morning and I found him light-headed wandering about the room, I was very uneasy; he knew me, however, and said, 'ah! papa!' but I went off at once for Dr. Tonge, the doctor who lives nearest. When I came back he seemed dropping into a heavy doze. I had to go very early to London, and he seemed in the same heavy doze when I left him. The rest you have heard; when I saw him again at 2 p.m. all the doctors were there, besides Hutton, who had come down with me; and it was clear there was no hope. He never showed the least spark of consciousness, till his breathing ceased with a sort of deep sigh. How fond you were of him, and how I like to recall this! He looks beautiful, and my main feeling about him is, I am glad to say, what I have put in one of my poems, the 'Fragment of a Dejaneira.'

☙❦

Kate Amberley fills in her journal after she has given birth to twins, one of whom was stillborn. Her description highlights the change in outlook that took place in the late twentieth century when it became the practice for a mother to be able to see and hold her stillborn child. (Miss Garrett was the midwife; Wee was Kate's nurse.)

## 2nd March, 1868

On finding it was a foot presentation Miss Garrett sent for Dr. Priestley but he was out, so did not come. The first child was born about 7.15 and the other about ¼ of an hour after, both foot presentations; the second never breathed but its heart beat for some time and Mama did all in her power to bring it to life and so did Miss Garrett but they did not succeed. I saw it one moment in Maude's arms but not again as I did not wish it at the time; but ever since I have been very sorry I did not see it and so grieved it did not live but at the time I felt I had one and did not at all realize I had lost anything. I hear it was the largest of the two and very dark and like Amberley – Lizzie dressed it in a nightgown and Mama had it sent down to Alderley unknown to me and buried in dear old Wee's grave. Mama did not tell me till sometime after as she waited for me to say something and I never liked to mention the subject. I was very glad I knew where it was.

Lord Amberley writes to his mother after the death of his wife Kate and, some days later, his only daughter Rachel, aged six, from diphtheria. He died two years later, aged thirty-four, leaving two sons, Frank and Bertrand Russell.

3rd July, 1874

My dear Mama,

I thought the cup of misery had been full enough, but it seems not. The child too had to go, and I have lost for ever the sweet caressing ways and the affectionate heart that might if anything could have been some consolation. And now I feel that the desolation is complete. Yet I think I must be almost dead to feeling, for Rachel's death seemed hardly to add to my sorrow. But I know how I shall feel it hereafter when I miss her. Of all the children she was the dearest to me, and so my two greatest treasures in the world are gone almost at one blow. It is cruel, unspeakably cruel! I know how you will feel for me dearest Mama.

Ever,
Amberley.

❦

Captain Robert Falcon Scott (1868–1912), the Antarctic explorer, writes his last letter to his wife Kathleen. Their only son, Peter, was aged three.

March, 1912

To my widow

Dearest Darling – we are in a very tight corner and I have doubts of pulling through – In our short lunch hours I take advantage of a very small measure of warmth to write letters preparatory to a possible end – the first is naturally to you on whom my thoughts mostly dwell waking or sleeping – if anything happens to me I shall like you to know how much you have meant to me and that pleasant recollections are with me as I depart – I should like you to take what comfort you can from these facts also – I shall not have suffered any pain but leave the world fresh from harness and full of good health and vigour – this is dictated already, when provisions come to an end we simply stop where we are within easy distance of another depot. Therefore you must not imagine a great tragedy – we are very anxious of course and have been for weeks but in splendid physical condition and our appetites compensate for all discomfort. The cold is biting and sometimes angering but here again the hot food which drives it forth is so wonderfully enjoyable that we would scarcely be without it.

We have gone down hill a good deal since I wrote the above. Poor Titus Oates has gone – he was in a bad state – the rest of us keep going and imagine we have a chance to get through but the cold weather doesn't let up at all – we are now only 20 miles from a depot but we have very little food or fuel

Well dear heart I want you to take the whole thing very sensibly as I am sure you will – the boy will be your comfort I had looked forward to helping you to bring him up but it is a satisfaction to feel that he is safe with you. I think both he and you ought to be specially looked after by the country for which after all we have given our lives with something of spirit which makes for example – I am writing letters on this point in the end of this book after this. Will you send them to their various destinations?

I must write a little letter for the boy if time can be found to be read when he grows up – dearest that you know cherish no sentimental rubbish about re marriage – when the right man comes to help you in life you ought to be your happy self again – I hope I shall be a good memory certainly the end is nothing for you to be ashamed of and I like to think that the boy will have a good start in parentage of which he may be proud.

Dear it is not easy to write because of the cold – 70 degrees below zero and nothing but the shelter of our tent – you know I have loved you, you know my thoughts must have constantly dwelt on you and oh dear me you must know that quite the worst aspect of this situation is the thought that I shall not see you again – The inevitable must be faced – you urged me to be leader of this party and I know you felt it would be dangerous – I've taken my place throughout, haven't I? God bless you my own darling I shall try and write more later – I go on across the back pages.

Since writing the above we have got to within 11 miles of our depot with one hot meal and two days cold food and we should have got through but have been held for four days by a frightful storm – I think the best chance has gone we have decided not to kill ourselves but to fight it to the last for that depot but in the fighting there is a painless end so don't worry. I have written letters on odd pages of this book – will you manage to get them sent? You see I am anxious for you and the boy's future – make the boy interested in natural history if you can, it is better than games – they encourage it at some schools – I know you will keep him out in the open air – try and make him believe in a God, it is comforting. Oh my dear my dear what dreams I have had of his future and yet oh my girl I know you will face it stoically – your portrait and the boy's will be found in my breast and the one in the little red Morocco case given by Lady Baxter – There is a piece of the Union flag I put up at the South Pole in my private kit bag together with Amundsen's black flag and other trifles – give a small piece of the Union flag to the King and a small piece to Queen Alexandra and keep the rest a poor trophy for you! – What lots and lots I could tell you of this journey. How much better it has been than lounging in comfort at home – what tales you would have for the boy but oh what a price to pay – to forfeit the sight of your dear dear face – Dear you will be good to the old mother. I write her a little line in this book. Also keep in with Ettie and the others – oh but you'll put on a strong face for the world – only don't be too proud to accept help for the boys sake – he ought to have a fine career and do something in the world. I haven't time to write to Sir Clements – tell him I thought much of him and never regretted him putting me in command of the Discovery.

Rudyard Kipling (1865–1936), novelist, poet and defender of the British Empire, writes to his son John, aged seventeen, in the second year of the First World War. John is training as an ensign in the Irish Guards before going out to the front. He had very bad eyesight and would normally have been rejected by the army, but Kipling, a strong, idealistic supporter of the war, had managed to get him a commission in the Guards.

Kipling to John at Warley:

4th March, 1915
(stinking wet and mild)

Dear old man,

Phipps and I had a look at the catalogues (A & N and Harrod's) last night to see what we could possibly find in the Games line which would be refined (but not too bally refined) and quiet and at the same time have *no* connection with War. . . . Do you think a *small* billiard-table (like the one we have here at Bateman's) could be put into one corner of the ante-room? It's simply dam silly of them not to allow for any means of recreation.

. . . as I lay awake wrestling with 'conflicting reports from various channels' I reviewed the facts and surroundings of your present life – how damnably and unrelievedly dull the surroundings were and what a wet and grey and muddy and depressing existence it was in itself: and I felt exceedingly proud of the way you'd stuck it without yapping. So I made a resolve that I'd write and tell you so in the morning. Young as I was when I began, and hard as my work was in that climate [India], I did not have to *live* absolutely alone. As you know I lived in my Father's house. It was only when my people went to the Hills for the summer and the house was shut up, that I had to live for a few weeks at the Club. But *you* have had to face a certain discomfort (which is inevitable) *plus* a certain loneliness of the spirit which is awfully hard to bear; and a certain sense of isolation which, as I remember, almost frightens a young man. And you have stood it like a white man and a son to be proud of. I haven't said much about it, but I've noticed it, and I think I can feel pretty well what is passing in your mind. It is an experience that you have got to go through by yourself (all the love in the world can't take it off your shoulders) but it may be some help to know that another man has had to face something of the same sort (I mean loneliness *plus* news of a pal's death; *plus* dirt; *plus* a general feeling that the world is a wicked place which it isn't) and respects you for the way you are taking your dose.

## 23rd March, 1915

Yesterday afternoon Mums and I went down to St Leonards to see old Mademoiselle *and* Rider Haggard. . . . [Mademoiselle] was immensely interested in your career. 'But *why*,' said she, 'is he in the Irish Guards?' I explained that our family blood was 'prudently mixed' in view of all international contingencies and that there was some Irish in the strain. Then she couldn't understand why you were in the Army at all. '*If* there is no compulsion,' she said, 'why should John enter the Army?' 'Precisely *because* there is no compulsion,' says Mother and after a while Mademoiselle tumbled to that idea too. She sent her very best greetings but kept on murmuring from time to time 'And *he* is in the Army'.

John writes to his father from 'somewhere in Brentwood'; 17th August 1915 was his eighteenth birthday.

## 5th July, 1915

I commanded my company and walked ahead with Kerry. He told me definitely that I would be the first ensign to go out to France after the 17th of August and I would have been too young then if I hadn't had a years service in the Brigade.

So going in early was a damned good move after all.

It is nice to have a month clear notice, so I can get every little thing all ready.

Kipling to John:

## 6th July

It is a comfort to get your notice in good time. Kerry, however, was wrong in one respect. It is not the mere fact of your having been in the Brigade for a year that has made you what you are. It is because you deliberately went into it for a purpose and gave yourself up to the job of becoming a good officer. (I have heard indirectly from another source that you are considered to be 'damned smart'.) Lots of men, as we know, go into the Brigade for a year and haven't made anything but a bloody show of themselves. *You* went in and you stuck it out without a whimper through that foul winter, and you shouldered any responsibility that was going and you laid yourself out to know and understand both your men and your profession. We are both more proud of you than words can say. It's a record that can't be beaten.

Kipling to John from Paris, where he was inspecting French military preparations and writing about them for the English papers. He had been on a 'little tour among the trenches in Alsace'.

## 22nd August

I hope you'll never get nearer to the Boche than I did. . . . I don't mind trenches half as much as going in a motor along ten or twelve miles of road which the Boches may or may not shell – said road casually protected at the worst corners with thin hurdles of dried pine trees. Also I hate to be in town with stone pavements when same is being bombarded. It's a grand life though and does not give you a dull minute. I found boric acid in my socks a great comfort. I walked 2 hours in the dam trenches. . . .

Don't forget the beauty of rabbit netting overhead against hand grenades. Even tennis netting is better than nothing.

Kipling to John from Paris again:

## 24th August

I have to go to the British Consulate . . . to get permission to leave France. I tell you, they look after the stray civilian pretty close here. It's necessary: for Paris is still fairly thick with spies.

Did I tell you how a soldier at Troyes (he knew all about 'me works') came up to me, and when I told him my name, uttered a long and friendly 'Ah-haa. God-dam'? It was the first time I'd ever heard the oath as a sort of *entente cordiale* greeting: and it fairly winded me for a second. Aren't the women good to our people everywhere. I've met hospitals all over the face of the country run by the English.

I'm *awfully* wondering where you are likely to be sent. If it is anywhere outside our present front – in the direction of the Argonne or that way, west of Soissons (which may be possible) I think you'll find it useful to chip in with my name occasionally among the French. This isn't swank but they all seemed to know me.

Dear love. I'm going out in a French taxi. They are burning petrol mixed with pee. At least that's how it smells.

> Daddo.

Kipling to John from Boulogne:

## 26th August

By the way the best dictionary for French is a dictionary in skirts.

Kipling to John from home:

## 28th August

Uncle Stan turned up last night. . . . he was dining with Kerry t'other day . . . Kerry said to him:- 'I've just discovered that I've a nephew of yours in my regiment – young Kipling. He's a very good boy and he's done very good work. All his work is good and thorough. I shall let him go out when he is eighteen because he's had a year's training and he knows his work.' . . .

> A heart full of love.
> Dad.

John to his parents:

## 29th August

Dear F –
Not having a letter for four days I get nine all in one post yesterday. . . .
Many thanks for Dad's letters.

His 'tips for the trenches' are rather quaint. Surely you know it is a standing order never to have anything over the top of a trench, even rabbit wires. If the Bosch comes, he has you like rabbits underneath it.

John to his parents:

25th September

Just a hurried line as we start off tonight. The front line trenches are nine miles off from here so it wont be a very long march.

This is THE great effort to break through & end the war.

The guns have been going deafeningly all day, without a single stop.

We have to push through at all costs so we won't have much time in the trenches, which is great luck.

Funny to think one will be in the thick of it tomorrow. . . .

They are staking a tremendous lot on this great advancing movement as if it succeeds the war won't go on for long.

You have no idea what enormous issues depend on the next few days.

This will be my last letter most likely for some time as we won't get any time for writing this week, but I will try & send Field post cards.

Well so long old dears.
    Dear love
    John.

John died in his first engagement sometime after 27th September at the Battle of Loos. His parents received news that he was wounded and missing in action in early October. His father wrote later: 'If any question why we died / Tell them, because our fathers lied'.

Raymond Asquith (1878–1916) was killed in battle in the First World War,
when his father was prime minister. His stepmother, Margot Asquith (1864–
1945), wrote about him in her autobiography.

It is a commonplace to say after a man is dead that he could have done
anything he liked in life and often an exaggeration; but of Raymond
Asquith the phrase would have been true. . . .

His death was the first great sorrow that occurred in my stepchildren's
lives after I married and an anguish to his father and me. My husband's
natural pride and interest in him had always been intense and we were
never tired of discussing him when we were alone: his personal charm
and wit, his little faults and above all the successes which so certainly
awaited him. Henry's grief darkened the waters in Downing Street at a
time when, had they been clear, certain events could never have taken
place.

When Raymond was dying on the battle-field he gave the doctor his
flask to give to his father; it was placed by the side of his bed and never
moved till he left Whitehall.

I had not realized before how powerless a stepwife is when her husband
is mourning the death of his child; and not for the first time I profoundly
wished that Raymond had been my son.

❧

In her biography of her mother, Clementine Churchill, Mary Soames
(b.1922) describes the death of Clementine's fourth child, Marigold
Churchill (1918–1921). At the beginning of August 1921, the children were
on holiday at Broadstairs in the care of their governess, Mlle Rose.

. . . from the start of their seaside holiday Marigold had not been very well;
and since in the last year she had been subject to 'throats' and coughs,
perhaps not enough significance was attached at first to what was in fact
the onset of a mortal illness. The local doctor was very good, but, alas for
the 'Duckadilly', the age of antibiotics had not yet dawned, and her painful
sore throat progressed into a fatal septicaemia. The child became really ill
about 14th August, but it was a day or two before Mlle Rose, stimulated
into action by the kind and watchful landlady of 'Overblow', sent for her
mother. Clementine left Eaton at once and rushed to Broadstairs; the

three elder children travelled to Scotland according to plan, with Bessie, Clementine's maid. By the time her mother arrived, Marigold was gravely ill. Winston came down from London; a specialist was sent for, but he could do nothing. . . .

On the evening of 22nd August, Clementine was sitting by Marigold's bedside; the child was sinking; suddenly she said to her mother: 'Sing me "Bubbles".' Clementine, summoning all the control she knew, began the haunting, wistful little song that Marigold loved so much; she had not struggled very far, when the child put out her hand and whispered, ' Not tonight . . . finish it tomorrow.' The next day Marigold died; she was two years and nine months old; both her parents were with her. Clementine in her agony gave a succession of wild shrieks, like an animal in mortal pain.

☙❧

Rosamond Lehmann (1901–1990) was a novelist. Her adored daughter Sally (1934–1958) died of polio in Jakarta, aged twenty-four, only a year after her marriage to Patrick Kavanagh. Lehmann describes her first sensation of communicating telepathically with her daughter, some days after Sally died. She is staying on the Isle of Wight the day before she hears of her daughter's death.

June 1958

Since Sally was nearly always in my thoughts it is no wonder that, as I prepared for bed in my hotel room, looking out over the sea towards the lights of the mainland opposite, another memory of her should have slipped, very quietly and clearly, into the forefront of my mind. Once, when she was five years old, as we walked together on the down above Compton in Berkshire where we spent the war years she said, without the slightest warning:

'One day . . . one day . . .'

'What about one day?'

'One day I might call you and call you and call you . . . over the whole world. Over the whole world, and you might not answer. What shall I do then?' Her voice seemed to toll. Taken aback, I quickly promised her that I would always answer.

'You mean you won't die?'

'I mean I won't die'
'Promise?'
'I promise.'
'That's all right then.' . . .

Yes, I was thinking, but not sadly, of . . . these things that night in 1958: something in their quality seemed to sum up the ground of her mysteriously simple nature. No, it was not unusual to have her thus in my mind's eye and ear: one's children, and indeed one's grandchildren, constantly stir about in one's imagination like an accompaniment to daily living. There was no premonition of disaster in the memories. On the contrary, I was happier than usual; not troubled, as I sometimes was, by my last sight of her, as the train drew away at Waterloo, looking intently at me from the window, not waving, white-faced.

*The following day Lehmann hears that Sally has died.*

Nowadays I measure my life by Sally, not by dates. There was the time before her birth; the time of her life span; the time I am in now, after she slipped away from us. The decision to write about it has not been easily arrived at; but I am not the first person, and shall not be the last, to undertake a similar testament; and, like others, I can only go forward in the hope that the great glimpse (what can I call it?) which overwhelmed me at the peak, or nadir, of my agony may taste as unquestionably to others, as it does to me, of reality . . .

*A fortnight later, Rosumund goes to stay with friends in the country where she experiences what she believes to be a telepathic communication with Sally:*

A blackbird was pouring forth his whole being just beyond my window; and from where I lay I could see elm tops moving against an intensely blue sky in billowing masses of unearthly greens and golds.

Suddenly, a clear high-pitched vibration, like the twang of a harp-string, crossed my ears. . . . At the same time a sort of convulsion or alarum struck me in the heart centre, followed by a violent tugging sensation in this region. As if attached to an invisible kite string that was pulling me, out, upwards, upwards, I began to be forcibly ejected from the centre of my body. I heard myself moan, felt a torrent of tears pour down my face, distinctly remarked to myself that this was like some very peculiar birth process . . . Then the humming faded out, and the song of the blackbird, swelled, swelled, as if it was being stepped up a hundredfold. . . .

Now I was with Sally. She was behind my left shoulder, leaning on it. Together we were watching Patrick. His face, only his face, confronted us: it was clearly recognizable but the whole scale of it was altered, expanded; and it was self-luminous, and transformed by an expression of dreaming beatitude. He was (we both knew) starting on a journey. I said: 'Aren't you going with him?' 'No,' she said, 'he's got to go alone.' . . .

Patrick's lit face vanished, but Sally and I remained together, wordlessly communicating. More than anything, it was like laughing together, as we always did laugh; like sharing the humour of a situation: his going off without her in some sort of state of disarray and unpreparedness. . . . She made some characteristic joke (I can't define it) about the muddle of his packing. I did not see her. I had the unaccountable impression that she was hiding her face, that I was forbidden to look round. There was no light, no colour, no external scenic feature: only close embrace, profound and happy communion; also the strongest possible impression of her individuality.

Then, with no shock or sense of travelling, I was back in my body, awake, cheerful as if I had just replaced the receiver after one of our long gossiping joking conversations.

꿍

Jan Morris describes the death of her daughter Virginia, aged two months.

We lost one child, but even then the desolation of the loss was tempered for me by a sense of continuous possession, and by that streak of perverse optimism I had preserved from my childhood. I felt she would surely come back to us, if not in one guise, then in another – and she very soon did, leaving us sadly as Virginia, returning as Susan merry as a dancing star. Her first little body is buried beneath a magnolia tree, cherished by sculpted cherubs, outside the door of the Saxon church at Waterperry in Oxfordshire: but her spirit left us, for the time being, on a hot May night in Hampshire.

We had returned from abroad, and had rented half a country house near Newbury. The baby, developing an unidentified virus within two months of her birth, had been taken from us to Newbury hospital, and we knew she was very near death. Elizabeth and I lay sleepless in our room overlooking the garden, too hot and too unhappy even to close our eyes. A great moon shone through the windows, and towards midnight a nightingale began to sing in the tree just outside. I had never heard an English nightingale before, and it was like hearing for the first time a voice from the empyrean. All night long it trilled and soared in the moonlight, infinitely sad, infinitely beautiful, and filling every corner of our room with its resonance. We lay there through it all, each knowing what the other was thinking, the tears running silently down our cheeks, and the bird sang on, part elegy, part comfort, part farewell, until the moon failed and we fell hand in hand into sleep.

In the morning the child had gone.

☙❦❧

Susan Hill (b.1942), novelist, whose daughter Imogen was born three months prematurely in 1984 and died at five weeks in hospital in Oxford.

Dr Tarnow-Mordi came into the room. Together we looked down at Imogen.

'She looks very old,' he said. I knew what he meant. She had gone smaller, looked wizened. Rather wise, but peaceful. And far, far away, miles beyond my reach now.

'Please can I hold her?' I said, and suddenly I knew it was urgent, and I longed to be as close to her as I could again, not so that I could do anything more for her now, but to ease her passing, have her go from me finally while she was in my arms, not lying in her impersonal, perspex box . . .

I bent down and held her fragile, minute body to me, kissed her head, her cheek, spoke to her, words I can't remember – but she could not hear. I stroked her cheek with my finger – the skin was so soft, it felt like nothing, as if it were not there at all.

'Mrs Wells – ' The voice seemed to come from somewhere far away. 'Mrs Wells – it's gone right down now.'

What? I glanced up. There was no reading on the monitor, and the line had gone flat – there was just a pulse, a bleep –

'It's gone down, Mrs Wells. Do you understand?' I looked at Imogen.

Her skin was very pale, but when I kissed her again, it felt just the same. Soft. Warm.

'Mrs Wells – ' Sister Di was holding my hand, bending beside me. I looked into her eyes. They were full of tears. 'That's only the ventilator you see now on the monitor. There isn't anything else. Imogen's heart has stopped.'

I sat for a long time, holding her. She looked no different. Just even further away from me – quite out of reach.

That quiet time immediately after she had died might have been seconds, minutes, hours. There was no time. After a death, when you are close to it, have witnessed it, the world seems to be suspended, time ceases to have any meaning at all, nothing beyond this room, this momentous event, exists.

Death seemed such a simple thing to me then, so easy, so . . . I cannot express or explain. It was the most important, the most significant thing in life, I felt in awe of it and yet quite peaceful, as though I were in the company of a familiar friend. Imogen was here, death was here, too – yet I did not really know what that meant. I was not afraid, I did not recoil, and I wanted this time to last forever, to hold on to it. Because here, now, I felt as if I were within reach of understanding the secret of the universe. I was 'at the still point of the turning world'.

All those things I thought and felt and knew, as I sat on, holding my dead infant and no one hurried me, they gave me all the space I wanted and needed. It was over now, there was no urgency about anything. Is it always like that at a death bed? I hope so.

# EPILOGUE

Richard Eyre (b.1943), director and writer.

Our parents cast long shadows over our lives. When we grow up we imagine that we can walk into the sun, free of them. We don't realise until it's too late that we have no choice in the matter; they are always ahead of us, forever old.

We carry them within us all our lives, in the shape of our face, the way we walk, the sound of our voice, our skin, our hair, our hands, our heart. We try all our lives to separate ourselves from them and only when they are dead do we find we are indivisible.

We grow to expect that our parents, like the weather, will always be with us. Then they go, leaving a mark like a handprint on glass or a wet kiss on a rainy day, and with their death we are no longer children.

# SOURCES

# BIBLIOGRAPHY

Abbott, Mary *Family Ties: English Families 1540–1920* (Routledge, 1993)

Alderley family *The Ladies of Alderley: being the letters between Maria Josepha Lady Stanley of Alderley and her daughter-in-law Henrietta Maria Stanley during the Years 1841–1850*, ed. Nancy Mitford (Chapman and Hall, 1938; Hamish Hamilton, 1967)

Amberley family *The Amberley Papers: The Letters and Diaries of Lord and Lady Amberley*, 2 vols, ed. Bertrand and Patricia Russell (Hogarth Press, 1937)

Amis, Kingsley *Memoirs* (Hutchinson, 1991)

Anderson, Michael *Approaches to the History of the Western Family 1500–1914* (Macmillan, 1980)

Aries, Philippe and Robert Baldick *Centuries of Childhood* (Jonathan Cape, 1962)

Arnold, Matthew *Letters of Arnold Matthew 1848–1888*, 2 vols, ed. George W.E. Russell (Macmillan, 1895)

Aspinall-Oglander, Cecil *Admiral's Wife; Being the life and letters of The Hon. Mrs. Edward Boscawen from 1719 to 1761* (Longmans, Green and Co., 1940)

Aubrey, John *Brief Lives chiefly of Contemporaries set down by John Aubrey between the Years 1669 and 1696*, ed. Richard Barber (Boydell Press, 1982)

Asquith, Margot *The Autobiography of Margot Asquith*, ed. Mark Bonham Carter (Eyre & Spottiswoode, 1962)

Becon, Thomas *The Catechism of Thomas Becon, S.T.P.*, ed. John Ayre (Parker Society, Cambridge, 1844)

Bell, Quentin *Elders and Betters* (John Murray, 1995)

Bessborough, Lady *Lady Bessborough and her Family Circle*, ed. Earl of Bessborough and A. Aspinall (John Murray, 1940)

Betjeman, John *John Betjeman Letters Volume One: 1926 to 1951* and *Volume Two: 1951 to 1984*, ed. Candida Lycett Green (Methuen, 1994, 1995)

Blundell, Margaret *A Lancashire Squire, The Life of Nicholas Blundell of Crosby 1669–1737* (Day Books, 2002)

Blundell, William *Cavalier: Letters of William Blundell to his Friends, 1620–1698*, ed. Margaret Blundell (Longmans, Green, and Co., 1933)

Boswell, James *Boswell for the Defence 1769–1774*, ed. William K. Wimsatt, Jr. and Frederick A. Pottle (Heinemann, 1960)

Boswell, James *Boswell: The Ominous Years 1774–1776*, ed. Charles Ryskamp and Frederick A. Pottle (Heinemann, 1963)

Boswell, James *Boswell: The English Experiment 1785–1789*, ed. Irma S. Lustig and Frederick A. Pottle (Heinemann, 1986)

Bradford, Sarah *Sacheverell Sitwell, Splendours and Miseries* (Sinclair-Stevenson, 1993)

Browne, Janet *Charles Darwin: Voyaging* (Jonathan Cape, 1995)

Browne, Janet *Charles Darwin: The Power of Place* (Jonathan Cape, 2002)

Bunsen, Baroness *The Life and Letters of Frances Baroness Bunsen*, 2 vols, ed. Augustus J.C. Hare (George Routledge and Sons, 1879)

Butler, Samuel *The Family Letters of Samuel Butler 1841–1886*, ed. Arnold Silver (Jonathan Cape, 1962)

Cadogan, William 'An Essay upon Nursing and the Management of Children, from their Birth to Three Years of Age' (1748) in *The Father of Child Care, Life of William Cadogan (1711–1797)*, Morwenna and John Rendle-Short (John Wright & Sons Ltd., 1966)

Cecil, David *The Young Melbourne* (Constable, 1939)

Cecil, David *Visionary & Dreamer, Two poetic painters: Samuel Palmer and Edward Burne-Jones* (Constable, 1969)

Chalmers, Patrick R. *Kenneth Grahame: Life, Letters and Unpublished Work* (Methuen, 1933)

Channon, Sir Henry *'Chips': The Diaries of Sir Henry Channon*, ed. Robert Rhodes James (Weidenfeld & Nicolson, 1967)

Chesterfield, Lord *The Letters of Lord Chesterfield: Letters to his Son, first published by his son's widow Eugenia Stanhope (1774) and the Letters to his Godson (1890)* (Eyre & Spottiswoode, 1932)

Clarke, Isabel C. *Maria Edgeworth: Her Family and Friends* (Hutchinson, 1949)

Cobbett, William *Advice to Young Men, and (incidentally) to Young Women, in the Middle and Higher Ranks of Life* (Mills, Jowett, and Mills, 1829)

Cobden-Sanderson, Thomas *The Journals of Thomas James Cobden-Sanderson 1879–1922*, ed. Richard Cobden-Sanderson (Richard Cobden-Sanderson, 1926)

Coleridge, Samuel Taylor *Letters of Samuel Taylor Coleridge*, 2 vols, ed. E.H. Coleridge (William Heinemann, 1895)

Coleridge, Samuel Taylor *Collected Letters of Samuel Taylor Coleridge*, 6 vols, ed. Earl Leslie Griggs (Oxford University Press, 1956–1971)

Coleridge, Sara *Memoir and Letters of Sara Coleridge*, ed. Edith Coleridge (Henry S. King and Co., 1873)

Connor, Eva G. (ed.) *Letters to Children* (Macmillan, 1938)

Constable, John *Memoirs of the Life of John Constable, Composed Chiefly of his Letters*, C.R. Leslie (Phaidon, 1951)

Cooper, Diana *Trumpets from the Steep* (Rupert Hart-Davis, 1960)

Cunningham, Hugh *Children and Childhood in Western Society Since 1500* (Longman, 1995)

Cunningham, Hugh *The Invention of Childhood* (BBC Books, 2006)

Cusk, Rachel *A Life's Work: On Becoming a Mother* (Fourth Estate, 2001)

Darwin, Charles 'A Biographical Sketch of an Infant', *Mind*, 2, 285–294 (1877)

Darwin, Charles *The Correspondence of Charles Darwin*, 15 vols, ed. Frederick Burkhardt *et al.* (Cambridge University Press, 1985–2006)

Darwin, Erasmus *The Letters of Erasmus Darwin*, ed. Desmond King-Hele (Cambridge University Press, 1981)

Dee, Dr John *The private diary of Dr. John Dee, and the catalogue of his library of manuscripts*, ed. J.O. Halliwell-Phillipps (Camden Society, old series, IX, 1842)

Defoe, Daniel *The Letters of Daniel Defoe*, ed. George Harris Healey (Oxford University Press, 1955)

Denbigh, Cecilia Countess of *Royalist Father and Roundhead Son* (Methuen, 1915)

Edgeworth, Richard Lovell *Memoirs of Richard Lovell Edgeworth, Esq., begun by himself and concluded by his daughter, Maria Edgeworth*, 2 vols (R. Hunter and Baldwin, Cradock, and Joy, 1820)

Elwes, Winefride and Richard Elwes *Gervase Elwes: The Story of His Life* (Grayson & Grayson, 1935)

Evelyn, John *The Diary of John Evelyn*, ed. E.S. de Beer (Oxford University Press, 1959)

Evelyn, John *Memoirs of John Evelyn, Esq. F.R.S.*, 5 vols, ed. William Bray (Henry Colburn, 1827)

Eyre, Richard *Utopia and other places: Memoir of a Young Director* (Bloomsbury, 2003)

Fell Smith, Charlotte *Mary Rich, Countess of Warwick (1625–1678): Her Family & Friends* (Longmans, Green, and Co., 1901)

Fielden, Jan (ed.) *Family Letters: Parents and Children* (Marginalia Press, 1994)

Fielding, Daphne *Mercury Presides* (Eyre & Spottiswoode, 1954)

Fletcher, Anthony and Stephen Hussey *Childhood in Question: Children, Parents and the State* (Manchester University Press, 1999)

Foreman, Amanda *Georgiana Duchess of Devonshire* (HarperCollins, 1998)

Furneaux, Robin *William Wilberforce* (Hamish Hamilton, 1974)

Gainsborough, Thomas *The Letters of Thomas Gainsborough*, ed. John Hayes (Yale University Press, 2001)

Gérin, Winifred *Elizabeth Gaskell, A Biography* (Oxford University Press, 1976)

Glendinning, Victoria *Vita: The Life of V. Sackville-West* (Weidenfeld & Nicolson, 1983)

Glendinning, Victoria *Rebecca West: A Life* (Weidenfeld & Nicolson, 1987)

Glendinning, Victoria *Trollope* (Hutchinson, 1992)

Godden, Rumer *A Time to Dance, No Time to Weep* (Macmillan, 1987)

Grove, Valerie *Laurie Lee: The Well-loved Stranger* (Viking, 1999)

Guest, Lady Charlotte *The Diaries of Lady Charlotte Guest, Extracts from her Journal 1833–1852*, ed. Earl of Bessborough (John Murray, 1950); see also Schreiber, Lady Charlotte

Halifax, Marquis of 'The Lady's New Year Gift: or, Advice to a Daughter' (1688) in *The Life and Letters of Sir George Savile, Bart, First Marquis of Halifax, Vol. II*, H.C. Foxcroft (Longmans, Green, and Co., 1898)

Hall, Ruth *Marie Stopes: A biography* (André Deutsch, 1977)

Hanawalt, Barbara A. *Growing up in medieval London: the experience of childhood in history* (Oxford University Press, 1993)

Hanawalt, Barbara A. *The ties that bound: peasant families in medieval England* (Oxford University Press, 1986)

Hare, Augustus *The Years with Mother*, ed. Malcolm Barnes (George Allen & Unwin, abridged edition, 1952)

Harley, Lady Brilliana *Letters of the Lady Brilliana Harley*, ed. Thomas Taylor Lewis (Camden Society, 1854)

Haydon, Benjamin *The Autobiography and Memoirs of Benjamin Robert Haydon (1786–1846), Vol. II*, ed. Tom Taylor (Peter Davies, 1926)

Hendrick, Harry *Children, childhood and English society 1880–1990* (Cambridge University Press, 1997)

Hervey, Lord *Lord Hervey's Memoirs*, ed. Romney Sedgwick (William Kimber, 1952)

Heywood, Colin *A History of Childhood: children and childhood in the West from medieval to modern times* (Polity Press, 2001)

Hill, Susan *Family* (Michael Joseph, 1989)

Holland, Lady *A Memoir of the Rev. Sydney Smith by his daughter, with a Selection from his Letters edited by Mrs Austin* (Longmans, Green, and Co., 1855)

Holles, Gervase *Memorials of the Holles Family 1493–1656*, ed. A.C. Wood (Camden Society, Camden Third Series, LV, 1937)

Holroyd, Michael *Augustus John* (Chatto & Windus, 1996)

Houlbrooke, Ralph *The English Family 1450–1700* (Longman, 1986)

Houlbrooke, Ralph (ed.) *English Family Life 1576–1716: An Anthology from Diaries* (Basil Blackwell, 1988)

Houlbrooke, Ralph *Death, Religion and the Family in England 1480–1750* (Oxford University Press, 1998)

Howard, Elizabeth Jane *Slipstream* (Macmillan, 2002)

Hughes, Ted *Letters of Ted Hughes*, ed. Christopher Reid (Faber and Faber, 2007)

Ilchester, Earl of *Henry Fox, First Lord Holland, His Family and Relations* (John Murray, 1920)

Irving, Laurence *Henry Irving: The Actor and his World* (Faber and Faber, 1951)

Italian visitor 'A Relation, or rather a True Account, of the Island of England; . . . about the year 1500' (Camden Society, XXXVII, 1847)

Josselin, Ralph *The Diary of Ralph Josselin 1616–1683*, ed. Alan Macfarlane (British Academy, 1976)

Keane, Fergal *Letter to Daniel: Despatches from the Heart* (Penguin, 1996)

Kipling, Rudyard *"O Beloved Kids": Rudyard Kipling's Letters to his Children*, ed. Elliot L. Gilbert (Weidenfeld & Nicolson, 1983)

Knapp, Oswald G. (ed.) *An Artist's Love Story told in the letters of Sir Thomas Lawrence Mrs. Siddons and her daughters* (George Allen, 1904)

Lawrence, D.H. *The Letters of D.H. Lawrence Vol. III October 1916–June 1921*, ed. James T. Boulton and Andrew Robertson (Cambridge University Press, 1984)

Lehmann, Rosamond *The Swan in the Evening: Fragments of an Inner Life* (Collins, 1967)

Leinster, Duchess of *Correspondence of Emily, Duchess of Leinster (1731–1814), Vol. I*, ed. Brian Fitzgerald (Dublin Stationery Office, 1949)

Lennox, Lady Sarah *The Life and Letters of Lady Sarah Lennox 1745–1826*, 2 vols, ed. Countess of Ilchester and Lord Stavordale (John Murray, 1902)

Lessing, Doris *Walking in the Shade* (HarperCollins, 1997)

Lipman, Maureen *You Can Read Me Like a Book* (Robson Books, 1995)

Locke, John *Some Thoughts Concerning Education*, ed. Rev. R.H. Quick (Cambridge University Press, 1889)

Locke, John *An Essay Concerning Human Understanding* (1690)

Londonderry, Marchioness of *Henry Chaplin, A Memoir* (Macmillan, 1926)

Lowndes, Marie Belloc *Diaries and Letters of Marie Belloc Lowndes 1911–1947*, ed. Susan Lowndes (Chatto & Windus, 1971)

Lyttleton, George *The Lyttelton Hart-Davis Letters, Correspondence of George Lyttelton and Rupert Hart-Davis 1955–56*, ed. Rupert Hart-Davis (John Murray, 1978)

Macfarlane, Alan *The Family Life of Ralph Josselin, A Seventeenth-Century Clergyman: An essay in historical anthropology* (Cambridge University Press, 1970); see also Josselin, Ralph

Macfarlane, Alan *Origins of English Individualism: Family, Property and Social Transition* (Blackwell, 1978)

Martin, Joanna *Wives and Daughters: Women and Children in the Georgian Country House* (Macmillan, 2004)

deMause, Lloyd *The History of Childhood: Untold Story of Child Abuse* (Jason Aronson Inc., 1974)

Mitford, Jessica *A Fine Old Conflict* (Michael Joseph, 1977)

Montagu, Lady Mary Wortley *The Complete Letters of Lady Mary Wortley Montagu, Vol. II 1721–1751* and *Vol. III 1752–1762*, ed. Robert Halsband (Oxford University Press, 1966, 1967)

Montague, Lady Mary Wortley *Letters of Lady Mary Wortley Montague, written during her travels in Europe, Asia, and Africa: to which are added Poems by the same author* (Didot, 1822)

Moore, Charlotte *George and Sam* (Viking, 2004)

Morris, Jan *Conundrum* (Faber and Faber, 1974)

Morris, William *The Collected Letters of William Morris, Vol. I 1848–1880*, ed. Norman Kelvin (Princeton University Press, 1984)

Mortimer, John *Murderers and Other Friends: Another Part of Life* (Viking, 1994)

Musson, A.E. and Eric Robinson *Science and Technology in the Industrial Revolution* (Manchester University Press, 1969)

Nelson, Lord *Letters from Lord Nelson*, ed. Geoffrey Rawson (Staples Press, 1949)

Nicholson, Virginia *Among the Bohemians: Experiments in Living 1900–1939* (Viking, 2002)

Nicolson, Harold *Harold Nicolson Diaries and Letters 1930–1939*, ed. Nigel Nicolson (Collins, 1966)

Orrery, Countess of Cork and (ed.) *The Orrery Papers*, 2 vols (Duckworth, 1903)

Paget family *The Paget Brothers 1790–1840*, ed. Lord Hylton (John Murray, 1918)

Palmer, Samuel *The Life and Letters of Samuel Palmer*, ed. A.H. Palmer (Seeley & Co., 1892)

Parker, William Riley *Milton, A Biography, Vol. I, The Life* (Oxford University Press, 1968)

Partridge, Frances *Frances Partridge, Diaries 1939–1972*, ed. Rebecca Wilson (Weidenfeld & Nicolson, 2000)

Partridge, Frances *Frances Partridge, Good Company: Diaries 1967–1970* (HarperCollins, 1994)

Paston family *The Pastons: a family in the Wars of the Roses*, ed. Richard Barber (The Folio Society, 1981)

Paston family *The Paston Letters: A Selection in Modern Spelling*, ed. Norman Davis (Oxford University Press, 1963)

Pembroke family *Pembroke Papers (1780–1794) Letters and Diaries of Henry, Tenth Earl of Pembroke and his Circle*, ed. Lord Herbert (Jonathan Cape, 1950)

Pinchbeck, Ivy and Margaret Hewitt *Children in English Society, Vol. I, From Tudor Times to the Eighteenth Century* and *Vol. II, From the Nineteenth Century to the Children Act, 1948* (Routledge & Kegan Paul Ltd, 1969, 1973)

Piozzi, Hester *Anecdotes of the Late Samuel Johnson, LL.D., during the Last Twenty Years of his Life* (T. Cadell, 1786); see also Thrale, Hester

Plowden, Alison *Women All on Fire: The Women of the English Civil War* (Sutton Publishing, 1998)

Pollock, Linda *A Lasting Relationship: Parents and Children over Three Centuries* (Fourth Estate, 1987)

Pollock, Linda *Forgotten Children: parent–child relations from 1500 to 1900* (Cambridge University Press, 1983)

Pückler-Muskau, Prince Hermann *A Regency Visitor: The English Tour of Prince Pückler-Muskau Described in his Letters 1826–1828*, trans. Sarah Austin, ed. E.M. Butler (Collins, 1957)

Ransome, Arthur *Signalling from Mars, The Letters of Arthur Ransome*, ed. Hugh Brogan (Jonathan Cape, 1997)

Raverat, Gwen *Period Piece* (Faber & Faber, 1952)

Redgrave, Corin *Michael Redgrave: My Father* (Richard Cohen Books, 1995)

Rich, Mary *Autobiography of Mary Rich Countess of Warwick*, ed. with introduction and notes by T.G. Croker (Percy Society, 76, 1848); see also Fell Smith, Charlotte

Robinson, Mary *Memoirs of The Late Mrs Robinson written by herself* (Cobden-Sanderson, 1930)

Ruskin family *The Ruskin Family Letters: The Correspondence of John James Ruskin, His Wife, and Their Son, John, 1801–1843*, 2 vols, ed. Van Akin Burd (Cornell University Press, 1973)

Russell, Bertrand *Bertrand Russell Autobiography*, 3 vols (George Allen & Unwin, 1967, 1968, 1969)

Russell, Bertrand *The Selected Letters of Bertrand Russell, The Public Years, 1914–1970*, ed. Nicholas Griffin (Routledge, 2001)

Ryder, Dudley *The Diary of Dudley Ryder 1715–1716*, ed. William Matthews (Methuen, 1939)

St Clair, William *The Godwins and the Shelleys: The biography of a family* (Faber and Faber, 1989)

Sage, Lorna *Bad Blood* (Fourth Estate, 2000)

Sampson, Anthony *The Scholar Gypsy* (John Murray, 1997)

Schreiber, Lady Charlotte *Lady Charlotte Schreiber, Extracts from her Journal 1853–1891*, ed. Earl of Bessborough (John Murray, 1952); see also Guest, Lady Charlotte

Sherry, Norman *The Life of Graham Greene*, 3 vols (Jonathan Cape, 1989, 1994, 2004)

Sitwell, Osbert *Laughter in the Next Room* (Macmillan, 1949)

Sitwell, Osbert *Tales My Father Taught Me* (Hutchinson, 1962)

Smith, Sydney *The Letters of Sydney Smith*, 2 vols, ed. Nowell C. Smith (Oxford University Press, 1953)

Soames, Mary *Clementine Churchill* (Cassell, 1979)

Spender, Stephen *Stephen Spender Journals 1939–1983* (Faber and Faber, 1985)

Stedman J.G. *Journal of J.G. Stedman, 1744–1797, Soldier and Author*, ed. Stanbury Thompson (Mitre Press, 1962)

Stewart, Agnes M. *The Life and Letters of Sir Thomas More* (Burns & Oates, 1876)

Stone, Lawrence *The Family, Sex and Marriage in England 1500–1800* (Harper & Row, 1977)

Stonor family *Kingsford's Stonor Letters and Papers 1290–1483*, ed. Christine Carpenter (Cambridge University Press, 1996)

Stubbs, John *Donne: The Reformed Soul* (Viking, 2006)

Thackeray, William *The Letters and Private Papers of William Makepeace Thackeray*, 4 vols, ed. Gordon N. Ray (Oxford University Press, 1945, 1946)

Thesiger, Wilfred *The Life of My Choice* (Collins, 1987; HarperCollins, 1991)

Thrale, Hester *Anecdotes of the late Samuel Johnson, during the last twenty years of his life*, ed. S.C. Roberts (Cambridge University Press, 1925)

Thrale, Hester *Thraliana : the diary of Mrs. Hester Lynch Thrale (later Mrs. Piozzi)*, ed. Katharine C. Balderston (Oxford University Press, 1942)

Thrale, Hester *Dr. Johnson's Mrs. Thrale*, ed. J.H. Lobban (T.N. Foulis, 1910)

Tomalin, Claire *Mrs Jordan's Profession* (Viking, 1994)

Trollope, Anthony *The Letters of Anthony Trollope*, ed. Bradford Allen Booth (Oxford University Press, 1951)

Trollope, Frances *Eleanor Frances Trollope: Her Life and Literary Work, from George III to Victoria*, 2 vols (Richard Bentley and Son, 1895)

Tynan, Kenneth *The diaries of Kenneth Tynan*, ed. John Lahr (Bloomsbury, 2001)

Uglow, Jenny *The Lunar Men* (Faber, 2002)

Verney, Lady Frances Parthenope (ed.) *Memoirs of the Verney Family during the Seventeenth Century, Vol. I* (Longmans, Green, and Co., 1907); *Vol. II* (Longmans, Green, and Co., 1904)

Verney, Lady Margaret Maria (ed.) *Verney Letters of the Eighteenth Century from the MSS. at Claydon House*, 2 vols (Ernest Benn, 1930)

Victoria, Queen *Dearest Child, Letters between Queen Victoria and the Princess Royal 1858–1861*, ed. Roger Fulford (Evans Brothers, 1964)

Victoria, Queen *Queen Victoria in her Letters and Journals*, ed. Christopher Hibbert (John Murray, 1984)

Walton, Isaac *Walton's Lives: The Lives of Dr. John Donne; Sir Henry Wotton; Mr. Richard Hooker; Mr. George Herbert; and Dr. Robert Sanderson, Vol. II* (Payne and Foss, and J. Mawman, 1817)

Waugh, Evelyn *The Letters of Evelyn Waugh*, ed. Mark Amory (Weidenfeld & Nicolson, 1980)

Wentworth family *The Wentworth Papers 1705–1739*, ed. James J. Cartwright (Wyman & Sons, 1883)

White, Antonia *Antonia White: Diaries 1926–1957*, ed. Susan Chitty (Constable, 1991)

Wilde, Oscar *The Letters of Oscar Wilde*, ed. Rupert Hart-Davis (Rupert Hart-Davis, 1962)

Wilson, Harriette *Harriette Wilson's Memoirs of herself and others* (Peter Davies, 1929)

Wodehouse, P.G. *Yours, Plum, The Letters of P.G. Wodehouse*, ed. Frances Donaldson (Hutchinson, 1990)

Woolley, Hannah *The Gentlewoman's Companion: Or a Guide to the Female Sex, for the guidance of mothers and governesses* ed. Caterina Albano (Prospect Books, 1999)

Wollstonecraft, Mary 'Thoughts on the Education of Daughters' (London, 1787)

Wollstonecraft, Mary *The Collected Letters of Mary Wollstonecraft*, ed. Janet Todd (Allen Lane, 2003)

Woodforde family *Woodforde Papers and Diaries*, ed. Dorothy Heighes Woodforde (Peter Davies, 1932)

Wood, Mary Anne Everett (ed.) *Letters of Royal and Illustrious Ladies of Great Britain, Vol. I* (Henry Colburn, 1846)

Wordsworth, William *The Letters of William and Dorothy Wordsworth*, 8 vols, ed. Ernest de Selincourt, Alan G. Hill *et al.* (Oxford University Press, 1967–1993)

Wynne family *The Wynne Diaries*, 3 vols, ed. Anne Fremantle (Oxford University Press, 1935, 1937, 1940)

# INDEX